YEMEN – U.S. RELATIONS:

THE EXTERNAL AND INTERNAL DYNAMICS

18th century - 2012

Dr. Moath A. Alrefaei

DEDICATION

This book is dedicated to all who have contributed to my academic journey. I extend my deepest gratitude to my noble family and esteemed instructors from the universities in Yemen, Malaysia, the United States, the Office of the Presidency of the Republic of Yemen, and the UN. To my beloved homeland, Yemen, and the United States, which I will forever cherish—this is for you.

YEMEN – U.S. RELATIONS:
THE EXTERNAL AND INTERNAL DYNAMICS

Abstract

The subject of Yemen-U.S. relations has become more important in view of the global war on terrorism and the need for stability in the Middle East. Currently, Yemeni-American relations are heading into the unknown due to a state of hostility and proxy war against the areas controlled by the Ansar Allah group in northern Yemen. Additionally, there is no American diplomatic representation in any Yemeni territory. Fourteen years ago, Yemen-U.S. relations were enjoying a wide bilateral partnership. Literature addressing Yemen-U.S. relations is inconsistent and seldom does it penetrate to the core of the dynamics that determine this relationship. The inconsistencies that permeate this relationship are often overlooked. In light of this, the key issues addressed by this book specially deals with the dynamics driving the bilateral relations between the two countries. The book's findings assert that Yemen-U.S. relations are governed by a wide variety of dynamics that can be broadly categorised as external and internal. These dynamics are fluid and often differ according to the ever-changing environment and circumstances. One stage of the relationship can appear completely different to the next.

However, the analysis of various dynamics provides a new interpretation of the systematic change in Yemen-U.S. relations and their future prospects. The wide range of dynamics that are characterized by plurality and overlap as well as dual influence are behind the instability and oscillation that characterized the relationship. The external dynamics such as the regional geo-strategic factors, the influence of the Cold War, the democratization and human rights agenda, and the global war on terrorism in the new international order appear to be a greater determinant of the relations between Yemen and U.S. Due to weak common internal interests between the two countries, the influence of internal factors is often described as marginal. This however changed after the 9/11 attacks, especially with the escalating threat of Yemen and U.S. homeland security by terrorist groups. The new security perspective gave the relationship a new direction. Various internal dynamics, such as Yemen's war against al-Qaeda, its economic and developmental needs, and Yemen's instability, were major factors that shaped the relationship over the 2001-2012 period.

However, the temporal limits of this book will not deal with the period of the Arab Spring and the current civil war. The book will provide a brief overview of the initial features of the crisis in 2011. The author prefers to address those phases as a topic for his next book. In fact, and to clarify the ambiguity of the U.S position on the Yemeni crisis 2013-2024, this book is considered important and basic to understanding the natural changes in the U.S policy towards the Middle East including Yemen. For instance, the future changes in the internal and external dynamics compared with those covered in this book, which in turn made U.S. policy seek to fail some states in the region instead of saving fragile states to not being failures.

This book stands out from others discussing the general state of Yemeni and American relations in two key ways. First, it avoids the conventional, chronological approach that often becomes tedious, opting instead for an analytical methodology that interprets changes in relations based on dominant factors. Second, it employs established scientific and methodological approaches from political science and international relations to ensure objectivity and enhance its scholarly integrity.

LIST OF ABBREVIATIONS

AAIA	Aden-Abyan Islamic Army
ABCFM	American Board of Commissioners for Foreign Missions
ACC	Arab Cooperative Council
AQAP	Al-Qaeda in the Arabian Peninsula
CPI	Corruption Perceptions Index
CS	Copenhagen School
EIU	Economist Intelligence Unit
FBI	Federal Bureau of Investigation
FYM	Free Yemeni Movement
GCC	Gulf Cooperation Council
GDP	Gross Domestic Product
GPC	General People's Council
GWOT	Global War on Terrorism
HDI	Human Development Index
IEF	Index of Economic Freedom
IJM	Islamic Jihad Movement
IOR-ARC	Indian Ocean Rim Association for Regional Cooperation
IR	International Relations
ISLAH	Yemeni Reform Group
ISIS	Islamic State began as an Iraqi organization
JMP	Joint Meeting Parties
KOY	Kingdom of Yemen
KSA	Kingdom of Saudi Arabia
LDCs	Least Developed Countries
NAM	Non-Aligned Movement
NF	National Front
NSB	National Security Bureau in Yemen
PDRY	People's Democratic Republic of Yemen

PRSY   People's Republic of South Yemen

PSS   Political Security Service in Yemen

RDP   Revolutionary Democratic Party

ROY   Republic of Yemen

SABA   Yemen News Agency

UAE   United Arab Emirates

UAR   United Arab Republic

UN   United Nations

U.S.   United States of America

USAID   United States Agency for International Development

USSR   Union of Soviet Socialist Republics

YAR   Yemen Arab Republic

YLP   Yemeni Liberal Party

MAP OF YEMEN

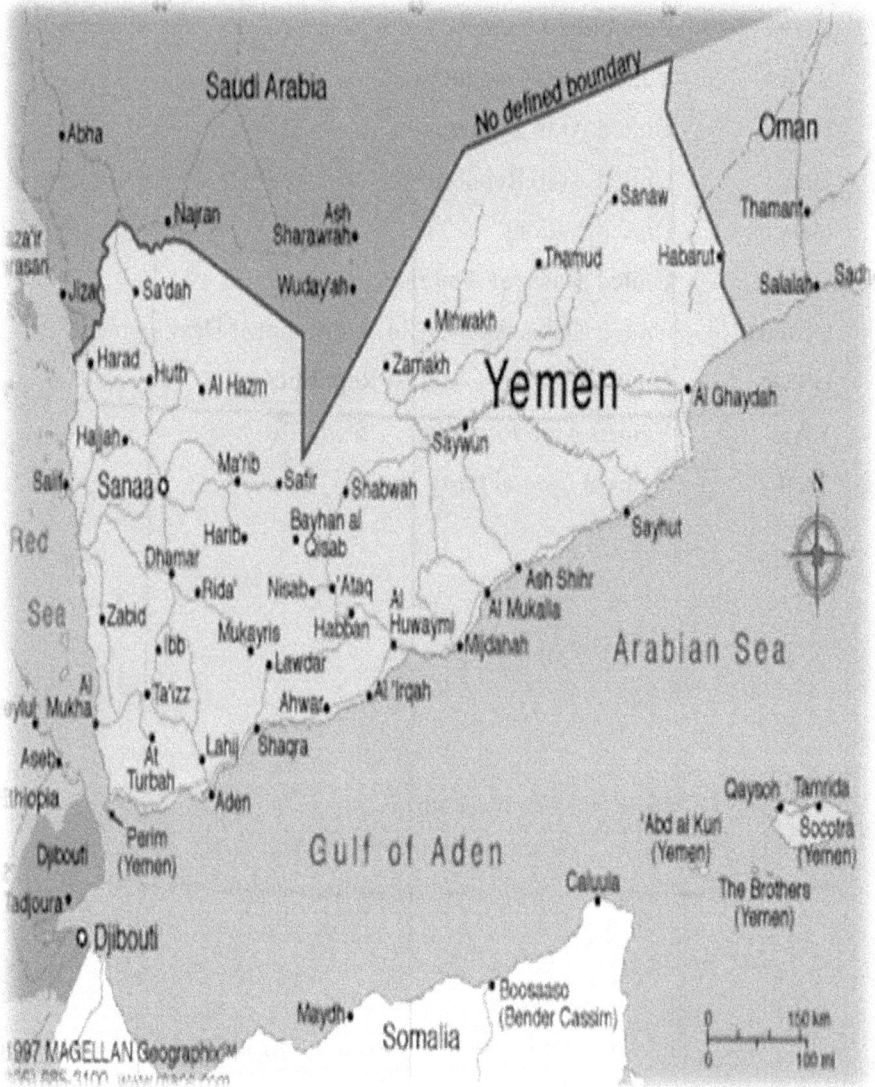

TABLE OF CONTENTS

CHAPTER ONE: INTRODUCTION.

CHAPTER TWO: THE EARLY YEARS OF YEMEN-U.S. RELATIONS

CHAPTER THREE: EXTERNAL DYNAMICS SHAPING THE RELATIONSHIP

CHAPTER FOUR: INTERNAL DYNAMICS INFLUENCING THE RELATIONSHIP

APPENDIX

LIST OF MAPS AND FIGURES

CHAPTER ONE:
INTRODUCTION

The historical and modern context of Yemen-U.S. relations is characterized by forms of oscillation and instability that varies from one stage to another. Furthermore, the bilateral relations between the two countries are governed by various external and internal dynamics characterized by complexity, diversity, and instability. These dynamics can be divided as external dynamics that come from the international and regional environment, while internal dynamics that pertain to the domestic environment of Yemen. Over the past decade, Yemen-U.S. relations have become particularly important. A wide variety of dynamics have given impetus to the importance of this relationship.

Yemen-U.S. relations are considered complex and unique. Studies in international relations attest to the difficulty of analysing and tracking the relations between small countries and great powers. The dilemma Yemen faces as a small power is finding the right approach for dealing with great power under its national constants and in the shadow of the contradiction of external and internal factors. In the same way, the U.S. also faced the contradiction of many factors with the same reaction. In addition, it experienced a political and security dilemma in its relationship with Yemen. In the global war on terrorism, the United States found that its security was linked to the security and stability of other weak countries such as Yemen. This supreme power does not have plenty of options, especially with the failure of military intervention and the lack of confidence in USAID. On the other hand, Yemen and the United States interact in an unstable and volatile environment, exacerbated by the New World Order and Yemen's strategic location in the Middle East—a region at the center of conflict and significant U.S. military presence.

Consequently, the U.S. foreign policy towards Yemen has been described as contradictory and schizophrenic.[1] Similarly, the Yemeni foreign policy towards

S has often been unexpected. In this context, this book attempts to deal with the bilateral relations by shedding light on the effects of the internal and external dynamics that shaped this relationship. Although several studies dealt with the issue of the mutual relations between the two countries, the various internal and external dynamics influencing those relations are still vague and unclear, considering that most studies were limited in describing the conduct of such relations.

The historical context of the Yemen-U.S. relations varied from one phase to another. The era of colonialism and the Cold War cast a shadow over the relations between the two countries as well as the importance of the role of Yemen's location and regional factors. In more recent times, the attack on the U.S. Navy destroyer *USS Cole* and the events of 9/11 ushered in a new phase, which was characterized by an increase of bilateral relations coupled with the absence of mutual trust. Thereafter, Yemen-U.S. relations entered a critical stage when Yemen was threatened with foreign and military intervention similar to that taking place in Afghanistan. However, with the presence of intense diplomatic activity between the two countries, Yemen became an important partner and ally to the U.S. in the so-called the Global War On Terrorism (GWOT).

Since the beginning of the third millennium, Yemen is one of the least developed countries (LDCs). It continues to experience enormous economic and development challenges. Moreover, Yemen is suffering from a number of internal conflicts such as the *Southern* movement, which advocates secession, the *Houthi* movement in the northern part of Yemen, and the on-going protests and demonstrations that are part of the so-called Arab Spring that swept across a number of Arab nations. At that time, U.S. is well aware that instability in Yemen threatens not only regional countries but also U.S. national and global security according to the Secretary of State, Hillary Clinton.[2] Accordingly, in the aftermath of 9/11, U.S. no longer relied heavily on a traditional strategy towards Yemen. America's relationship with Yemen went beyond dealing with the government, and into having relations with other parties, organizations, and tribal leaders.

According to the inadequacy of available literature, the need for a new model is a requirement in order to better interpret the corridors of Yemen-U.S. relations in addition to shedding light on the significant shift after the events of 9/11. In an attempt to fill this lacuna, this book depends on the analysis of the factors that shape the relationship and their influence in order to explore and explain the nature of Yemen-U.S. relations. It attempts to provide an alternative model for interpreting and justifying the inconsistencies that permeate this relationship.

1.1 Purpose of the book

The book aims to examine the dynamics that shape Yemen-U.S. relations. There are four significant objectives of this book. Firstly, it attempts to explain the historical context of the bilateral relations between the two countries and the basic factors in that period. Secondly, this book determines and explores the main external dynamics that shape the relationship in the context of international and regional issues. Thirdly, the book aims to explore and explain the main internal dynamics that influence this relationship and interpret the change after the events of 9/11. The book traces and interprets the changes in Yemen and U.S. foreign policies towards each other in accordance with the changes in the domestic, regional, and international security environments. Finally, it aims to provide the overall findings of the Yemen-U.S. relations that are effected by various dynamics in addition to the future prospects of the Yemen-U.S. relations.

To achieve the book's goals, there is a main question: "What are the internal and external dynamics driving Yemen-U.S. relations?" In order to addresses this question, the following four sub-questions help to elaborate, namely what is the nature of the factors that contribute to enhance or weaken the bilateral relations? What is the main dynamic that governing the two countries' stands towards the critical turning points in their relationship? To what extent has the emergence of terrorism from Yemen made internal dynamics the main factors that form Yemen-U.S. relations? Finally, how can a change in the dominant factor explain the change in US foreign policy towards Yemen during the Arab Spring, especially the shift from supporting stability to creating chaos?

1.2 New-Realism and Securitization Approaches.

Researchers studying the relations between a Great state and a small state often face difficulties in determining the theoretical framework. Some aspects of analytical frameworks reflect the doubts surrounding the determination of the applicable core theories in International Relations (IR) to interpret the relations between Great states and small states. Some Scholars, Singer and Wildavsky, argue that world politics is different between the North and South in terms of the structure of the political system, development, and foreign interests.[3] Therefore, the core assumptions of the theories of International Relations might be applicable in one region but not in the other. By the same token, other scholars argue that theories such as the Neo-realism and Neo-liberalism, for example, are designed to interpret the power and industrial state and are not suitable for many developing countries.[4] Although both currents have their criticisms of the major theories in IR, they fail to provide a new model or approach.

To circumvent this dilemma, this book adopted a conventional IR model that assumes that all states are fundamentally comparable.[5] Therefore, it will be based on the norms of the Neo-realism and the Securitization Approach according to the concepts of the Copenhagen School as a conceptual framework of the book. Such theories provide an explanation for the state's behavior, whether great or small, in line with achieving its national interest and solving the security problem pertaining to inter-state relationships. This section justifies the application of the two theories in addition to explaining the importance of their arguments in order to achieve the objectives of the book.

Firstly, realism is among the oldest theories that explain the behavior of states. It emerged in the 1940s and presently remains the dominant paradigm in international relations and security studies. Its main argument emphasizes that states are in the pursuit of power and aim to protect their vital interests in order to exist and survive in a competitive environment.[6] From the perspective of realist, the state is the main actor in IR and the sovereignty of the state is paramount to any cooperation, alliance, and international institutions.[7] The action and reaction between states could be characterized as power politics.[8] The concepts of realism developed in the post-Second World War period and are the most influential in scientific circles and among governments as well.

The contributions of Kenneth Waltz namely Structure Realism or Neo-realism assume that the structure of political systems is characterized by anarchy and competition.[9] As a result, he argues that states in IR are motivated by self-help and survival.[10] This means that it cannot rely on other states or institutions to guarantee its survival. In fact, neo-realists believe that any cooperation between states may prove difficult to achieve. This is because, in trying to gain power, a state may upset the role of another state and the absolute trust between states is impossible, even between allies.[11] In addition, cooperation among states will not happen unless the states involved make efforts to make it happen. This will depend on the individual states themselves.[12]

Furthermore, the concept of the national interest, which is seen as being central to the development of realism, provides researchers with the tools to realize the state's behavior in IR. Beyond morality, the term aims to encapsulate the point that states act in IR based on their interest.[13] Morgenthau stressed that the essential endeavor of foreign policy is to ensure, *"the integrity of the nation's territory, of its political institutions and of its culture"*.[14] The concept of national interest expanded to include various other interests of the state. According to Waltz, the state's foreign policies are not limited to achieve their survival only, but also other interests such as gaining wealth, prosperity, and influence.[15] In this context, some realists considered that morality should ensure that people are aware of a government's policies. A government's interests can be divided into "high and low policies." The government's interest in internal matters such as health, environment, and welfare for example are considered "low politics".

The assumptions of the realists present a model capable of explaining the interactions between Yemen and U.S. regarding mutual issues and interests, inconsistent policies, and their security cooperation in its various stages. It represents a solid base to illustrate how the key dynamics under study affected the relationship between the two countries such as the influence of the change of the international system on the behavior of each country towards the other, whether in the post-Second World War and the post-Cold War. Unlike other theories in IR, neo-realism explains the security cooperation between the two countries on the one hand, and the complete lack of success of that cooperation on the other. Even in the new international order, this theory explains the U.S. position against exporting the Yemeni democratic experiment to its neighbors. Even after competing states transformed into hegemonic powers, like the U.S. policy in the Arabian Peninsula after the post-Cold War, it attempted to control resources, raw materials, as well as its industries.[16]

The book also uses the securitization approach to articulate the internal dynamics and its effect on Yemen-U.S. relations, especially after the 9/11 attacks. Neo-realism is unable to deal with some issues and factors such as the emergence of terrorist groups and Yemen's internal challenges in various aspects of development, economy, and politics. Scholars of the securitization approach attempted to bridge the gap of the concept of security in the traditional theories, which depicts and confines the security concern of the state in the military threats of other states.[17] The most important contribution in this field was by scholars of the Copenhagen School (CS) who expanded the concept of security and offered an alternative approach for articulating security issues. Barry Buzan indicates that the concept of security was "too narrowly founded", so he attempts to present a new framework of security.[18] Including the military sector, the concept of security threats importantly expands to other four sectors namely the political, economic, societal, and environmental.[19]

The process of securitization of any non-military issue is accomplished through three stages in which normal issues are securitized. Firstly, to identify an existential threat as Wæver suggested or to identify a potential threat as Olaf Corry argued.[20] Secondly, this threat requires a plan of action and finally it becomes an urgent issue in the state's policy.[21] Moreover, non-traditional threats are not only considered as a security concern in the sub-state level, but are also considered security concerns in the regional and international level. The CS developed regional studies to focus on the security dynamics of the region.[22] In the post-U.S. war on terrorism in 2001, this approach has been widely used to articulate non-military issues such as immigration, health, political dissidence, and others.[23] Furthermore, the securitization approach is capable of describing the states foreign policy towards the securitized issues in other state, for instance, "*a process of using foreign aid to advance the donor governments' national security*".[24]

Accordingly, this book depends on certain norms from the securitization approach to fill the vacuum in traditional theories including neo-realism. It helps to understand the major changes in Yemen-U.S. relations after the 9/11 attacks and how the internal factors came to shape the relationship. The alternative approach of the security concept provides researchers the ability to articulate the new security perspective adopted by the international community including the U.S. and the securitization of Yemen's internal challenges. It assists in tracing and following changes in the rules of the game between Great states and small states. More pointedly, it explains why and how U.S. policy-makers considered certain internal factors in Yemen as threats to their homeland security such as the weakness of the government, economic and social challenges, and the potential of Yemen becoming a failed state.

1.3 Yemen-U.S. Relations in Literature Review

The subject of Yemen-U.S. relations is considered to be among the current and vital issues in Middle Eastern regional affairs. The literature on Yemen-U.S.

relations may appear multiple and varied. Nevertheless, the perception among many of those interested in Yemen-U.S. affairs is that the related studies remain few, insufficient, and predominantly address generalities. After the rise of al-Qaeda in Yemen as a force that threatens international interests, Yemen has become an important subject in the fields of international relations and strategic studies. The first problem faced by researchers is the lack of English literature on the dynamics and systems of governance in Yemen.[25] This section attempts to cover the available studies on Yemen-U.S. relations and brings to the fore the potential contributions of this dissertation.

The available literature that addresses Yemen-U.S. relations can be classified into two namely the general and literature that directly addresses this relationship. The general literature is that which is widely available and popular. It helps to understand the U.S. policy towards a number of states, including Yemen. Most of the studies have implicitly covered the U.S. foreign policy on Yemen although they may not specifically name Yemen. It explains the attitude and objectives of U.S. vis-à-vis the general attitude and objective of other countries including Yemen according to its geographical position or cultural identity.

Some studies address Yemen through the U.S. relationship with the third world.[26] Such studies focus on the factors that govern U.S. foreign policy toward the third world. These factors have changed throughout the various stages of U.S. foreign policy such as isolation, and their involvement in the Cold War and the post–Cold War. Among the general characteristics of such studies is that they don't specifically focus on Yemen, or its regional states. However, they help explain what determines U.S. foreign policy towards third-world countries.

Regionally, many researchers consider Yemen to be a part of three groups namely the Middle East, Arab Countries, and the Horn of Africa. They have studied the general features of the U.S. foreign policy and its objectives, external determines, and reactions according to the countries under these categories.[27] These studies predominantly address issues such as the Arab-Israeli conflict and democratization and terrorism in the region. The discourse is general in nature and fails to specifically study the U.S. position towards Yemen. Such studies fail to properly present the reality of the relations between the two countries and overlook the dynamics that govern those relationships.

In contrast, the literature that directly addresses the bilateral relations between Yemen and U.S. can be divided into two parts namely comprehensive studies and limited studies. Comprehensive studies cover all aspects and issues between the two countries in a specific period. In many cases, the comprehensive studies are based on a description of a massive collection of historical sequences of events. These studies do not offer an in-depth interpretation of the factors behind such events, as will be seen later.

A number of dissertations have adopted the overall trend in the study of Yemen-U.S. relations. The doctoral dissertation by Ahmad al-Madhaji titled *"Yemen and the United States, A Study of a Small Power and Super-State Relationship 1962-1994"*, is one of these. Undoubtedly, the examination of the relations between a Great power with a small state raise questions such as how a small power has maintained a degree of freedom to manoeuvre in deciding its foreign policy to the extent that a great power and small state benefited from their relations.[28] It tried to answer the above questions and to cover the different stations of diplomatic relations between the two countries; U.S. recognition of YAR 1962, severance of diplomatic relations 1967, restoration of relations 1972, and the Yemen unification in 1990 which coincided with the first Gulf War 1991.

In spite of the wide variety of sources used in al-Madhaji's dissertation, it did not use a theoretical framework and failed to cover the 1994 War in Yemen and the events that followed. Furthermore, Yemen-U.S. relations have been studied from a limited framework al-Madhaji emphasizes the relationship of a great power with an emerging nation that spanned three decades. The relationship was shrouded in Cold War politics and was constrained by the United States' role in the Arab-Israel conflict. It reflects the degree of freedom that an emerging state enjoys in determining its foreign policy.[29] However, this book is characterized by coherence and cohesion in addition to the adoption of a wide variety of sources, both primary and secondary.

In the period between the unification of Yemen in 1990 and the 9/11 attacks in 2001, Yemen-U.S. relations have witnessed a change in their relations, particularly in four crucial turning points. Bakeel al-Zandani explained the diplomatic positions between the two countries in this four events namely the Yemeni unity in 1990, the Iraqi invasion of Kuwait in 1990, the Yemeni Civil War in 1994, and the attacks of September 11. The main argument in his dissertation assumes that the economic, social, and political problems in Yemen led to the convergence of interests between the U.S. Administration and the Yemeni government in their war on terror.[30] In addition, he argues that *"U.S.-Yemen relations were transformed in the latter half of the 1990s up to 2003 for several reasons, among them is the strained American-Saudi and Saudi-Yemen relations, and the rise of terrorism".*[31]

Regardless of the limited temporal and objective framework, the main weakness of Bakeel's work is weak primary sources, particularly interviews and similar to the study of Salwa Dammaj ignores the theoretical framework. Dammaj's work is also considered within the comprehensive category in the litterateur of Yemen-U.S. relations. Her master thesis is close to context of al-Madhaji's dissertation in that she focused her study on the relationship between a great power and a small state. She states that the study reflects an example of relationships between a great power and a small country.[32] In general, Dammaj's study contained an introduction and reviews of the historical background in chapter one and two, and then explored factors that effected Yemen-U.S. relations. It was limited to Yemen's strategic position, democracy and human rights, and economic cooperation as internal factors, and Gulf security and normalizing relations with Israel as external factors.

Her study ignores several effective internal and external factors such as Great powers rivalry, U.S. interest in the Horn of Africa, al-Qaida in Yemen, and the region rivalry i.e. the Gulf Cooperation Council as well as the internal challenges of Yemen. Dammaj's study did not address the role of these dynamics in her analytical framework, although they briefly described a number of factors related to Yemen-U.S. relations. Her next chapter focused on U.S. and Yemen relations as represented in three events namely the unification of Yemen 1990, the position of both countries toward the Second Gulf War 1991, and the bombing of the *USS Cole* in 2000. Finally, the last chapter discussed the first year of relations in the aftermath of September 11, including the security and military cooperation.

Other limited studies are based on specialized studies on particular events, or aspects in the relationship. These kinds of studies often cover a number of important factors but neglect other factors in addition to providing a limited picture of the dynamics of relations. Many studies in this category address particular aspects such as the historical and diplomatic to name a few. Contemporary security issues in Yemen-U.S. relations have had the lion's share of attention followed by other mutual issues, as will become evident later.

Historically, '*Yemen and the Western World*' is a unique chronicle written by Eric Macro who addressed the revolution in Yemen and focused on commercial, political and military rivalry in South-West Arabia from 1571 to 1967. It has been recognized by the Great powers that Yemen is situated in a significant and strategic location. The ancient Great powers such as Portugal, Dutch, France, Turkey, Italy, Germany, and U.S. still sought a foothold in Yemen. This book presents the historical background of Yemen's relationship with the outside world and internal politics with special attention awarded to the affairs of South-West Arabia.

According to Eric Macro, the objective of his book was to show the alteration between political and military rivalry and trade activities in the 18th and 19th centuries.[33] Eric Macro also referred to the roots of the commercial relations between Yemen and the United States and the U.S. activities in the Red Sea between 1798 and 1840. The first United States vessel to call at one of the Arabian ports at the entrance of the Red Sea thus beating the enterprise captained by Richard Cleveland in 1797 was in 1796 by Captain Joseph Ropes.[34] Despite the importance of this book from a historical perspective, it focuses more on Yemen's relationship with European countries rather than with U.S.

Another book covering the first half of the twentieth century is titled *'The United States Activity in Yemen between the Two World Wars (1918-1939)'*, written in Arabic by Madeehah Darweesh. It is limited to a study of the American National Archive and highlights the activities of the U.S. Consulate in Aden.[35] This book helps to understand the activity of the U.S. missions in the region, at that time when the consulate of Aden was the only American consulate in the region.

Recently published literature still addresses the relations between Yemen-U.S. relations in the modern history, particularly, in the twentieth century, during the World Wars I and II, and in the Cold War era. One of these studies is titled *'Al-Alaqat al-Yamaniyah al-Amrikiyah 1904-1948, 'a'hd al-imam Yahiya Hamid al-Din'*, which was written in Arabic by Mohammed Jabarat in 2008.[36] He studied the relations between the Kingdom of Yemen (KOY) and the United States during the reign of Imam (King) Yahiya Hamid Al-Din. His book is a systematic historical study that attempts to shed light on Yemen-U.S. relations during the first half of the twentieth century.

In spite of his study being based on never before referred to documents, the result of the study did not highlight any new findings in the period between 1904 and1948. Jabarat's conclusion indicated the relations which started in 1910 as natural relations that often led to failure with the exception of the signing of the Treaty of Amity and Commerce in 1945. Furthermore, there was a shortcoming evident in the book's literature referring to its limited Arabic sources and did not include any English literature.[37]

The studies that address Yemen-U.S. relations in the Cold War era, in terms of security, often focused on a special aspect or dimension. Security was the most prominent in such literature. During the years 1962-1967, the revolution and the following crisis in north Yemen (Yemen Arab Republic- YAR), represented an important stage in Yemen's history on the regional or international level.

Due to the international competition in the Cold War era, several researchers were interested to study this period and presented the different roles of the great powers (U.S., UK, and USSR). Alexander Wieland's article titled *'Anglo-American Relations and the Yemeni Revolution, September 1962-February 1963' in 2009'* argued that the contradiction between the American and British position toward the Yemeni revolution produced tensions between London and Washington. The fact that the Yemeni revolution produced tensions between London and Washington should not have been a surprise since the leaders of both countries namely Prime Minister Harold Macmillan and President John F. Kennedy were close. The relationship deteriorated during the course of events in 1962.[38]

Alexander explained the different perspectives of the UK and the U.S. regarding their interactions with Yemen from September 1962 to February 1963. He emphasized that the British position toward Yemen was shaped by regional interests with some international implications. On the contrary, U.S. foreign policy was largely conditioned by international interests with regional implications. In short, one paragraph summarized his article *"The question which has gone largely unanswered, therefore, is why the British and Americans failed to see eye to eye in Yemen during the period 1962-63? Simon C. Smith argues that the root cause of the Anglo-American antagonism lay in the conflict between specific UK and U.S. (regional interests)."*[39]

Furthermore, Dana Adams Schmidt explained the war between the Yemeni Republic and the Yemeni Royalists and their alliances. In his book *'Yemen: The Unknown War'*, he described the revolution, the origins of the republic, the beginning of royalist resistance, and the role of outside powers. During the course of negotiations between Saudi Arabia, Egypt, and the royalists and republicans, Yemen-Saudi relations were studied via the efforts of the U.S. to restore peace.[40]

On the other hand, some scholars have studied the Yemen crisis of 1962-1967, from a narrow perspective. They did not directly address U.S.-Yemen relations, but their work reflected the pivotal role of the regional factor in Yemen-U.S. relations. Saeed Badeeb's work agreed with Dana Schmidt about the description of the U.S. foreign policy in the conflict on Yemen as schizophrenic. Saeed addressed this issue in chapter five of his book, *'The Saudi-Egyptian Conflict over North Yemen, 1962-1970'*. He examined the role of the United States in this war, and he confirmed that the U.S. amply demonstrated its mediatory and military role in Yemen from the beginning of the conflict.[41]

Additionally, Jesse Ferris in his doctoral *'Egypt, the Cold War, and the Civil War in Yemen, 1962-1966'*, examines Egypt's foreign policy and its relations with the United States through the lens of their positions in the Yemeni Civil War. Due to Egypt's five years of intervention in Yemen and the Saudi role to drag Washington to the point of confrontation with Egypt, U.S.-Egyptian relations were terribly affected, and this stage is considered the worst level in their relations since 1952.[42]

Furthermore, Christopher McMullen addressed this issue in his book *'Resolution of the Yemen Crisis, 1963: A Case Study in Mediation.'* He distanced himself from the historical writings of the 1963 Yemen crisis. The scope of his book attempted to bring to the fore the process of negotiations during the mission of John F. Kennedy's envoy, Ambassador Ellsworth Bunker. Although Christopher's work did not directly address the relationship between Yemen and the U.S., it illustrated one aspect of the U.S. intervention in Yemen and its position that was seeking to mediate between the conflicting parties.[43]

A new era has emerged with the advent of 1967. Southern Yemen ended the era of British colonial rule and established a new country in the southeast Arab peninsula called the "People's Republic of South Yemen (PRSY)". Two years later, a radical Marxist wing of National Front (NF) gained power and changed the country's name to the People's Democratic Republic of Yemen (PDRY). North Yemen ended the civil war between Republicans and Royalists and started to build the stability of the Yemen Arab Republic YAR. The aftermath of 1967 represented a new political dilemma faced by U.S. foreign policy. The People's Democratic Republic of Yemen PDRY gained fame as the only country in the Middle East that adopted the Marxist-Leninist ideology.

South Yemen's motivation to transform its foreign policy to a strategic alliance with the Soviet Union has been analysed by researchers. Al-Jahny Shiry in his doctoral dissertation, titled *'South Yemen and the Soviet Union, 1967-1986: A Study of a Small Power in an Alliance,'*[44] brought out some internal factors that shaped South Yemen's foreign policy and presented the influence of its alliance on the region during 1967 and 1986. He did not address the relations with the U.S. and limited his study to the Soviet Union, but he presented an analysis of the framework of South Yemen in its relations with other countries.

By the same token, the impact of the 1967 revolution on south Yemen foreign policy has been studied by Fred Halliday in his book, *'Revolution and Foreign Policy, the Case of South Yemen 1967-1987'*. This study addressed three aspects namely the international implications of the revolution, the historical events in the Arabian Peninsula, and the foreign policies of the third world states. Halliday specifically referred to Washington's stance on the crisis in 1968 and the causes of a rupture in Aden-Washington relations. His study points out the disputes between the U.S. and South Yemen manifested in at least three events in which contradiction was evident. One was the Arab-Israeli issue, another the Indian Ocean which had become an area of U.S.-Soviet rivalry, and the third was the Horn of Africa in which the PDRY supported the Eritrean guerrillas and Somalia. While the issues varied, South Yemen-U.S. relations were almost continuously hostile throughout the post-1967 period.[45]

Another security issue in Yemen-U.S. relations depends on the mutual events after the 9/11 attacks. After the U.S. announced its war on terrorism, there was a clear change in its method of dealing with Yemen. Therefore, recently, many studies, books, articles and international conferences have focused on counter-terrorism in the Republic of Yemen (ROY) and its influence on Western states. In spite of this international focus on Yemen, Yemen's relations with the U.S. suffered from a lack of academic resources. The studies, as will be noted, were based on the description of the relationship as a result of the two countries' positions without regard to the dynamics that shaped those attitudes or relationships.

However, there are a number of studies that have focused on the issue of security in the Yemen–U.S. partnership to counter terrorism and its related issues. Some of these studies deal with the U.S. perspective and its foreign policy. For example, Richard Rosthauser brought out the American official response to some terrorist operations in Yemen such as the *Yemen Hotel* bombing in 1992, the *USS Cole* bombing in 2001 and the U.S. Embassy bombing In Sana'a in 2008.[46] Richard Rosthauser 2010, in his dissertation, titled *'Terrorism Conflict: How the United States Responds to al-Qaeda Violence and Expressed Grievances'* shows al-Qaeda's grievances in these events as well as provides a brief section on the negotiation between U.S. and Yemen. This study included many of the events and details, but it was limited to secondary sources with the exception of certain statements by U.S. officials. It also ignored the conflict between the positions of Yemen with the U.S.

Ahmed al-Zandani examined the impact of George W. Bush's discourse on Arab countries after the events of 9/11 event until 2005.[47] He selected Syria, Egypt, and Saudi Arabia as case studies. The study's findings may be applied to Yemen, particularly, the Egyptian model. He emphasizes that the American demands revolved around three major issues namely waging war on "terrorism," applying liberal democracy and liberal economy. Consequently, these countries were incapable of fully consenting to the American demands because of the internal pressures. As a result, he adds, *"the selected states opted to maneuver as they reluctantly respond to the Bush demands."*

From a different perspective, new published books and dissertations all address terrorism and its impact on the country from the Yemeni perspective. For instance, Noha Abdullah al-Sadsy 2005 in her master dissertation, studied the change in Yemen foreign policy towards U.S. after the events of 9/11. She explored terrorism in Yemen and their national measures. The study is limited to Yemen's internal issues and covered just four years of its partnership with U.S. in the war on terrorism.[48] Furthermore, Nabiel al-Razaqi, in his published doctoral dissertation 2010, assessed the influence of the phenomenon of terrorism on Yemen's national security. He addressed the changes in Yemen's relations with the great states including the U.S., which are considered as threats to Yemen national security.[49]

By the same token, several other articles, conferences, and reports dealt with one of the aspects such as the development, economy and others that are adopted by each of the two countries. In general, these literatures often reflect the agenda of the foreign policy of one without the other such as the above work mentioned, namely al-Sadsy and al-Razaqi. They do not reflect the nature of relations between the two countries and provide the point of view of one party.

The above criticism also corresponds to the following studies. The master thesis by Abad al-Ghany al-Shamcri 2008 was based on the study of U.S. foreign policy towards the experience of democracy in Yemen. Although its analysis of the factors behind the U.S. foreign policy on this issue, he did not indicate the impact of such attitudes on the relationship.[50] In the same way, the master thesis of Daniel R. Mahanty 2010 discusses how the security concern on al-Qaeda in Yemen changed the standards of U.S. aid to Yemen.[51] He criticizes the national security policymakers because they ignored the standards of development and economic aid such as aid effectiveness. His description of this issue is aid for the dilemma of security. Despite the importance of such studies, they do not address Yemen-U.S. relations and do not explain the impact of U.S. aid in those relations.

In summary, the literature hitherto discussed, whether general or, did not provide explanations of the questions under consideration in the current study. For example, the change in the global system and its ideology and agenda, the national and regional conflicts, and the social and economic challenges that threaten the Yemeni regime were not discussed. These factors were not subjected to evaluation and comparison in previous studies. Furthermore, these include some events which were brought out in the post-Cold War era and created new phases in the Yemen-U.S. relations. These events are yet to be addressed.

Although the above studies are written from the view of the overall relations and specific aspects, it seems that there is a lack of studies that focus on the external and internal dynamics in different phases of Yemen-U.S. relations. Moreover, the vital external or internal dynamics are very different from one stage to another, i.e., Cold War, post-Cold War, and the aftermath of 9/11. This study argues that the traditional view of the main factors that shaped the relationship between the two countries changed in the post-Cold War era. For instance, this study emphasizes the stability of Yemen as an objective of the U.S. foreign policy, not only because of the importance of the stability of Yemen's neighbors, but also for the protection of the U.S. national security and international security.

1.4 Significance of the Book

The existing studies have not rigorously focused on the external and internal dynamics in Yemen-U.S. relations. On the subject of the early literature, there are insufficient studies covering Yemen-U.S. relations, particularly, on the period of the global war on terrorism, and on the assessment of the role of internal and external dynamics. As a result, this book differs as it can be considered the first work that examines the dynamics and their transformations that shaped the two countries' relations. It is based on the wider range of constraints and dynamics influencing the Yemen-U.S. relations. In addition, it tries to fill the lacuna in the literature on bilateral relations after 9/11. The book also highlights the future of Yemen and U.S. relations in the light of a careful analysis of the external and internal drives of the relations between the two countries.

The subjects tackled in this research are crucial as they deal with one of the most critical issues in foreign policy and the dilemma of security. It might be the first book that attempts to provide a new interpretation of the inconsistencies that permeate Yemen-U.S. relations and as such explores and explains the role of different dynamics, which shaped the two countries' relations in different stages. Furthermore, the book provides a good example of shifts in the international relations, in particularly in the security environment following the events of 9/11.

The book considers Yemen as a case study for the reflection of various factors on international relations and the security dilemma in this era. This increases the importance of the study for several reasons. First, the significance of the book includes a practical implication. Second, it reflects an example of the war on terrorism from the perspectives of the great powers and a small and developing state. Finally, the Republic of Yemen occupied a global significance within the context of GWOT, as it recently represented a battlefield for the war against al-Qaeda in the Arabian Peninsula AQAP that threatened international interests.

Furthermore, the book adopts a qualitative approach. This approach relies on data collected from different resources, and systemic methods to analyze it. The resources are divided into primary and secondary resources. The book relied on a wide variety of primary resources such as documents, published and unpublished minutes of meetings, official statements, etc. Many published documents represent studies by many researchers that can be referred to for re-examination. In addition, some recent documents and correspondences were not previously available.[52]

The book includes several personal interviews with government officer, in particular in what concerns security in addition with experts in the development and economic sectors. It also includes an interview with a member in the Jihadist groups in Yemen and the *Houthi* movement. The book also focuses on various reports issued by the decision-making centres in many agencies, both in the United States and Yemen, especially those reports that were submitted to the White House or the U.S. Congress by the Department of State, Defence Department. Announcements, official statements as well as statistical data are also other primary resources.

The book also relied on enormous secondary resources such as books, articles, theses, scientific researches or periodicals, and news. Such resources are available in Malaysia, Yemen, and the U.S.

1.5 Chapterisation

The book is divided into five chapters. Chapter two examines the evolution and history of Yemen-U.S. relations from the beginning of the 18th century until the early 60s of the 20th century. It evaluates the dynamics of these relations, both those which enhanced or declined their relations during three phases of time namely the colonial era, WW I and II, and the period of Imam Ahmed's rule.

Chapter three of the book attempts to identify the external dynamics that shaped Yemen-U.S. relations. The first section examines the strategic location and regional factors includes the contradiction of Yemen and U.S. policies on regional issues. In the second section, it studies the improvement of Yemen-U.S. relations due to the influence of the Cold War. The following two sections discuss the effect of Yemen-U.S. relations according to two external dynamics namely democratization and the human rights agenda and the global war on terrorism.

Chapter four determines the role of the internal factors that influence Yemen-U.S. relations. This will be examined by looking at the factors of the Jihadist groups emergence in Yemen, the influence of the strategic Yemen-U.S. partnership against al-Qaeda in Yemen, Yemen's economic and development needs, in addition to the Yemen internal conflict and the potential of becoming a failed state.

Chapter five draws important conclusions and highlights how changes in factors have shaped Yemeni-American relations and its role in anticipating the future of relations.

[1] For further reading, Saeed M. Badeeb. *The Saudi-Egyptian Conflict over North Yemen, 1962-1970* (Boulder, Washington DC: Westview Press and American-Arab Affairs Council, 1986). And see, Dana Adams Schmidt. *Yemen: The Unknown War* (London: Bodley Head, 1968).

[2] Michele Kelemen. "Clinton: Yemen Instability Threatens World." *NPR news* (January 4, 2010), accessed 12/3/2011, http://www.npr.org/templates/story/story.php?storyId=122226355

[3] Mohammed Jamal Al-Khraisha. "Evaluating Theories of Liberal Hegemony and Small States in US-Jordanian Relations since 2000." (PhD Thesis, Nottingham Trent University, 2010), pp. 67-68.

[4] Ibid., p. 69.

[5] MauriceA East. "Foreign Policy-Making in Small States: Some Theoretic Observations Based on a Study of the Uganda Ministry of Foreign Affairs." *Policy Sciences* 4, no. 4 (1973), p. 491.

[6] Robert Owen Keohane. *Neorealism and Its Critics* (New York: Columbia University Press, 1986), pp. 211-212.

[7] Mohammed Jamal Al-Khraisha. "Evaluating Theories of Liberal Hegemony and Small States in US-Jordanian Relations since 2000.", pp. 67-68 And see, Charles W. Kegley. *Controversies in International Relations Theory: Realism and the Neoliberal Challenge* (New York: St. Martin's Press, 1995), pp. 1-24.

[8] Peter Hough. *Understanding Global Security* (London: Routledge, 2008), p.3.

[9] Kenneth Waltz. *Man, the State, and War* (New York: Columbia University Press, 1959), p. 160.

[10] Kenneth Waltz. *Theory of International Politics* (New York: Random House, 1979), pp. 79-101.

[11] Andrew Jones. "Comparatively Assess Neo-Realism and Neo-Liberalism. Whose Argument Do You Find the More Convincing and Why?." *E-IR Articles* (2007), accessed 3/6/2010, http://www.e-ir.info/

[12] Steven L. Lamy. "Contemporary Mainstream Approaches: Neo-Realism and Neo-Liberalism." In *The Globalization of World Politics: An Introduction to International Relations*, (ed.) John Baylis, Steve Smith, and Patricia Owens. (New York: Oxford University Press, 2008), p. 133.

[13] Peter Hough. *Understanding Global Security*, p. 3.

[14] Hans J. Morgenthau. "Another 'Great Debate': The National Interest of the United States." *The American Political Science Review* 46, no. 4 (1982), p. 973.

[15] Jack Donnelly. "Realism." In *Theories of International Relations*, (ed.) Scott Burchill and Andrew Linklater. (Houndmills, Basingstoke: Palgrave, 2005), p. 42.

[16] Robert O. Keohane. *After Hegemony: Cooperation and Discord in the World Political Economy* (Princeton, NJ: Princeton University Press, 1984), pp. 31-39.

[17] Peter Hough. *Understanding Global Security*, p. 9.

[18] Barry Buzan. *People, States and Fear: The National Security Problem in Unternational Relation* (Sussex: John Spiers, 1983), pp. 8-20.

[19] Marianne Stone. "Security According to Buzan: A Comprehensive Security Analysis." *Security Discussion Papers Series* (2009), accessed 6/9/2011 http://geest.msh-paris.fr/IMG/pdf/Secur-ity_for_Buzan.mp3.pdf, p. 4.

[20] Olaf Corry. "Securitzation and 'Riskization': Two Grammars of Security" (paper presented at the 7th Pan-European International Relations Conference, Stockholm: September, 2010), p. 10.

[21] Barry Buzan, Ole Wæver and Jaap De Wilde. *Security: A New Framework for Analysis* (Boulder, CO: Lynne Rienner Publishers, 1998), p.43.

[22] Catherine Charrett. "Taking on the Normative Dilemma of Writing Securitization: A Critical Approach" (Masters Dissertation, London School of Economics, 2008), pp.2-9.

[23] Matt McDonald. "Securitization and the Construction of Security." *European Journal of International Relations* 14, no. 4 (2008), pp. 1-36.

[24] Jaroslav Petřík. "Securitization of Official Development Aid: Analysis of Current Debate." In *International Peace Research Conference* (Leuven, Belgium: Conflict Resolution and Peace-Building Commission, 14-19 July, 2008), accessed 3/2/2010, https://is.muni.cz/www/52839/pub03.pdf.

[25] John Anthony. "Introductory." (paper presented at the Yemen Headlined: Contemporary Myths And Empirical Realities, Washington, DC: December 10, 2009), p. 2.

[26] For instance, Ted Hopf. *Peripheral Visions: Deterrence Theory and American Foreign Policy in the Third World, 1965-1990* (Ann Arbor: University of Michigan Press, 1994), pp. 170-190. Also refer to, Robert S. Snyder. "The US And Third World Revolutionary States: Understanding the Breakdown in Relations." *International Studies Quarterly* 43, no. 2 (1999), pp. 265–290.

[27] For instance, Katerina Dalacoura. "US Democracy Promotion in the Arab Middle East since 11 September 2001: A Critique." *International Affairs* 81, no. 5 (October, 2005), pp. 963–979.

[28] For further more example see, Kari M. Hiepko-Odermann. "Latvian-American Relations in the 20th Century: The Study of a Great Power and a Small State." (PhD Thesis, Freie Universität, 2009).

[29] Ahmed Noman Kassim Almadhagi. *Yemen and the United States: The Study of a Small Power and Super-State Relationship 1962–1994* (London, New York: I.B.Tauris Publishers, 1996), p. 1.

[30] Bakeel A. aL-Zandani. "US-Yemen Relations in a Changing World: A Study of Four Major Events in US-Yemen Relations." (Master Thesis, Long Island University, 2003), p. i.

[31] Ibid.

[32] Salwa A. Dammag. "A Study Yemen-United States Relations 1990-2002." (Master Thesis, University of Malaya, 2005), p. 3.

[33] Eric Macro. *Yemen and the Western World, since 1571* (New York: Praeger, 1968), p. 1.

[34] Ibid., p. 23.

[35] Madeehah Darweesh. *Nashat Al-Americi Fi Al-Yemen Ma Bayn Al-Harbain Al-Alamytiene 1981-1939, Men Waqea Al-Ershief Al-Consulia Al-Americia Fi Aden* (Al-Qahera: al-Hayaa al-Aamma lel-Ketab, 2002), p. 15.

[36] Mahmud Hamlan Jabarat. *Alaqat Al-Yamaniyah Al-Amrikiyah 1904-1948, 'Ahd Al-Imam Yahiya Hamid Al-Din* (Amman: Moaassat Alamam Zaied, 2008).

[37] Ibid., pp. 315-17.

[38] Alexander R. Wieland. "Anglo-American Relations and the Yemeni Revolution, 1962-1963." *Cold War Sudies* (2009), accessed 18/2/2011, www2.lse.ac.uk/IDEAS/publications/workingPapers/wiela-nd.pdf, p. 5.

[39] Ibid., p. 7.

[40] Dana Adams Schmidt. *Yemen: The Unknown War*, p. 16.

[41] Saeed M. Badeeb. *The Saudi-Egyptian Conflict over North Yemen, 1962-1970*, p. 61.

[42] Jesse Ferris. "Egypt, the Cold War, and the Civil War in Yemen, 1962-1966." (PhD Thesis, Princeton University, 2008), p. 349.

[43] Christopher J. McMullen. *Resolution of the Yemen Crisis 1963 a Case Study in Mediation* (Washington DC: University Press of America, 1985).

[44] Shiry Al-Jahny. "South Yemen and the Soviet Union, 1967-1986: A Study of a Small Power in an Alliance." (PhD Thesis, George Washington University, 1991).

[45] Fred Halliday. *Revolution and Foreign Policy the Case of South Yemen 1967-1987* (New York: Cambridge University Press, 1990), pp. 79-80.

[46] Richard Rosthauser. "Terrorism Conflict: How the United States Responds to Al-Qaeda Violence and Expressed Grievances." (Master Thesis, University of Denver, 2010), pp. 74-162.

[47] Ahmed al-Zandani. "Political Discourse of George W. Bush and Its Impact on the Policies of Selected Arab Countries of the Middle East, 2001-2005." (PhD Thesis, International Islamic University Malaysia, 2009).

[48] Noha Abdullah al-Sadsy. "Ath'er Th'aherat Al-Erhab Aldoaly A'la Alsyasah Al-Yemeniah Ak'ab Ah'dath' Alhadie Ashar Men September." (Master Thesis, Cairo University, 2005).

[49] Nabiel al-Razaqi. *Ath'er D'aherat Al-Erhab A'la Al-A'mn Al-Q'aomy Alyemeni* (Sana'a: Markaz Abady Llderast wa Alnasher, 2010).

[50] Abad al-Ghany al-Shameri. "Alsiasah Alk'argiah Tegah Altagrabah Aldemok'ratiah Alyemeniah 1990-2006." (Master Thesis, Sana'a University, 2008).

[51] Daniel R. Mahanty. "The Aid for Security Dilemma: The Distortive Impact of US National Security Interests on Development Assistance." (Master Thesis, Georgetown University, 2010).

[52] Some documents have been published recently by the American National Archive, or leaked by others such as *Wikileaks* website, which published hundreds of documents on Yemen and its relationship with the United States in different areas.

CHAPTER TWO:
THE EARLY YEARS OF YEMEN-U.S.
RELATIONS

2.1 Introduction

The chronological background of Yemen-U.S. relations has been subjected to actions of colonial powers. These powers sought to maintain their global affluence by dominating the strategic location and resources of the colony states. A good example of such actions was the Portuguese occupation of the Strait of Hormuz and the Yemeni Island Socotra in 1506, and the Island of Bahrain in 1515 and the Straits of Malacca between 1511 to 1641.[1] Subsequent to the colonial era, colonial powers, namely Great Britain and the Ottoman Empire, expressed their colonial interests in the design and application of their respective foreign policies which have effectively affected both U.S. and Yemen after their respective independence.

In this context, the colonial policy between the 16th and 20th centuries prevented Yemen from establishing global relations with other nations including U.S. whereby American traders were prevented access and Christian missions were prohibited from establishing relations with Yemen. The end of World War I saw a change in global politics and represented the starting point of a new relationship, which included new factors that affected the relationship. The Yemen-U.S. mutual diplomatic relationship began after World War II and was affected by the interests of American allies in the region as well as the change of leadership in Yemen.

This chapter highlights the historical background of Yemen-U.S. relations from the beginning of the 18th century through to the mid-20th century. Despite the weakness of the bilateral relations between the two countries during this period, this chapter aims to identify the early external and internal factors that strengthened or weakened the relationship. The time frame that is the subject of scrutiny in this book can be organized into three interrelated sections. Section one covers the origins of relationship whereby Yemen was under British and Ottoman colonial rule. Section two discusses Yemen-U.S. relations during World War I and II after the independence of North Yemen while the South remained colonized. Section three focuses on the period after the mutual recognition between Yemen and U.S. in 1946. It highlights the factors behind mutual diplomatic relations and its development during the Imam Ahmed period.

Map 2.1: The Colonial Arab States

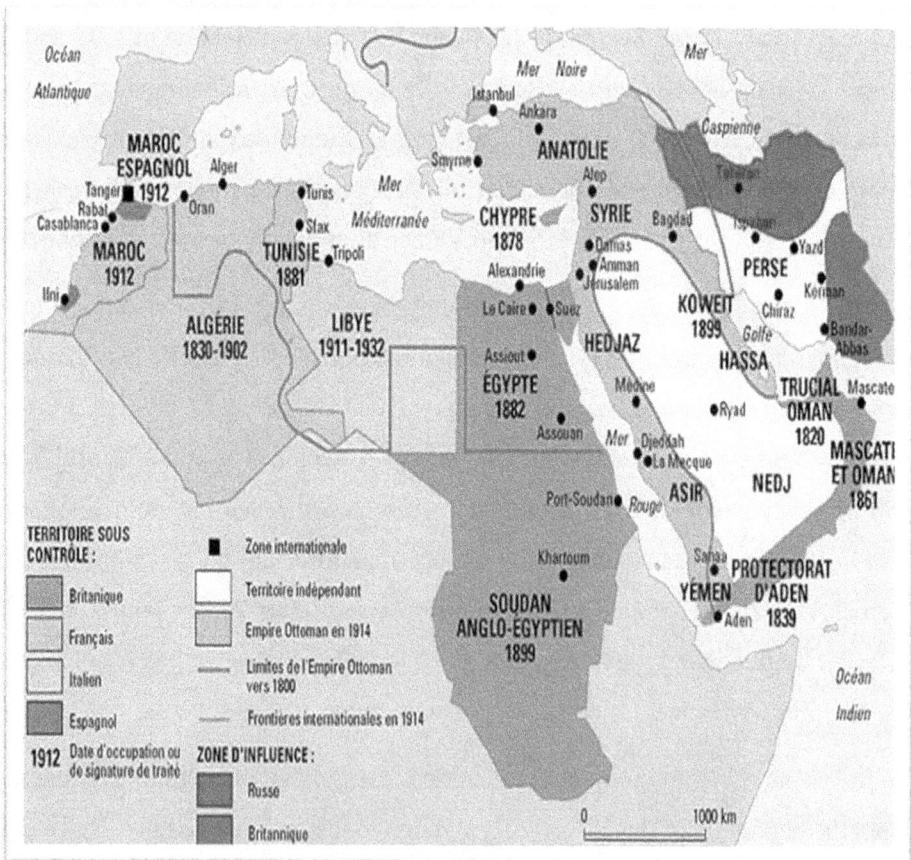

Source: Wordpress. accessed 12/11/2011,
http://bobblincoe.files.wordpress.com/2011/05/frenchcolonial.jpg.

2.2   The Relationship under British and Ottoman Colonial Rule

Yemen-U.S. relations can be traced back to the 18th century, twenty years after the declaration of the independence of the United States of America while Yemen remained colonized until the early 20th century. In modern history, the British Empire occupied Aden harbor in South Yemen in 1839, and then expanded to establish what became known as the 'Aden Protectorate'. This forced the Ottoman Empire to settle in the northern part of Yemen in 1872. Thus, colonization by British and Ottoman divided Yemen into two parts, North and South.[2] North Yemen became independent in 1918 which coincided with the establishment of the Kingdom of Yemen that lasted until 1962. Southern Yemen remained under British colonial rule until 1967.

While Yemen remained colonized, two factors initiated and formed Yemen-U.S. relations. Yemen-U.S. commercial relations began in 1798 and were further supported by American missionaries in the late 19th century. Regardless of the early trade exchange between the two countries, official relations and direct correspondence remained non-existent until the early twentieth century. The following discussion attempts to bring to the fore the shape and form of early Yemen-U.S. relations up till the independence of North Yemen in 1918. It also endeavors to explore how the colonial powers attempted to prevent the establishment of this relationship.

Commercial interests form the oldest identifiable motive that attracted the attention of American merchants towards Yemen. Trade between Yemen and the U.S. can be traced back to as early as the eighteenth century. The Yemeni coffee internationally known as 'Mocha Coffee' and leather were the most important Yemeni products exported to U.S., while America's exports to Yemen include kerosene and cotton textiles.[3] Such trade exchange was affected through U.S. ships such as *Recovery* which was the first American ship to reach the port of Mocha in 1798.[4] *Recovery* was also the first American ship to reach an Arab port in the Red Sea.[5] Mocha coffee became well known and was in high demand in the U.S. more so than Brazilian coffee.[6] In its second trip in 1801, *Recovery* returned from the port of Mocha with 326,000 tons of coffee. The success of such American trips opened the door to greater bilateral trade. This resulted in a notable increase in maritime trade. In 1809 the ship named *Ulysses* returned to U.S. with two million pounds of Yemeni coffee on board. In 1826, when famine spread throughout Yemen, an American vessel named *Ann* carried tons of food to Mocha.[7]

English merchants competed with the Americans in regards to coffee exports from Yemen. They attempted to impede the Yemen-U.S. coffee trade by offering to buy Yemeni coffee at higher prices. This lead American merchants to offer prices higher than those offered by the British which eventually led them to monopolize the Yemeni coffee trade.[8] Such commercial competition motivated the American merchants to extend their official presence in the port of Mocha by establishing the United States Commercial Centre. This allowed the Americans to raise the U.S. flag on Yemen territory for the first time. Furthermore, American merchants attempted to persuade the Imam of Yemen to accept their offer to open the first U.S. factory in Yemen.[9] The Imam was not enthusiastic of this idea due to the absence of any mutual official recognition of the relationship between the two countries despite the promises made by American merchants of official government recognition.[10]

In spite of America's increasing economic presence in Yemen, Yemen-U.S. commercial relations did not lead to the development of political relations between the two countries as might have been expected. The Ottoman and British empires constituted the main reason that delayed the development of Yemen-U.S. political relations during the eighteenth century. The U.S. commercial relations with Yemen depended on monopolizing the Yemeni coffee market for more than half a century. Eric Macro emphasized that in spite of the short period of Yemen-U.S. trade relations, it was enough to enhance the British ambition in controlling Eastern and Southern Arabia. The Britain-Yemen coffee trade was overthrown by the American merchants; an event that led further enflamed British colonial interests in the region.[11]

In 1820, out of its quest to enhance its regional influence, warships belonging to the British Empire reached the shores of the Red Sea and bombarded the Port of Mocha. Nineteen years later, Britain occupied the Yemeni city of Aden on the coast of the Arabian Sea.[12] Some of the generals of the British Navy urged their leaders to occupy Aden for several reasons among them were to prevent the penetration of Ottomans, to exploit the strategic location of the city of Aden which would represent an important commercial center for the British Empire, to enable them to use its ports to supply their ships, and to protect the trade route between Britain and its colonies in India.[13]

Great Britain was not the only stumbling block impeding the emergence of Yemen-U.S. relations, the Ottoman Empire likewise played an important role in the region and competed with British ambitions in Yemen. From 1818 to 1841, the western coasts of Yemen were under the control of Muhammad Ali Pasha, who ruled Egypt and was the most important Ottoman military leader. Pasha led a coup against the Ottomans and attempted to expand his influence by deploying his army in the Arabian Peninsula. Accordingly, Britain was aware that its commercial and military interests were threatened and quickly reacted by bombarding the port of Mocha in 1820 as a means to emphasize its influence on the western coasts of Yemen.[14] In 1839 it colonized Aden and established further consolidated its power and regional importance. After the opening of the Suez Canal in 1869, the strategic importance of the western coasts of Yemen grew, and with it the southern coasts. In light of its growing importance, the Ottoman Empire increased its efforts to control the parts of Yemen that overlook the Red Sea.[15] The two Empires divided Yemen and its coasts between them. It is possible to say that from the mid-nineteenth century to the World War I, Yemen became a place of conflict between the two great powers, Britain and Ottoman.[16]

As a consequence of imperial competition for Yemen, Yemen-U.S. commercial relations were forced to take on an indirect nature; that is, American goods were delivered to Yemen through Aden and Masqat in Oman, while Yemeni goods were passed to U.S. ships through ports in Aden and Jeddah. The U.S. was aware of the intense rivalry between the British and the Ottomans and as such it attempted to maintain good relations with one or the other rival powers in Yemen. The U.S. State Department appointed an American trader who was residing in Aden as an Honorary Consul in 1879, but the official consulate opened in Aden in 1895.[17] The funding of the U.S. consulate in Aden was to facilitate trade and provide consultation services to the American merchants in Yemen as well as to serve the U.S. interests in the region. At the time, U.S. diplomatic missions were very limited in the region. The U.S. administration valued its presence in the region through its consulate in Aden, which also represented the Arab peninsula and the southern parts of the Red Sea.[18]

American Missionaries in Yemen

The importance of the American missionaries as part of U.S. foreign policy was no less important than its commercial interests. According to Glenn Hastedt, *"The missionaries in the Middle East and their patrons at home worked diligently to influence government policy and enjoyed mixed success. Missionaries themselves received consular or diplomatic appointments in Athens, Beirut, and Constantinople. Encouraged by an ABCFM lobbyist,[19] Secretary of State Daniel Webster wrote Porter in 1842 that missionaries should be assisted 'in the same manner' as merchants".[20]* U.S. missionary bodies had a presence in Yemen by the end of the 19th century. These included the American Dutch Reformed Church, which received a response in the region in general.[21]

Yemen-U.S. relations improved through the efforts of American missionaries especially when Dr, Samuel Zwemmer, a member of the Arab delegation that belongs to the American Dutch Reformed Church, visited Sana'a in the period between 1892 and 1895.[22] Another American preacher, Charles F. Camp, settled with his family in the Yemeni town *Manakha* in 1905. Charles F. Camp was later killed by a Turk and his wife left Yemen.[23] At the beginning of the 20th century, the Dutch Reformed Church in the United States was met with a hostile Turkish campaign in Yemen. American missionaries in the Ottoman territory represented one of the thorny issues in the U.S.-Ottoman relations.[24] The official attitudes of the Ottomans towards the American missionaries represented a point of pressure on the U.S. at that time, the Turks' involvement in the killing of Charles K. Moser formed part of the reaction towards the U.S. and its missionaries for supporting the Armenian issue.[25]

Therefore, in 1910 the U.S. sent its consul in Aden, Charles K. Moser, to participate in the investigating with the Imam of Yemen, who expressed his willingness to cooperate with the American envoy.[26] Meetings between the administration of Imam Yahiya and the U.S. strengthened relations between both countries. The Imam of Yemen offered greater protection to American nationals than the Ottomans did. These joint negotiations provided the opportunity for U.S. to strengthen its ties with Yemen.

Accordingly, the U.S. counselor suggested signing a peace treaty with Imam of Yemen 'Yahiya'. However, Yemeni leaders were not interested in a treaty with the U.S. because of the great distance separating the two countries and the absence of wide economic benefits between Yemen and the U.S.[27] There was however a notable change in political attitudes after the First World War which merits an examination to the internal and external factors that helped bring about this change.

2.3   The Relationship between WW 1 and II

With the end of the First World War, the Ottoman Empire withdrew its troops from North Yemen's territories. On the other hand, the U.S. adopted a foreign policy more open than ever before. Its new foreign policy and the withdrawal of the Ottomans paved the way for a new configuration in Yemen-U.S. relations but there was no mutual diplomatic recognition between Yemen and the U.S. until the end of the Second World War. However, several factors hindered the development of relations between the two countries. Firstly, as a result of the colonial legacy both countries had adopted the policy of isolation. Another factor was the involvement of Yemen in conflicts with American allies in the region, whether with Britain in Southern Yemen or with the Kingdom of Saudi Arabia in the north.

The third factor is the continuation of British colonial rule in Southern Yemen, as well as the U.S. obligation to remain neutral in issues concerning Yemen. As a result, relations between the two countries remained unofficial. Despite such obstacles, the relations between the two countries, in this period, witnessed a new phase characterized by a degree of political openness and an increased presence of U.S. companies, in addition to the U.S. commitment to maintaining the stability of Yemen and the region. Furthermore, direct communication between decision-makers from both countries resulted in joint construction and development projects in Yemen.

In addition to the aforementioned factors, this section highlights the emergence of new factors after the WW I. In subsequent discussion, it examines the influence of those factors particularly the independence of North Yemen, the change of U.S. foreign policy after WW I and the Yemen response as well as the American stance concerning Yemen's conflict with Britain and Saudi Arabia.

First of all, due to the change in the international environment, Yemen adopted an open policy towards the U.S. On 31 October 1914, the Ottoman Empire declared its support of Germany against France, Italy, and England. After four years, the Ottoman Empire was defeated by England and its allies, which led the Ottomans to withdraw its troops from Yemen.[28] In November 1918, Imam Yahya of Yemen became the legitimate heir of the Ottoman Empire

Yahya Muhammad Hamid ed-Din

in Yemen and established the Kingdom of Yemen (KOY).[29] As Imam Yahiya also inherited the Ottoman hostility with Britain, he asked Britain to hand over all occupied territories. In response, Britain offered to recognize the independence of the KOY in exchange for their non-interfering in the 'Aden Protectorate' but the Imam refused to abandon any part of Yemen.[30]

The foreign relations of the monarchy in Yemen were characterized by isolationism, suspicion, and caution.[31] Its foreign policy, especially with the Western world, was built to avoid the western greediness that surrounded the Arab World at that time.[32] With regard to his relations with U.S., Imam Yahiya was aware that U.S. had no colonial ambitions. Furthermore, he was also aware that the White House had liberal designs for the world. The U.S. had become an international influence after its victory in the World War I. As such, Yemen proposed open relations directly with the U.S. President Woodrow Wilson, especially after he announced the famous 14 Principles.

In his speech to the Congress on January 18, 1918, President Woodrow Wilson provided a set of principles known as 'Wilson's Fourteen Points', which were considered to be a new approach to international diplomacy.[33] Yemen was interested in the 14 principle that refers to *"The Turkish portion of the present Ottoman Empire should be assured a secure sovereignty, but the other nationalities which are now under Turkish rule should be assured an undoubted security of life and an absolutely unmolested opportunity of autonomous development, and the Dardanelles should be*

Woodrow Wilson

permanently opened as a free passage to the ships and commerce of all nations under international guarantees".[34]

As a result of the transition in the U.S. foreign policy from nationalism to internationalism, Imam Yahiya sent a letter to President Woodrow Wilson appealing for U.S. support for the liberation of the Arabs in general and Yemen in particular. He expressed *"For the Sake of humanity, use your authority to grant recognition for the rights of Imam in Yemen and the Arab independence".*[35] There was no reaction from the U.S. regarding the Imam's letter.[36] This could be due to America's commitment to neutrality as the British position toward the Imam was antagonistic. In 1919, the American consul in Aden visited the Imam with a vision aiming at paving the way for the presence of U.S. oil companies in Yemen.[37] U.S. companies did not have a presence in Yemen until 1920 when the Standard Oil Company made a geological investigation for oil.

In another development, the Imam exploited the tour of Amin al-Rihani, an American of Syrian origin, to Yemen in 1920-22. Al-Rihani carried a letter from the Imam to the American consul in Aden.[38] Imam Yahiya's letter addressed the topic of development and the establishment of official relations between Yemen and the U.S.

In 1926 and 1927, Yemen-U.S. relations flourished due to several factors. First, important U.S. traders visited Yemen and actually began commercial projects in Yemen, including Niton Houlberg, a representative of the Houlberg Kidde Corporation of Aden and New York, in 1926.[39] The American Millionaire Charles Crane met the Imam in Sana'a in January 1927 and offered to develop Yemen at his own expense.[40] The second factor was the geological survey by Karl Marx who claimed the possibility of oil in many areas in Yemen.[41] Furthermore, U.S. companies began the construction of roads, namely Sana'a-Hodeida road.[42] Finally, the Imam used Charles R. Crane as a mediator and sent with him to the American Consul in Aden a draft of a treaty that addressed bilateral trade between the two countries.

It is evident that America did not have key interests in Yemen to encourage it to recognize the Imam's rule. The major objective of the Imam's foreign policy was to achieve the independence of Yemen through its recognition by great powers. Although American presence in Yemen was increasing, this did not lead to official recognition. Even though there were repeated visits by the consul in Aden in 1910, 1919, and again in 1927, Imam Yahiya did not receive official U.S. recognition. It was clear that U.S. was seeking to maintain semi-official relations so that it could remain neutral in a turbulent region.

U.S. Neutrality Towards Yemen's Border Disputes

The second factor that affected the relationship is the U.S. neutrality towards Yemen's border disputes with Britain and Saudi Arabia. The colonial legacy and its policy to stabilize the region are the reasons that stand behind its neutral policy towards Yemen's disputes. In fact, the colonial legacy affected the nature of the foreign policy of states that gained independence. Yemen was not the only country that adopted a foreign policy of isolationism after its independence, according to Akira Iriye *"Too often American foreign policy in the nineteenth century has been described in simplistic terms as geographical isolation, withdrawal from European politics, continental expansion and the like"*.[43] The American founders, particularly George Washington and Thomas Jefferson, had supported the isolation and neutrality of America; they believed in *"a conduct friendly and impartiality towards the belligerent powers"*.[44] By the same token, Monroe's doctrine clearly opposed European greed in Latin America, and thus, Monroe himself stood behind the American rejection of imperialism, particularly the European rivalry in Arabia.[45]

According to such interpretations, U.S. had committed itself to neutrality regarding Yemen. This hampered the development of the future prospective relations between Yemen and the U.S. In 1927, the correspondences between the Secretary of State and its Consulate in Aden demonstrated that both American merchants and the Consul sought enhanced relations with Yemen regarding commercial interests. However, the Secretary of State advised the consul to reaffirm that it was important to maintain the unofficial relations with Yemen and hoped to further develop commercial relations and it is not disposed at this time to proceed to ending the formal treaty. The Secretary of State's justification to Mr. Clark based its position on *"The unsettled political situation and the resulting uncertainty as to the permanency of the political entities so far established as well as amongst the more obvious reasons which have led the Department to this position".*[46]

The domestic dimension was the most important factor that shaped the Yemen foreign policy towards U.S. With the U.S. or without it, Yemen was looking for recognition by the great powers in order to consolidate its internal stability, reduce the British influence, and liberate Yemen from colonial rule.[47] In 1927, Yemen signed a treaty of friendship and commerce with Italy, which was considered to be the most challenging action to Britain in the region, at that time.[48] In a similar development, Yemen was the first Arab country to have signed a treaty of friendship and commerce with Moscow on November 1, 1928.[49]

During the course of Yemen's involvement in the war against Britain in 1927, it took control of certain areas of the so-called 'Aden Protectorate'. In response, Britain bombarded many cities in Yemen and moved to isolate Yemen on the global front. Britain moved to re-align its interests with the Italians through a bilateral agreement in 1927 in which it was agreed that Italy would not interfere in the internal affairs of Yemen. Thus, Britain then moved to hinder Yemen's relations with other great powers, particularly the U.S. and the Soviet Union.[50]

In spite of this, the U.S. foreign policy continued its commitment to neutrality in Yemen's wars with its neighboring countries in spite of Yemen's successive calls for American help. During the period between 1927 and 1934, Yemen was engaged in two wars with Britain and Saudi Arabia. It was defeated in both wars. Britain succeeded in persuading U.S. to prevent the arrival of weapons to Yemen.[51] The Kingdom of Saudi Arabia also succeeded in obtaining a loan from the U.S., which was in the form of weapons, such as personnel carriers and machine guns.[52] For its support in the Yemen-KSA war, Saudi had given concessions to U.S. oil companies. The position of the great powers differed during the war between Yemen and KSA. Italy, France, and Britain sent military ships to the western coast of Yemen around *Hodeida Port*. Italy announced its support to Yemen, while Britain declared its neutrality and then it sought to play the role of a mediator between Yemen and Saudi Arabia.

In the war of 1934, U.S. had urged all parties to find peaceful solutions. Washington pushed for stability in the region as a means to protect its interests.[53] In regards to the 1943-44 wars between Yemen and Britain, Yemen sought American help, but the U.S. State Department considered the conflict to be outside of its concerns. It preferred to postpone its involvement in this and other conflicts in the Arabian Peninsula until the end of World War II.[54] This vision did not continue in the U.S. after World War II, when U.S. along with the Soviet Union had become the two strongest great powers at the top of the international system.

It is possible to say that Yemen-U.S. relations declined during the period between 1927 and the end of WWII.[55] This was an expected outcome given its neutrality towards Yemen's wars in 1934 and 1944. Several other reasons contributed to the deteriorating of relations. First, failure to develop relations saw U.S. companies stop operations in Yemen which included the construction of roads and harbors. Secondly, Yemen-U.S. commercial relations had been affected by the Yemen-Italy treaty.[56] Thirdly, both Crane and Twitchell shifted their interests to the KSA.[57] As mentioned earlier, Britain played a big role in blocking Yemen's relations with foreign countries. In addition, according to the confidential reports of American companies the lack of oil had reduced American commercial interests in Yemen.[58]

2.4. The Establishment of Official Bilateral Relations

During World War II, the U.S. foreign policy changed from nationalism to internationalism. It adopted a policy of openness towards other states. A noticeable shift in the U.S. foreign policy was the substitution of the Monroe Doctrine with the Marshall Plan and Eisenhower Doctrine. Thus, the U.S. became more determined to improve and ensure their interest around the world, including the Middle East. According to Roger Trask, *"Only since the end of World War II the Middle East has become a major concern in United States foreign policy. The region was little known to the American before 1945".*[59]

The Arab Peninsula is an important part of the Middle East. The Kingdom of Yemen KOY and Saudi Arabia were the most prominent nations in the Arabian Peninsula because they were the first independent Arab States in modern history.[60] American foreign policy was no longer affected by the multi-polar international order. Therefore, it is hard to say that, the competition of colonial states in the Arab Peninsula affected the expansion of U.S. relations with other parts of the world, particularly in the Arab World.

This section explores the factors behind the mutual diplomatic recognition between the two countries and traces the evolution of their relations until the end of the Kingdom of Yemen. The first factor examined is the impact of changes in the international and regional environment. The second factor is the shift in Yemen's foreign policy following an unsuccessful coup attempt in 1948.

After World War II, the international and regional environment changed with the emergence of new factors in Yemen-U.S. relations such as the end of the U.S. isolation policy, the change of the international system, decline of the British influence in Yemen and enhanced the U.S.-Saudi relationship. As a result, Yemen-U.S. relations expanded and it was possible for the U.S. to officially recognise Yemen. It could be argued that the transformation of the U.S. position towards recognizing Yemen was driven by its policy of openness towards other states and increased U.S. interests in the region. In turn, U.S. recognition enhanced Yemen's international presence and fostered its development.

Imam Yahiya realized that his policy of isolation led to popular discontent, recession, and economic decline.[61] Yemen observed the changes taking place worldwide, particularly the rise of U.S. global influence and the massive aid provided to revive the European economy through the Marshall Plan as well as the prosperity of Saudi Arabia by oil revenues through investments by U.S. companies.[62] On one hand, the Imam of the Kingdom of Yemen sought to obtain political support and to give his rule international legitimacy, while on the other he sought financial aid to spur development.[63]

As a result of the Imam's efforts in the establishment of mutual relations with the U.S., Yemen was able to secure a loan of an estimated one million dollars in May 1946.[64] Yemen's leaders were more interested in establishing diplomatic relations between the two countries. Delegates from the Imam of Yemen were repeatedly sent to Aden to meet the U.S. consul Mr Clark in January 1945. They confidentially asked him to visit Sana'a to discuss ways to develop the relations between the two countries, mostly, trade exchange, the assignment of American experts including medical officers, and economic and cultural assistance from the U.S.[65]

While Yemen was governed by internal dynamics, U.S. was governed by external dynamics. U.S. was taking into account its allies' interests in the region, in particular Britain and Saudi Arabia. Furthermore, U.S. anticipated a beneficial future of relationship with Yemen. It took into account the geographical location of Yemen as it extended from the Arabian Peninsula to the Horn of Africa. Therefore, in the aftermath of Clark's visit to Sana'a in April 1945, the Secretary of State urged, in his memorandum, President Harry S. Truman to recognize Yemen. He emphasized that *"In view of American interest in near-by countries such as Saudi Arabia and Ethiopia, and also in view of possible future developments in the Yemen, it is the Department's belief that the United States should indicate to the Imam its readiness to extend formal recognition to the Government of the Imam (already in treaty relations with the British and with Saudi Arabia) and to establish a channel for the exchange of diplomatic correspondence. This measure, it is believed, should precede any decision on Yemeni requests for assistance".*[66]

Even though both Saudi Arabia and Britain already recognized the independence of Yemen, U.S. took into account the non-objection of both Britain and Saudi Arabia on its proposal to recognize Yemen. According to al-Madhaji

"Washington realized that by neglecting Yemen, the U.S. long-term interests in Saudi Arabia might be threatened, and established formal relations without British objection because the latter wanted to stabilize the balance of power in the Arabian Peninsula".[67] The U.S. State Department received a briefing of no objection by the United Kingdom and the Kingdom of Saudi Arabia on November 19, 1945.[68] President Truman sent a letter to the King of

Harry S. Truman

Yemen to confirm the willingness of U.S. government to discuss such an agreement as well as designate the Honorable William Eddy, the United States ambassador in Saudi Arabia as his representative.[69] On March 4, 1946, diplomatic relations were established with the Kingdom of Yemen and the U.S. recognized Yemen as an independent nation.[70] William A. Eddy's mission was concluded May 4, 1946, when the U.S. and Yemen approbated on a treaty of friendship and commerce.

Within the framework of the consolidation of Yemen-U.S. relations, Prince Saif al-Islam Abdullah arrived at Washington in July 1947.[71] He met the

President of the United States, Harry Truman, and the Secretary Marshall to whom he handed three letters. The main objectives of Prince Abdullah's visit was to gain U.S. support for Yemen's membership in the UN, procure modern weapons, secure more loans and to negotiate on the issue of granting petroleum exploration rights to American companies.[72] The U.S. documents indicate American support of Yemen's accession to the United Nations in the General Assembly held on September 30, 1947. In addition, a surplus property agreement was struck in Cairo in May 1947, which extended a line of credit of up to one million dollars for Yemeni purchases of American surplus, although Yemen did not make such purchases.[73]

Another potential factor that affected the U.S. policy towards Yemen was The Yemeni Liberal Party movement (YLP).[74] The enlightened elites in Yemen were aware of the long-term consequences of the U.S. recognition. In this context, YLP asked the U.S. not to recognize Imam Yahiya. The YLP through a telegraphic message sent to President Harry Truman, on February 27, 1946, emphasized that Yahiya's government was the cause of the failure to fulfill the aspirations of the people of Yemen.[75] The U.S. administration ignored YLP's message and overlooked the significant role of the YLP as a new movement, which was to renounce any local or international support, particularly from the Kingdom of Saudi Arabia.[76] Unexpectedly, this movement -YLP- was behind the opening of a series of revolutions in Yemen, the first revolution was in 1948.

Relations during Imam Ahmed's Rule[77]

The change of leadership in Yemen after the coup attempt in 1948 forced many of the alterations to Yemen's existing foreign policy, which, in turn, reflected on the nature of relations between Yemen and U.S. In 1948, the YLP carried out a coup and was able to assassinate Imam Yahiya, but the coup failed when Crown Prince Ahmad succeeded to regain control of Yemen thus succeeding his father as the ruler of Yemen.[78] Some researchers associate the establishment of Yemen-U.S. relations with the revolution of 1948. Al-Madhaji argues that *"the official U.S.*

approach to Yemen exacerbated the hostility of both the internal and external enemies of the ruling family. The establishment of formal relations between Yemen and the United States played on this conflict and was a factor behind the 1948 revolution and the assassination of Imam Yahiya on 17 February 1948".[79]

Imam Ahmed ruled Yemen from 1948 until 1962. In this period, the U.S. did not support the YLP against him. President Truman requested the new regime to abide by the previous bilateral treaties, specially the treaty of 1946.[80] U.S. foreign relations towards Yemen appeared to be liberated from the dominance of Britain over Yemen's affairs, as Britain was supportive of the 1948 revolution.[81] Despite the fact that Imam Ahmed welcomed Truman's requests, bilateral relations froze for several years till 1950. Between

Ahmed bin Yahya

1950 and 1955, U.S. companies pursued oil and mineral exploration, and the study of the ancient civilization of Yemen.[82] According to a secret document issued by the U.S. State Department in 1951, the strategies of the U.S. policy towards Yemen were based on the following nine policies:[83]

1. Preventing, where possible, the spread of Communist influences in Yemen and the Near East generally and promoting the stability of the area.

2. Assisting in the orderly development of the economy and public welfare of Yemen.

3. Giving friendly counsel as the occasion may warrant to all parties to any dispute involving Yemen and encouraging prompt solution of the controversy.

4. Observing the utmost respect for Yemen's sovereignty, independence and local customs.

5. Promoting the modernization of the country.

6. Encouraging sound American enterprise to establish business and developmental interests in Yemen.

7. Extending loan assistance on the basis of normal banking procedures.

8. Disseminating American cultural media in Yemen and inviting Yemeni students and leaders to the United States.

9. Fostering philanthropic (but non-religious) enterprise of public interest. In all our efforts to carry out our policies in Yemen, U.S. should be very careful to serve as a guide or partner and avoid injuring Yemeni sensibilities by appearing to dominate them.

In spite of the proposed sensitivity to Yemeni sensibilities, several factors contribute to the decline of Yemen-U.S. relations. U.S. foreign policy was subjected to the wishes of other countries be it Saudi Arabia or Britain and the traditional rivalry of North Yemen.[84] Some studies go further in asserting that the U.S. was engaged in the internal issues of Yemen through Saudi Arabia, particularly with regards to Imam Ahmed's appointment of his son Bader as a crown prince instead of his brother Prince al-Hassan. Both Saudi Arabia and the U.S. were not convinced of Prince Bader as a successor of Imam Ahmad, because the Prince maintained a good

Muhammad Al-Badr

relation with President Jamal Abdul Nasser, the president of Egypt who adopted nationalism.[85]

Finally, Imam Ahmad appointed Prince Bader as secretary of state and who was instrumental in making changes to Yemeni foreign policy.[86] Among his contributions was Yemen's accession to the Non-Aligned Movement (NAM), the expansion of relations with Arab and socialist countries, Yemen's refusal to participate in the Baghdad Pact.[87] Yemen also rejected the conditional aid that accorded with the Eisenhower Doctrine.[88] This point related with the U.S.-USSR competition in and around Yemen forms the subject of the next chapter in which the external dynamics that shaped Yemen-U.S. relations is discussed including the influence of the Cold War.

2.5 Conclusion

Although Yemen-U.S. relations can be traced back to the 18th century in the form of bilateral commercial trade and the presence of American missionaries, initial formal relations were not fulfilled until the end of World War II. Even with intensive mutual correspondence during the period between World War I and II, the relations remained unofficial. U.S. traders and missionaries encouraged American presence in Yemen, while the need for certain U.S. products and the search for anti-colonial powers urged Yemen to establish ties with U.S. However, the obstacles proved greater than the motives to establish official relations.

Certainly, the colonial legacy was a stumbling block to the development of relations between the two countries, starting from the competition of colonial powers over the coasts of Yemen through to the British and Ottoman occupation of Yemen. Following the independence of North Yemen in 1918, Great Britain sought to build a wall of separation between the mutual interest of Yemen and the U.S., while Yemen was actively seeking to be recognized by the U.S. and obtain economic assistance in addition to the reduction of British influence.

In more modern times, U.S. chose to remain apart from the political struggles of the then great powers. It pursued this course even after emerging as a great power after the First World War. In line with this policy, U.S. preferred to maintain unofficial relations with Yemen in addition to adopting a neutral stance in regards to Yemen's conflicts with its neighbors. The end of World War II led to official U.S. recognition of Yemen in 1946, especially after the U.S. became convinced of the importance of strengthening America's relations with countries that have potential importance in the world map. According to the view of the U.S., Yemen enjoys a strategic geographical location, and its stability is necessary for maintaining American interests in the region as well as future relationships. On the other hand, Yemen sought to strengthen its regional influence and receive economic assistance by improving its relationship with U.S.

Generally speaking, U.S. was governed by external dynamics, while Yemen was governed by internal dynamics. In the aftermath of 1948 YLP revolution, Imam Ahmed became the King of Yemen and adopted an open foreign policy. U.S. was closely watching his foreign policy. The U.S. decided to adopt a policy based on achieving Yemen's stability and in the process to not appear as if it was dominating Yemen. The U.S. policy failed after it objected to Imam Ahmed's choice of the Crown Prince. This led to a decline in Yemen-U.S. relations for a number of years.

The historical background of Yemen-U.S. relations was subject to changes in the internal and external affairs of both Yemen and the U.S. The mutual interest formed the basis of bilateral relations which saw a degree of success. However, the obstacles proved greater than the motives and eventually led to the distancing of both nations. Yemen managed to secure international recognition from the U.S. while the U.S. manages to secure its interests in the region for a number of years. The following chapter explores the significance of external factors in defining Yemen-U.S. relations.

[1] The Strait Hormuz is a narrow, strategically important sea lane between the Gulf of Oman in the southeast and the Persian Gulf.

[2] Mohamed Ali Albahr. *Tareekh Al-Yemen Almoaser* (Cairo: Madbouly Maktabah, 1990), p. 61.

[3] Madeehah Darweesh. *Nashat Al-Americi Fi Al-Yemen Ma Bayn Al-Harbain Al-Alamytiene 1981-1939, Men Waqea Al-Ershief Al-Consulia Al-Americia Fi Aden*, p. 54.

[4] Mocha is a seaport city in Yemen, located to eastern side to the Red Sea.

[5] Eric Macro. *Yemen and the Western World, since 1571*, p. 23.

[6] Salwa A. Dammag. "A Study Yemen-United States Relations 1990-2002.", p. 21.

[7] Eric Macro. *Yemen and the Western World, since 1571*, p. 26.

[8] Salwa A. Dammag. "A Study Yemen-United States Relations 1990-2002.", p. 21.

[9] 'Imam of Yemen' is Religious title given only to the kings of Yemen at that time.

[10] Eric Macro. *Yemen and the Western World, since 1571*, pp. 23-24.

[11] Ibid., p. 27.

[12] Federal Research Division. *Country Profile: Yemen* (Washington DC: Library of Congress, 2008) accessed 28/03/2011, http://memory.loc.gov/frd/cs/profiles/Yemen.pdf, pp. 1-10.

[13] Najmey Abd Al-Majeed. "Almo'arek'h Hamzah Ali Lok'man W'a Eshamateh F'i Ketabat Tarik'h Aden." *14 October News* (19 May, 2006).

[14] For further reading; Najwa Abdul altif Motah'er. "Se'ra'a Alk'how'a Ala'a Tehama (1818-1849)." (Master Thesis, University Sana'a, 2005).

[15] Najmey Abd Al-Majeed. "Almo'arek'h Hamzah Ali Lok'man W'a Eshamateh F'i Ketabat Tarik'h Aden." *14 October News* (19 May, 2006).

[16] Paul Dresch. *A History of Modern Yemen* (Cambridge: Cambridge University Press, 2000), p.1-6.

[17] FOI, Swedish Defence Research Agency. "Yemen in Crisis – Consequences for the Horn of Africa." by Alexander Atarodi. (Stockholm: Division of Defence Analysis, March 2010), accessed 6/1/2011, http://www.nai.uu.se/research/nai-foi%20lectures/YemenIn-Crisis_AlexanderAtarodi.pdf, p. 31.

[18] Madeehah Darweesh. *Nashat Al-Americi Fi Al-Yemen Ma Bayn Al-Harbain Al-Alamytiene (1981-1939), Men Waqea Al-Ershief Al-Consulia Al-Americia Fi Aden*, pp. 27-145.

[19] ABCFM is American Board of Commissioners for Foreign Missions. For further reading, Charles A. Maxfield. "The 'Reflex Influence' of Missions: The Domestic Operations of the American Board of Commissioners for Foreign Missions, 1810-1850." (Dissertation, Union Theological Seminary, 1995).

[20] Leo P. Ribuffo. "Religion." In *Encyclopedia of American Foreign Policy*, (ed.) Richard Dean, Fredrik Logevall and Alexander Deconde. (New York: Facts On File, 2004), p. 375.

[21] Mahmūd Hamlān Jabārāt. *Alaqat Al-Yamaniyah Al-Amrikiyah 1904-1948, 'Ahd Al-Imam Yaḥyá Ḥamid Al-Din*, pp. 312-313.

[22] Ali Al-Ghifari. *Al-Deplumasia Al-Yemenia 1900-2000* (Sana'a: Dar al-Affaq lel-Tebaah we al-Nashr, 2000), p. 181.

[23] Nazeeh Mu'ayyed al-Azem. *Rehlah Fi Al-Arabia Al-Saeda* (Beirut: al-Tanweer, 1986), p. 230.

[24] For further reading; Cagri Erhan. "Ottoman Official Attitudes Towards American Missionaries." *Council on Middle East Studies CMES* (2007), accessed 5/4/2011, http://opus.macmillan.yale.ed-u/workpaper/pdfs/MESV5-11.pdf

[25] Jabarat. *Alaqat Al-Yamaniyah Al-Amrikiyah 1904-1948, 'Ahd Al-Imam Yahiya Hamid Al-Din*, p. 313.

[26] Ibid., p. 313.

[27] Nazeeh Mu'ayyed al-Azem. *Rehlah Fi Al-Arabia Al-Saeda*, p. 230.

[28] Farok' O'thman A'bad'ah. *Alh'okm Al-Ottmani F'i Al-Yemen 1872-1818* (Cairo: al-Haia'ah al-A'amah ll-Ketab, 1986), pp. 425-426.

[29] Mohammed Zakarya. "Al-Sera'a Alothmani Alinglizy F'i Al-Yemen." *14 Octoper News* (April 2, 2007).

[30] For further reading about the conflict Yemeni British; Sai'ed Most'afa Salem. *Albah'r Alah'mar W'a Aljoz'er Al-Yamniah Tarik'h Wa K'ad'iah* (Sana'a: Dar Almith'ak' LelNash'er Wa Altwzia'a, 2006).

[31] "Yemen F'i Al-A'ser Al-H'adith." *Algomhoriah News* (2010), accessed 6/2/2011, http://www.algom-horiah.net/atach.php?id=32076

[32] For example; Egypt, Iraq, Palestine and South Yemen have been subjected to British colonialism, while the French occupation was in Syria, Lebanon, Tunisia and Algeria, in addition to Libya and Ethiopia have been colonized by Italia. See the Map 2.1: The Colonial Arab State.

[33] Susan L. Carruthers. "International History, 1900-1945." In *The Globalization of World Politics; an Introduction to International Relations*, (ed.) John Baylis and Steve Smith. (New York: Oxford University Press, 2001), pp. 56-57.

[34] Congressional Record. *Wilson's Fourteen Points an Address to a Joint Session of Congress* (Wikispaces, January 8, 1918) accessed 23/3/2011, http://worldhistoryiispa.wikispaces.com/file/vie-w/14pts2.pdf

[35] Ali Al-Ghifari. *Al-Deplumasia Al-Yemenia 1900-2000*, p. 181.

[36] Richard H. Sanger. *The Arabian Peninsula* (Ithaca: Cornell Univ Press, 1954), p. 38.

[37] Robin Leonard Bidwell. *The Two Yemens*, no. 1 (London: Longman, 1983), p. 112.

[38] Almadhagi. *Yemen and the United States: The Study of a Smallpower and Super-State Relationship 1962–1994*, p. 13.

[39] Ibid.

[40] Ali Al-Ghifari. *Al-Deplumasia Al-Yemenia 1900-2000*, p. 182.

[41] Adnan Tarseesi. *Ardh Saba Wa Al-Hadharah Al-Arabia Al-Mub* (Beirut: Dar al-Fiker al-Muasir, 1985), p. 44.

[42] Albahr. *Tareekh Al-Yemen Almoaser*, pp. 39-40.

[43] Akira Iriye. *From Nationalism to Internationalism : US Foreign Policy to 1914* (London; Boston Routledge and K. Paul, 1977), p. 1.

[44] Manfred Jonas. "Isolationism." In *Encyclopedia of American Foreign Policy*, (ed.) Richard Dean Alexander DeConde and Fredrik Logevall. (New York: Charles Scribner's Sons, 2002), p. 338.

[45] For further reading; Joshua Reuben Clark. *The Monroe Doctrine* (New York: Committee for the Monroe Doctrine, 1928).

[46] US Department of State. *The Secretary of State's Dispatch to the Consul of Aden* (Washington DC: Foreign relations of the US, 1927) accessed 12/3/2011, http://images.library.wisc.edu/FR-US/EFacs/1927v03/reference/frus.frus1927v03.i0032.pdf, pp. 825-827.

[47] Almadhagi, *Yemen and the United States: The Study of a Smallpower and Super-State Relationship 1962–1994*, p16.

[48] Albahr, *Tareekh Al-Yemen Almoaser*, pp. 32-33.

[49] Andrej Kreutz. "Russia and the Arabian Peninsula." *Journal of Military and Strategic Studies* 7, no. 2 (2004), accessed 30/12/2010, http://www.jmss.org/jmss/index.php/jmss/article/download/184/201, pp. 6-7.

[50] Albahr. *Tareekh Al-Yemen Almoaser*, pp. 30-36.

[51] Jabārāt. *Alaqat Al-Yamaniyah Al-Amrikiyah 1904-1948, 'Ahd Al-Imam Yahiyá Hamid Al-Din*, p. 306.

[52] Richard H. Sanger. *The Arabian Peninsula*, p. 71.

[53] Almadhagi. *Yemen and the United States: The Study of a Smallpower and Super-State Relationship 1962–1994*, p. 18.

[54] Jabārāt. *Alaqat Al-Yamaniyah Al-Amrikiyah 1904-1948, 'Ahd Al-Imam Yaḥyá Ḥamid Al-Din*, p. 307.

[55] Albahr. *Tareekh Al-Yemen Almoaser*, p. 90.

[56] Jabārāt. *Alaqat Al-Yamaniyah Al-Amrikiyah 1904-1948, 'Ahd Al-Imam Yaḥyá Ḥamid Al-Din*, p. 309.

[57] Royal Embassy of Saudi Arabia. *Saudi-US Relations* (Washington DC: Royal Embassy, 2008) accessed 8/4/2011, http://www.saudiembassy.net/files/PDF/Brochures/DFS_us-saudi_relations.pdf, p. 4.

[58] Jabārāt. *Alaqat Al-Yamaniyah Al-Amrikiyah 1904-1948, 'Ahd Al-Imam Yaḥyá Ḥamid Al-Din*, p. 311.

[59] Roger R. Trask. "United States Relations with the Middle East in the Twentieth Century: A Developing Area in Historical Literature." In *American Foreign Relations, a Historiographical Review*, (ed.) Gerald K. Haines and Samuel Walker. (Westport, Conn: Greenwood Press, 1981), p. 293.

[60] Fred Halliday. *The Middle East in International Relations. Power, Politics and Ideology* (New York: Cambridge University Press, 2005), p. 7.

[61] Albahr. *Tareekh Al-Yemen Almoaser*, pp. 54-73.

[62] Ali Al-Ghifari. *Al-Deplumasia Al-Yemenia 1900-2000*, p. 182.

[63] Mojeeb Alrahman Ahmed. *Al-Yemen Wa Al-Dwoal Al-Kobra', Derasah Tah'liliah Tawthekiah,* (Sana'a: Wkalat Alanba'a Al-Yamniah Saba, 2003), p. 21.

[64] Ibid., p. 23.

[65] US Department of State. *The Consul at Aden (Clark) to the Secretary of State* (Washington DC: Foreign relations of the US, January 17,1945), accessed 4/5/2011, http://images.library.wisc.edu/FRUS/EFacs/1945v08/reference/frus.frus1945v08.i0016.pdf, p. 1312.

[66] US Department of State. *Memorandum by the Acting Secretary of State to President Truman* (Washington DC: Office of the Historian, May 1, 1945), accessed 4/5/2011, http://images.library.wisc.edu/FRUS/EFacs/1945v08/reference/frus.frus1945v08.i0016.pdf, p. 1314.

[67] Almadhagi. *Yemen and the United States: The Study of a Smallpower and Super-State Relationship 1962–1994*, p. 18.

[68] US Department of State. *Memorandum by the Acting Secretary of State to President Truman* (Washington DC: Office of the Historian, November 16, 1945), accessed 4/5/2011, http://images.library.wisc.edu/FRUS/EFacs/1945v08/reference/frus.frus1945v08.i0016.pdf, p. 1315.

[69] US Department of State. *President Truman to the King of Yemen 'the Imam Yehiya Bin Mohamed Hamid-Ud-Din'* (Washington DC: Foreign relations of the US, November 19, 1945), accessed 6/3/2011, http://images.library.wisc.edu/FRUS/EFacs/1945v08/reference/frus.frus1945v08.i0016.pdf, p. 1317.

[70] "A Guide to the United States' History of Recognition, since 1776: Yemen." *Office of the Historian* (2011), accessed 3/6/2012, http://history.state.gov/countries/yemen

[71] Prince Abdullah is the son of the King of Yemen, Imam Yahiya.

[72] US Department of State. *Yemen, Visit of Prince Saif Al-Islam Abdullah to the United States, Editorial Note* (Washington DC: Foreign relations of the US, 1947), accessed 2/1/2011, http://images.library.wisc.edu/FRUS/EFacs/1947v05/reference/frus.frus1947v05.i0019.pdf, pp. 1344-1345.

[73] Ibid.

[74] The Yemeni Liberal Party (YLP) is referred to in other studies as the Free Yemen Party (FYP). It is a revolutionary movement that consists of Yemeni citizens and soldiers who reject the Monarchy regime's policy in Yemen such as isolation and backwardness in all fields.

[75] Wakalt al-Anbaa al-Yemenia, Saba. "Al-Yemen Fi Ma'et A'mm." (Sana`a: Markez Al-Bah'ath wa Al-Derasat Saba, 2000), p. 138.

[76] Mojeeb Alrahman. *Al-Yemen Wa Al-Dwoal Al-Kobra', Derasah Tah'liliah Tawthekiah*, p. 22.

[77] Imam Ahmed ruled Yemen from 1948 until the revolution of 1962. The period of his rule was exceptional in the Yemen-US relations because he adopted an independent policy to improve relations with the countries that did not have good relations with US. Furthermore, he was the last ruler of the Kingdom of Yemen.

[78] For Further reading about Movement of year 48 and the reasons of failure, Fernando Carvajal. "Imamic Yemen's Sacred National Charter (1948): Failed Interpretations of an Established Social Compact." (paper presented at the Middle East PhD Students International Conference State, Society and Economy in the Modern Middle East, London, 7-8 May 2011), accessed 3/12/2012, http://www.soas.ac.uk/lmei/events/ssemme/file67890.pdf

[79] Almadhagi. *Yemen and the United States: The Study of a Smallpower and Super-State Relationship 1962–1994*, p. 19.

[80] Mojeeb Alrahman. *Al-Yemen Wa Al-Dwoal Al-Kobra', Derasah Tah'liliah Tawthekiah*, p. 30.

[81] Jabārāt. *Alaqat Al-Yamaniyah Al-Amrikiyah 1904-1948, 'Ahd Al-Imam Yaḥyá Ḥamid Al-Din*, p. 306.

[82] Albahr. *Tareekh Al-Yemen Almoaser*, pp. 90-97.

[83] US Department of State. *US Policy toward Yemen; Policy Statement Prepared in the Department of State* (Washington DC: Foreign relations of the US, February 8, 1951), accessed 2/1/2011, http://images.library.wisc.edu/FRUS/EFacs2/1951v05/reference/frus.frus1951v05.i0020.pdf, pp. 1192-1198.

[84] Almadhagi. *Yemen and the United States: The Study of a Smallpower and Super-State Relationship 1962–1994*, pp. 20-22.

[85] Mohamed Aglan Ga'id. "Al-Alaqat Al-Yemenia Al-Ameicia 1990-1998." (Master Thesis, Baghdad University, 1999), p. 23.

[86] Albahr. *Tareekh Al-Yemen Almoaser*, p. 97.

[87] For further more reading about Baghdad Pact and its role on the US secretary and small state at Middle East; Thomas D. Wahlert. "US National Security Strategy - the Magnitude of Second and Third-Order Effects on Smaller Nations: The Cases of Lebanon During the Cold War and Pakistan During the Global War on Terrorism." (Project, US Army War College, 2004).

[88] For further more reading; Salim Yaqub. *Containing Arab Nationalism: The Eisenhower Doctrine and the Middle East* (Chapel Hill, N.C.: University of North Carolina Press, 2004).

CHAPTER THREE:
EXTERNAL DYNAMICS SHAPING
THE RELATIONSHIP

3.1 Introduction

To gain a better understanding of the inconsistencies that permeate Yemen-U.S. relations, identifying and analyzing the less apparent dynamics that shape this relationship is required. Over the past nine decades of bilateral relations, internal and external factors have dominated the approach of a wide range of foreign policy makers in both countries. External dynamics are the focus of attention in this chapter. The chapter addresses the most important factors at the root of the changes in the international and regional environments. They are considered the most influential factors in the progress of the bilateral relations between the two countries. It can be argued that Yemen's importance rests on its ability to impact U.S. interests in the region because of the comparatively poor U.S. presence in Yemen.

This chapter examines a variety of influential external dynamics and their role in the formation of Yemen-U.S. relations such as the strategic location and the regional factors, the Cold War, and the new agenda of the international system, namely the spread of democracy and human rights in addition to the global war on terrorism (GWOT). The first section highlights the influence of the geo-strategic factor, which created a specific agenda in the foreign policy of both countries. The second section examines the implications of changes in the international political system from a multi-polar to a bilateral system known as the Cold War era. Following this, the next two sections discuss the role of the democratization agenda and the global war on terrorism in shaping Yemen-U.S. relations. In order to realize the aforementioned objectives, several issues and events that constitute turning points in the relationship between Yemen and the U.S. are highlighted and closely examined.

3.2 The Strategic Location and Regional Factor

It is difficult to address Yemen-U.S. relations without considering regional politics. Middle Eastern politics is fundamental for understanding the relationship between the two countries. This is due to the fact that the United States of America considers the Middle East a priority in its foreign policy. As for Yemen, it considers Middle Eastern issues as part of its own issues, and as such Middle Eastern politics forms a central part of its foreign policy.[1] In the regional framework of the above fact, this section reviews the reasons behind the importance of this region for both countries in terms of strategic location and the importance of energy sources. Moreover, the implications of regional political trends in shaping the foreign policy of each country towards the other are highlighted. It also highlights the role of the main regional actors such as Saudi Arabia and Israel.

First of all, to realize geographical significance of Yemen's region in U.S. foreign policy requires a broader understanding of the framework of international relations among Middle Eastern countries and its significance with the world powers. Sometimes, the term the Middle East is expanded to include all Arab countries as well as Turkey, Israel, Iran and Eritrea. At other times, the term does not include the Arab countries in North Africa but expands eastward to include Pakistan and Afghanistan.[2]

According to the geographical extension of Yemen in the region, Yemen shares borders with eight countries bordering the Red Sea.[3] Yemen also overlooks the Gulf of Aden and shares the Arabian Sea with Oman. The Arabian Sea represents a link between the Strait of Hormuz and the Red Sea and overlooks the Indian Ocean. Yemen and Arab countries such as Oman and the (UAE) are Arab members of the Indian Ocean Rim Association for Regional Cooperation (IOR-

ARC).[4] Yemen is a part of the Arabian Peninsula and represents the southern flank of the Gulf Cooperation Council countries (GCC).[5] Yemen also has historical and geographical extensions with the Horn of Africa countries. Yemen faced many challenges in its attempt to join the GCC and as a result looked towards the Horn of Africa and established the Alliance of Sana'a as a political alliance with Sudan and Ethiopia.[6] Finally, Yemen is a member of the Arab League and is influenced by the nature of relations with other regional countries such as Iran and Turkey.

There is no doubt that Yemen occupies a strategic location in the region, and this region itself occupies a strategic location in global interests including those of U.S. Due to Yemen's control of Perim Island in Bab el Mandeb, Yemen controls the maritime link between the Red Sea and the Arabian Sea.[7] Moreover, Yemen and Egypt only control the entrances of the Red Sea through the Suez Canal and the Bab el Mandeb. Thus, Yemen is a link between the countries of the Indian Ocean, Red Sea countries, and the countries of the Mediterranean.[8] Accordingly, Yemen is among the selected countries that control and oversee the third important maritime strait and maritime route in the world.[9] This rout is important to shorten the sea routes that connect the eastern continents with western continents. Furthermore, approximately 22.4 million barrels per day of oil go through the three straits in this region, i.e. Straits of Hormuz 15.3, Bab el Mandeb 3.8 and Suez Canal 3.3.

In light of this, the geo-strategic importance of Yemen carries positive connotations in the framework of its relations with the outside world, but sometimes it represents a negative connotation. This fact will be clear through close scrutiny of Yemen-U.S. relations. There is little doubt that U.S. duly recognized the geographical importance of Yemen. This formed the first impetus for the U.S. foreign policy to maintain friendly relations with Yemen. A large number of official American documents, whether ancient or modern, confirmed this fact. For example, in 1951, secret U.S. documents stressed that *"the geographical position of Yemen, situated at the southern narrows of the Red Sea, gives it a certain strategic value which we wish to remain in friendly hands."*[10]

Moreover, when Rogers, the Secretary of State, visited Yemen to resume Yemen-U.S. relations in 1972, his telegram to President Nixon indicated that *"Yemen has a strategic location at the tip of the Arabian Peninsula makes it an important country in this part of the world."*[11]

Map 3.1: The Oil Trade through International Straits

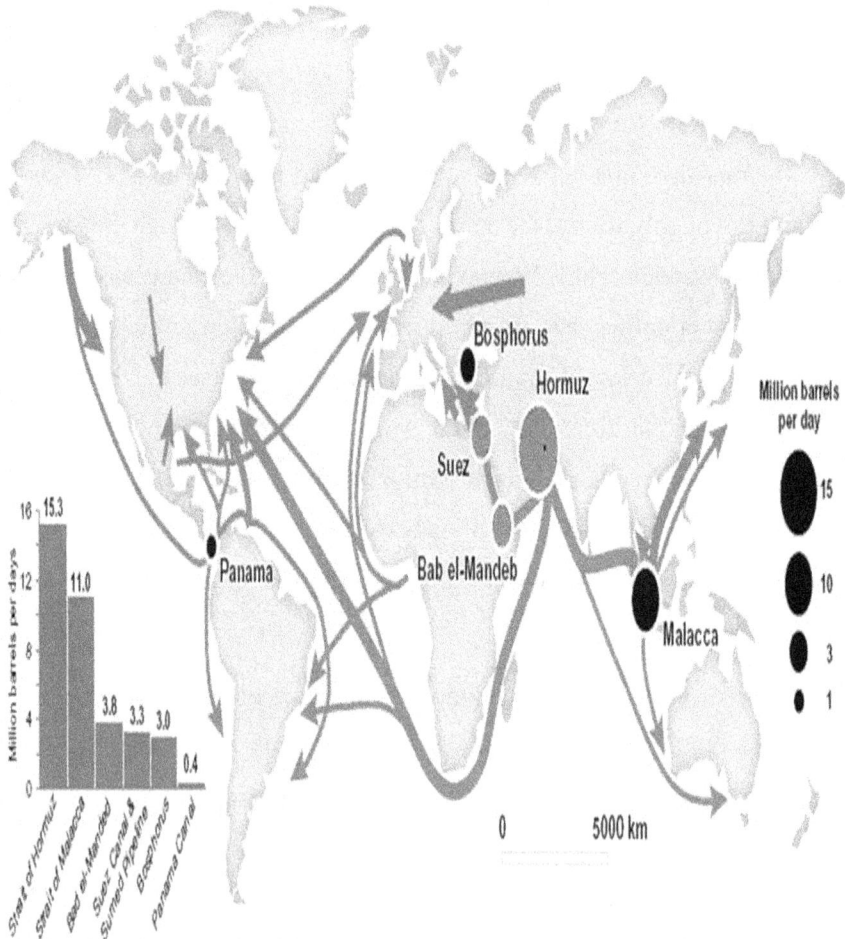

Source: "Maritime Chokepoints Critical to Petroleum Markets." Today in Energy (March 2, 2011), accessed 3/7/2011, http://205.254.135.7/todayinenergy/detail.cfm?id=330.

Recognizing the importance of Yemen's position on the global map, international maritime navigation is only one of many dimensions of it strategic geographic location. The natural resources of this region represent another important dimension. Yemen's oil production exceeded 300 thousand barrels per day. In 2010, in the Middle East, including the Arab countries in Africa, oil production was estimated at 32344 thousand barrels per day, and the reserves were estimated at approximately 865700 million barrels.[12] The Middle East produces 36.49 percent of global oil production and retains 59.47 percent of global oil reserves.[13] Similarly, the region retains 44.8 percent of the global gas reserves and produces 618.2 billion cubic meters.[14]

Accordingly, the U.S. commonly associates its interests in Yemen with its geographical location and proximity to Saudi Arabian oil reserves. More recent U.S. documents echo this fact. The 2010-2012 USAID strategy report on Yemen mentions that *"Yemen has become increasingly central to the U.S. foreign policy interests. Its strategic location features a long porous land border with Saudi Arabia, a critical U.S. ally, and a lengthy maritime border facing the oceanic chokepoint to the world's most heavily used sea lanes."*[15]

Having discussed Yemen's strategic location important in the region, the second key factor is associated to the implications it carries on the U.S. policy in the region and its compatibility or incompatibility with Yemen's politics. In fact, four out of five of American's vital goals in the region are related to the geo-strategic position enjoyed by Yemen namely to secure Israel's territories, obtain oil-energy, to ensure free maritime movement, and to prevent other powers from usurping regional control.[16] In contrast, the Yemeni foreign policy is based on a set of national, Arab, Islamic, and international principles. Its first goal is maintaining the independence of Yemen and its sovereignty and then attempts to achieve the unity of the Arabs, its territorial integrity and independence, solve Arab internal conflicts, and prioritizes the Palestinian issue.[17]

Given the differing concerns of each country's policy, disagreements on regional issues are expected. This section discusses the incompatibility between each country's policies, particularly concerning Yemen, and examines the evolution of American regional hegemony. It also explores the roles of Saudi Arabia and Israel in U.S. policy and the impact of the Gulf War.

Firstly, Yemen rejects any non-Arab military presence or bases in its territories and in the region, which, in turn, led to the Yemen-U.S. disputes around three regional issues. In the Gulf War in 1991, former Yemeni President Saleh sought to persuade the Gulf States to allow an Arab mediation to negotiate with Saddam to lead Iraq to withdraw his forces from Kuwait, and in case Saddam refused, the Arab countries will form a unified Arab army against him. Saudi Arabia rejected the Yemeni proposal. Yemen opposition turned the region into a major U.S. military base and voted against any military strike in the UN.[18] But Yemen paid a high price for this decision. The U.S. threatened Yemen that it would reject UN resolution no. 678.[19] Accordingly, Yemen relations with U.S. and also with Gulf states deteriorated to the lowest levels.

Ali Abdullah Saleh

Secondly, Yemen perceives piracy operations in the Gulf of Aden as a form of foreign military presence to counter-piracy and is uncomfortable with such a presence. Some Yemeni analysts argue that U.S. stands behind the piracy phenomenon to enhance its military presence.[20] Yemen foreign policy attempts to activate the role of the Red Sea countries to secure regional maritime trade. Moreover, Yemen attempted to prevent a unilateral U.S. act by providing logistic facilities in its strategic islands to other supreme powers such as China and

Russia.[21] In any case, Yemen agrees with the U.S. policy that in order to achieve regional stability, Yemen must first become stable. In addition, Yemen appreciates U.S. support of Yemen's influence over the Horn of Africa. However, in spite of this, it must be remembered that Yemen foreign policy is in contrast with that of the U.S. concerning several regional issues.

Map 3.2: The U.S. Military Bases in the World

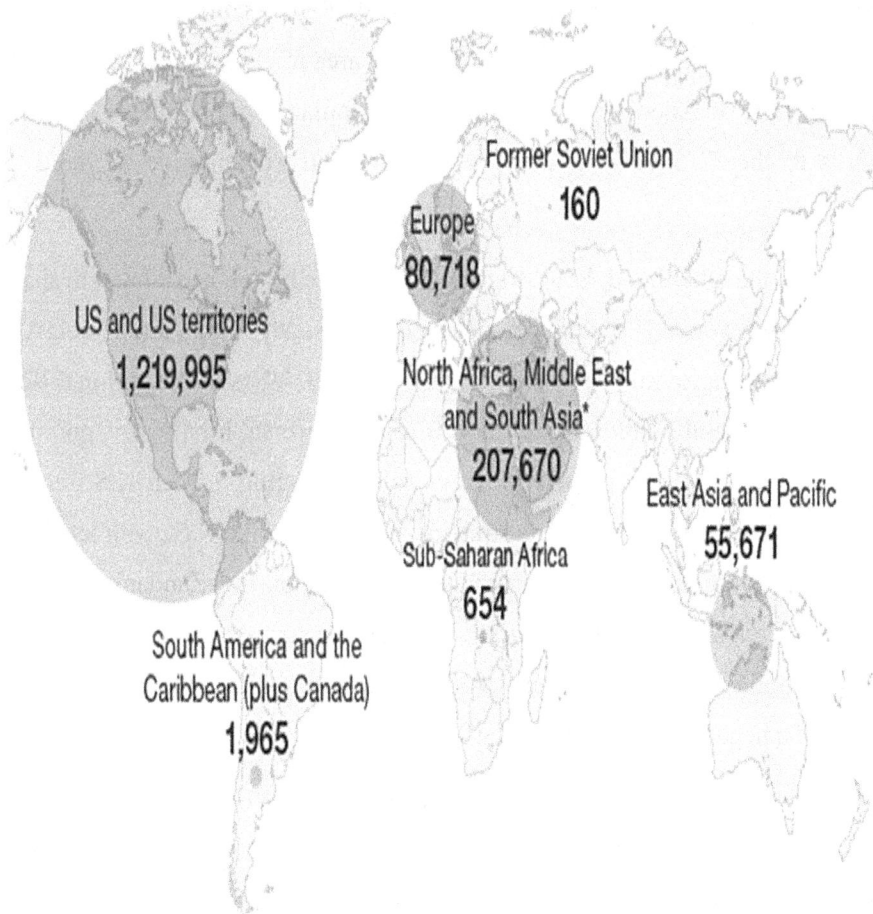

Former Soviet Union
160

Europe
80,718

US and US territories
1,219,995

North Africa, Middle East
and South Asia*
207,670

East Asia and Pacific
55,671

Sub-Saharan Africa
654

South America and the
Caribbean (plus Canada)
1,965

Source: The Defense Manpower Data Center (DMDC). Flg as Sep (2011), accessed 10/1/2012, http://www.bbc.co.uk/news/world-us-canada-16433138

Finally, Yemen's strategic location invites American interference. It has attempted on several occasions to establish a military presence on Yemen's ports and islands. This has however been met with continuous failure because of Yemen's rejection of a non-Arab military presence and the constant threat of terrorist operations. In 1991, the U.S. military was in Aden as part of the U.S. intervention in Somalia codenamed the *Benevolence Operation*. It was forced to return early because of an explosion in the *Aden Hotel*. Another American experiment was in 1998 when it forced a presence on *Socotra* Island. The people's reaction was greater than expected.[22] Although U.S. was satisfied with a treaty for military assistance that enabled it to move in the area freely and receive oil supplies from the port of Aden, terrorist's operations similar to those that transpired in regards to the *USS Cole* in 2000 were sufficiently obstructive to force their relocation.

On the other hand, U.S. strategic allies in the region had a hand in shaping the relations between U.S. and Yemen, especially Saudi Arabia and Israel. As we will see later, improving Yemen's relations with U.S. allies in the region reflected in positive bilateral relations with the U.S. and vice versa. Firstly, it is possible to argue that Saudi Arabia played an active role in shaping Yemen-U.S. relations. Saudi Arabia took advantage of its strategic alliance with the U.S. to direct Yemen-U.S. relations according to its interests in the region. Al-Zandani argues that Riyadh is the American gate to Sana'a. The U.S. foreign policy has been subjected to Saudi policy towards Yemen.[23] As hitherto discussed, Saudi has constantly exercised a negative effect on Yemen-U.S. relations.

For example, it shaped the U.S. stance on the Yemen civil war of 1962-1967 and then managed to affect the U.S. containment policy towards South Yemen. Such policies led to improving the U.S. relations with North Yemen, but Saudi Arabia controlled the U.S. military aid, which incited Yemen to acquire arms from the Soviet Union. Saudi Arabia also helped to isolate and contain democracy in Yemen and prevent it from spreading to other countries. Through the current chaos in Yemen, U.S. thinks that Saudi intelligence plays an important role in the fight against terrorism in Yemen.

An interesting question worthy of contemplation is why U.S. would allow Saudi Arabia to dictate its relations with Yemen. This can be explained through the framework of the regional U.S. strategy that is based on America's allies to ensure its interest in the region. As mentioned above, the U.S. chose Iran –during Shah Iran's rule- and Saudi Arabia as strategic allies. Joseph Sisco emphasized that the common interest between the U.S. and Saudi Arabia had to be the upper hand of the moderate forces in this region.[24] Moreover, America was aware of the fact that maintaining its interest in such a complex and mysterious country would be an expensive endeavor.[25] It is worth noting, however, that the U.S. and the KSA interests concerning Yemen are not absolutely compatible. Examples of diverging interests are American recognition of YAR after the 1962 revolution, the Yemeni unification in 1991, and its position regarding the Yemeni civil war in 1994. The United States prioritized its international interests over the interests of its regional allies.

Concerning the KSA purpose, it attempts to adjust American relations with Yemen in order to prevent Yemen from becoming a regional powerhouse while at the same time ensuring that it does not turn into a failed state.

Saudi Arabia believes that strengthening of bilateral relations between U.S. and Yemen will strengthen the Yemeni political and economic situation in the region. Saudi Arabia is also aware of the magnitude of the threat if Yemen were to turn into a failed state as a country in chaos is difficult to manage. It was outcome of the misunderstanding of the founder of Saudi Arabia King Abdul-Aziz ibn-Saud precept. On his deathbed, he said, *"The good or evil for us* -the Saudi royal family- *will come from Yemen."*[26] On the other hand, Yemen does not have a problem with improving its relations with Saudi Arabia. However, there remain many thorny issues between the two countries such as labour and border disputes that have led to many wars.[27]

Second, the other American influence in the region is the Zionists. Israel is a strategic ally to the point that U.S. believes that the protection of Israel is the first goal in the region.[28] The U.S.-Israel alliance is interpreted differently. Some analysts believe that the U.S. support for Israel is merely a form of human sympathy.[29] This approach is unable to interpret the 101-billion-dollar annual support and the more than 40 U.S. vetoes in the interest of Israel. On the other hand, some analysts exaggerate Israeli influence on U.S.[30] Regardless of the differences, the two parties, the Democrat and Republican, believe that Israel plays a strategic role in maintaining America's interest in the region.[31] Therefore, U.S. foreign policy considers the Arab-Israel peace as a crucial issue.

Consequently, Yemen along with other Arab countries severed relations with U.S. because of its unfair support for Israel in the Arab-Israel war in 1967.[32] Once again, the Six-Day War stopped the relationship and U.S. aid, but the U.S.-USSR competition caused U.S. relations with Yemen to resume. The U.S. Secretary of State William P. Rogers visited Sana'a in 1972 to restore relations. He announced that Yemen-U.S. relations would be based on Yemen's acquiescence to the U.S. policy in the region.[33]

The U.S. attempts to normalize Yemen-Israel relations. On the contrary, the Yemen foreign policy considers the liberation of Palestine a crucial issue in the region, which cannot be abandoned. As a consequence, Yemen and other Arab countries implemented a policy of complete boycott against Israel. In spite of this, a number of political events demonstrated Yemen's readiness to normalize relations with Israel which helped to improve relations between Yemen and the U.S. and vice versa. In the late 1990s, aiming to improve relations with the U.S., Yemen accepted an offer to attend international conferences where Israel was a participant and allowed Yemeni Jews—who held Israeli passports—to visit Yemen. However, Israeli criminal practices against the Palestinian people led Yemen to reconsider attempts to normalize relations.[34]

3.3 The Influence of the Cold War on Bilateral Relations

Though the importance of recognizing that Yemen-U.S. relations are formed by external regional dynamics, it is also important to address the framework of international politics. Over half a century ago, the Cold War had profound global implications. Therefore, this section attempts to identify the nature of this factor by inspecting three dimensions. Firstly, it examines the change of U.S. foreign policy towards Yemen through American fear of the strengthening of Yemen-USSR relations. Secondly, it discusses the effect of competition between the two great states on Yemen foreign policy and its orientation towards U.S. The section will also shed light on the change in the relations between U.S. and North Yemen, after South Yemen became a unique Communist state in the Arabian Peninsula.

In the shadow of the Cold War era, the two great powers U.S. and USSR attempted to extend their influence throughout the world. The Middle East, particularly the Arabian Peninsula had its importance in the balance of power between the two countries. Yemen was the cornerstone of that conflict because the Soviets succeeded in attributing South Yemen into the Eastern bloc, while the Americans succeeded in containing North Yemen.[35] There is no doubt, in this historical conflict, the importance of Yemen increased in the context of regional geo-politics. According to Roger Trask, *"The emergence of the Middle East as a major arena of Cold War conflict, the critical importance of its oil resources, and the Arab-Israeli dispute have forced the region..."*[36]

The initial U.S. foreign policy towards Yemen was affected by competition with the Soviets over Yemen. According to the U.S. State Department strategy toward Yemen, which was developed in 1951, the first goal was *"Preventing the spread of Communist influences in Yemen and the Near East generally and promoting the stability of the area."*[37] The nature of U.S.-USSR policies regarding Yemen have taken two phases; before and after the independence of South Yemen. The first phase was a U.S.-USSR competition to deepen bilateral relations with North Yemen and worked to block other competitors, while South Yemen remained colonized. During this phase, U.S. suspicions about Soviet ambitions in Yemen were strengthened under the USSR arms deals with North Yemen in addition to the involvement of Egypt, with support from the Soviets, to change the Yemeni regime in the 1962 Revolution.[38] Thus, U.S. sought to improve its relations with North Yemen as a reaction to Soviet policy towards Yemen. Their approach can be regarded as a pre-emptive policy.

Although the Yemen-USSR trade agreement in 1956 was not the first bilateral agreement between Yemen and USSR, the U.S. viewed the Yemen-USSR agreement as inconsistent with the directions of its policy in the Near Eastern countries. The United States' considerable concern was twofold: the U.S. feared the proliferating of arms sales by the USSR to the Near Eastern countries, and it also feared the growing influence of the USSR in the Arabian Peninsula.[39] The rest of the Arab World was linked to arms agreements with Western countries. In other words, Yemen would be the only state with good relations with the Soviet bloc. In 1957 the USSR military equipment arrived to Yemen as well as the establishment of USSR military in Sana'a. Moreover, Yemen had received technical and economic aid from the USSR bloc.[40]

Accordingly, the U.S. was gravely concerned with the ambitions of the USSR bloc in Yemen and the Arabian Peninsula. That convergence between Yemen and USSR created a debate inside the corridors of U.S. policy. In the context of consultations, the memorandum of the Office Director of the Near Eastern Affairs Wilkins on January 2, 1957, concluded three reasons *"Firstly, the desire to increase ability to raid the Aden Protectorate. The lack of a Yemen Air Force would appear to preclude any major Yemeni offensive action against the Protectorate –Aden-. Then, the flattery of Yemen by the Soviet Union and Egypt give the impression that they consider Yemen as a major Arab power. Finally, the Yemen desire to gain from both sides in the East-West conflict."*[41]

Therefore, the U.S. foreign policy interacted with Yemen in accordance with the conclusion of the above memorandum. One aspect of the shift in U.S.

foreign policy towards Yemen is in aid.[42] From 1959-1962 U.S. provided an estimated 42.7 million dollars of assistance to Yemen, of which 32.2 million was a grant.[43] As part of diplomatic negotiations, U.S. opened negotiations with regional actors. U.S. sought to convince Yemen on the dangers of Communism in the region through direct negotiations as well as through Saudi Arabia, which had maintained fraternal relations with Yemen at that time. In addition, U.S. sought to limit British influence and persuade the parties to settle disputes peacefully.

According to the extensive correspondence between Secretary Dulles and Wilkins-the director of the Office of Near Eastern Affairs- with the two U.S. ambassadors in KSA and Egypt, Secretary Dulles advised the embassy in Cairo to inform the Diplomatic Mission of Yemen that: *"The Department likewise is aware of the problems which exist between Yemen and the United Kingdom and has, in recent talks with the British, emphasized the desirability of a peaceful settlement."*[44] It is clear that the U.S. policy aimed to achieve two goals, namely to maintain regional stability and thus prevent USSR arms deals with Yemen.

Another controversial U.S. position concerned the recognition of (YAR) after the successful revolution on September 26, 1962, under the leadership of the first President of (YAR), Abdullah al-Sallal. American diplomacy was at a crossroads with respect to the civil war in Yemen between Republicans and the Royalists during 1962-1967.[45] Although American public opinion urged the U.S. leaders to respect the aspirations of the Yemeni people towards a better future, the U.S. recognition of Yemen Arab Republic (YAR) was hesitant.[46] Such policy

Abdullah al-Sallal

opened the way for Communist states to assert their influence in Yemen. The Communist bloc states, including China, were early to recognize Yemen Arab Republic (YAR) and offer both military and political assistance.[47] The Arab allies of the USSR such as the United Arab Republic (UAR) recognized the Yemen Arab Republic (YAR) immediately after the revolution while Egypt was involved in the civil war in Yemen. Egypt sent thousands of troops to support republicans and also participated in bombarding cities in Saudi Arabia which sheltered the royalists.[48]

U.S. had been monitoring with deep concern the series of declarations of the Eastern bloc countries pertaining to their recognition of Yemen Arab Republic (YAR). The Americans feared the permanent presence of Communist countries in the Middle East.[49] But at the same time, the U.S. was fully aware of the concerns expressed by Britain and Saudi Arabia regarding the future implications of the Yemeni revolution.[50] America's allies in the region, Britain, Saudi Arabia, and Jordan, sought to counter the revolution by providing military and political support to the royalists.[51] Moreover, the British considered the revolution of 1962 as a direct threat to their rule in Aden. By the same token, the royal regimes in the Arabian Peninsula were considering the Yemeni republican revolution as a threat to their existence.[52]

However, U.S. sought to strengthen its relationship with Yemen and in the meantime tried to achieve a balance between the contradictory interests of U.S., its allies Britain and Saudi Arabia, and Yemen's interests. The U.S. foreign policy was designed to ensure the stability of the region. Hence, the recognition of the new regime in Yemen is a dilemma in itself, as expressed by the State Department Executive Secretary Brubeck, *"Our immediate concern is less with what transpires inside Yemen than the prospect that our failure to recognize the new regime will lead to escalation of the conflict endangering the stability of the whole Arabian Peninsula. Likewise, failure to recognize will result in termination of an American presence in Yemen and is likely to lead to a considerable increase in the Soviet influence."*[53]

Consequently, it is obvious that the U.S. fear of Yemen-USSR rapprochement of relations urged it to recognize Yemen Arab Republic (YAR). The American recognition of YAR came on December 18, 1962, three months after the Yemeni revolution in spite of the objections voiced by its allies in the region. President Kennedy was obliged to preserve Saudi sovereignty and as such proposed that the United States call for a quaternion conference for Egypt, Yemen, Saudi Arabia, and Jordan to discuss matters pertaining to ending the war and the withdrawal of troops from Yemen.[54] According to the extensive correspondence between the concerned parties, American efforts aimed to put pressure on Yemen to declare its commitment to all the international obligations assumed by the previous government.[55] U.S. hoped that such an act would reassure Britain and Saudi Arabia in particular. By this, the U.S. appeased the immediate concerns of its allies Britain and Saudi Arabia.[56]

In terms of the impact of the Cold War on the Yemeni foreign policy, if the repercussion of the Cold War has made U.S. foreign policy closer to Yemen, it has made the Yemeni foreign policy closer to the U.S. and the USSR alike. Several reasons stand behind the Yemen policy to gain from both blocs. First, Yemen foreign policy has adopted a good relationship with various powers even before the Cold War. Due to the sensitivity of Yemen to the dominance of one of the great powers, the Yemeni foreign policy sought to create a balance between the interests of the great powers in Yemen.

John Kennedy

Long ago, Yemen enhanced its relations with the USSR by reviving a 1928 treaty of friendship and commerce and by ratifying a new trade agreement in March 1956. Efforts were directed toward the expansion of economic and trade relations on the basis of equality and mutual benefit. Furthermore, the visit of Crown Prince Bader, the Minister of Foreign Affairs, to the Soviet Union in June 1956 represented an added step towards strengthening relations between the two countries.[57] Furthermore, Yemen signed trade and technical agreements with some communist countries, such as the German Democratic Republic, Poland, Romania, Czechoslovakia, and China.[58]

Second, Yemen needs to strengthen its military capabilities through arms deals, while American maintains their reservations on this issue. U.S. thought that the military support to Yemen may lead to war and represent a threat to Britain. At the same time, it thought that the Soviets sought to ignite a war in the region, taking advantage of Yemen's recourses for the benefit of the Eastern bloc.[59] From the standpoint of Yemen, the arms deals with the Soviets was a good option, especially considering that North Yemen engaged in border disputes with the strategic allies of U.S. in the region, whether the United Kingdom and Saudi Arabia. Furthermore, Yemen was aware U.S. had military-supported Saudi Arabia.[60] Finally, in any case, the competition between the two camps represented a golden opportunity to achieve its interest and receive support.

Despite the change of Yemeni leadership after the revolution on September 26, 1962, the main gist of the foreign policy of Yemen did not change. By obtaining U.S. recognition, Yemen forged closer bilateral relations with U.S. Yemen was aware that U.S. recognition was a gateway for the recognition of the rest of NATO states as well as the adoption of a representative of Yemen to the United Nations (UN) who would replace the current royalist representative.[61] Therefore, Yemen had the desire to end the international conflict on its issues so Yemen accepted by issuing a statement reassuring all international parties of its commitment to its obligations. On December 19, 1962, the U.S. announced the recognition of the Yemen Arab Republic.[62] This announcement came a day after

Yemen declarations on 18 December. Sana'a declared that, *"YAR is still committed to this policy which includes its respect of its international obligations, hoping to live in peace and harmony with its neighbours, as well as cherishing this hope with the U.S."*[63]

However, the civil war again made the government of Yemen refer to the USSR bloc and Egypt, while the royalist insurgents were supported by Saudi Arabia.[64] Eventually, the U.S. paved the way for the United Nations to play the mediator role and prevent the possibility of the conflict intensifying.[65] Once again, U.S. got involved in Yemeni issues in order to prevent the Soviets from strategic opportunities. At this time, however, the relations did not improve during the Yemeni Civil War 1962-1967 leading to severance of ties until the 1970s.

The second phase of the influence of the Cold War was when Southern Yemen declared independence in 1967 and became a Communist state. As a result, Southern Yemen became a military base for the Soviets, while North Yemen became a key part of American policies in the region such as their containment policy. The implications of this phase again cast a shadow on bilateral relations between the two countries.

Despite that U.S. was eager to quickly recognize the independence of South Yemen (PDRY); the relations between the two countries were also half-hearted and were quickly severed.[66] Some reports have warned of Soviet ambitions in South Yemen.[67] According to the South Yemeni government, the U.S. policy attempted to change its political regime.[68] On October 24, 1969, the U.S. listed the regime of the PDRY amongst the terrorist countries,[69] prompting South Yemen to break off its relations with the United States, and requesting all Americans to depart within twenty-four hours.[70] America's failures in South Yemen can be attributed to two factors. Firstly, U.S. failed to prevent the infiltration of Communist ideology into South Yemen because it depended too heavily on Britain. Secondly, the absence of U.S. aid to South Yemen left Aden in urgent need of economic and military assistance, which the Soviets promised to grant.[71]

When the Soviets succeeded in finding a foothold in the region, American policy and its allies were forced to develop strategies to address this threat. The containment of the Soviet Union in the Arabian Peninsula was the main dynamic which transformed the Middle East and Yemen into a major concern for U.S. foreign policy.[72] As such, U.S. found itself forced to maintain a better relationship with North Yemen, in accordance with its strategy to prevent the expansion of Communist influence in the region. It seems that the U.S. policy to counter the Communist threat involved North Yemen in the line of confrontation with the South along with a plan to stage an internal coup. This policy was applied in both Saudi Arabia and Yemen. According to J. E. Peterson, *"the U.S. would have to see changes in Aden but apparently it did not regard the PDRY stance as threatening enough to justify active intervention ... Containment was a better and less risky option".*[73]

The major changes in the foreign policy of North Yemen after the dependence of South Yemen was the nature of the interests it sought to achieve. It was often feared that North Yemen would be the subject of Communist expansion. This fact was caused by South Yemen and USSR provocative policy in the region. With Soviet support, the PDRY became a catalyst for many of the dilemmas and border disputes with the countries of the region. Moreover, the armament of Aden by the Eastern Bloc raised many concerns in all of the U.S., North Yemen, and the rest of the Arabian Peninsula.[74] The report from Secretary of State William Rogers to President Nixon confirms that the leaders of the YAR welcomed the strengthening of bilateral relations to contain Soviet and Chinese Communism in the PDRY, as well as to address developmental problems.[75]

Consequently, the two countries were eager to resume their diplomatic relations. Yemen welcomed the resumption of relations and extended an invitation to the U.S. Secretary of State William Rogers to visit YAR on July 1, 1972. According to U.S. objectives, Rogers announced that, *"this visit is an opposition campaign for the Soviet Union to stop its expansion in the region"*[76], as well as it aims at strengthening the U.S. authority in the Middle East and the Gulf states.

According to the memoirs of Muhsin al-Aini, the then Prime Minister of Yemen and Minister of Foreign Affairs at that time, Sana'a goals were not far from Washington's, but the other motive was its need for U.S. development aid.[77]

In contrast to the rule of President Saleh, which began in 1977, President Ibrahim al-Hamdi's tenure from 1973 to 1977 was marked by a balanced and cautious policy in dealings with the world powers. Ibrahim al-Hamdi's approach to foreign policy during his presidency in North Yemen was indeed characterized by a strategic balancing act. By maintaining positive relations with the United States, he sought to counterbalance the influence of the Soviet Union during a period when the Cold War heavily influenced the political landscape of the Middle East. This approach allowed him to leverage economic and military assistance from the U.S., which was crucial for strengthening North Yemen's regional position.

Al-Hamdi's pragmatism in foreign affairs, particularly with the U.S., was indicative of his broader political strategy. He aimed to secure benefits for North Yemen while ensuring that the country retained its sovereignty and avoided the pitfalls of over-reliance on any single foreign power. His leadership style, more moderate and open to Western influences compared to some of his

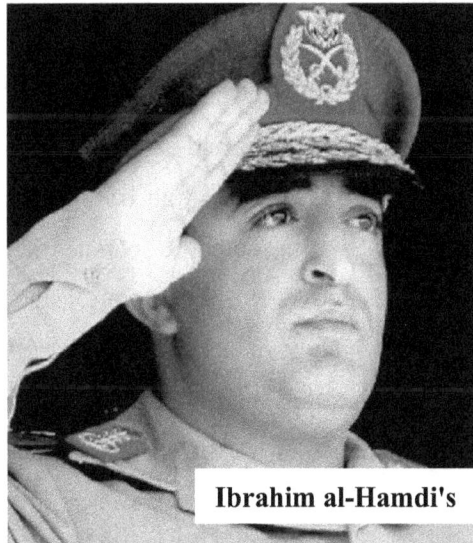

Ibrahim al-Hamdi's

contemporaries, facilitated this balanced approach. However, his awareness of public perception and the importance of national autonomy meant that he also maintained a degree of independence from U.S. influence to avoid negative perceptions among his populace. Overall, al-Hamdi's foreign policy was a nuanced endeavor to navigate the complexities of international relations during a turbulent time, seeking benefits while maintaining national integrity and autonomy.

As a result, the bilateral relations developed and U.S. development aid resumed. North Yemen grew from receiving less than two USD million in 1973 to 16.4 million annually during 1977-1982. The initiation of military and security cooperation was another form of strengthening mutual relations between the two countries during the Cold War. This cooperation was aimed to change the ruling class in South Yemen, which has led to two proxy wars between the north and south. As will be discussed in the next chapter, another purpose for this cooperation was to reduce the spread of Communist ideology in the Arab societies through the U.S. long-term strategy, which was based on the creation of radical Islamic currents that denounced Marxist ideology.

At that time, U.S. adopted a new policy based on supporting regional allies economically and militarily in order to play the role of the international law enforcer.[78] President Nixon asked his allies to assume greater responsibility in the defence of world freedom.[79] Israel and Iran were considered America's hand in the region. Similarly, to some extent, Saudi Arabia was another hand of the U.S., particularly in the Arabian Peninsula. But under such circumstances, the U.S. relationship with Iran and Saudi Arabia underwent significant changes. Saudi-U.S. relations froze after the Arab-Israel war in 1973 and the fall of the Shah of Iran in

1979. U.S. then opted to pursue the principles set by Presidents Carter and Reagan which were based on the idea of self-defence of its interests in the Middle East. In the fall of 1979, President Carter decided to establish a new security framework in the region. The U.S. strategy strengthened America's naval presence in the Indian Ocean including units for rapid intervention. In January 1980, President Carter announced that any attempt of any external force to

Jimmy Carter

control the Gulf is an assault on the America's interest, and such aggression will be met by any suitable means, including military response.[80]

Such a strategy has given special attention to Yemen and the on-going war between North Yemen and the Communist South. U.S. suspected that the Communists would set up camp along the coast of Aden and Ethiopia.[81] The administration of President Reagan was consistent with the principle of Carter. It also sought to strengthen the defence systems in the southeast NATO's countries, Turkey and Greece and become offensive in order to counter any threat to the Arabian Peninsula in addition to strengthening the military relationship with North Yemen as part of its containment policy. It seems that the collapse of the Soviet Union prevented the oil war, especially, when USSR leaders held that the U.S. policy threatened to turn the region into a barrel of gunpowder.[82]

Although the first inter-Yemeni proxy war did not last long, it was enough to confirm the impact of the Cold War era as a key factor in the outbreak of the war.[83] The U.S. gave the KSA the upper hand to lead the anti-PDRY campaign whether by supporting the NUF in the territories of North Yemen, or by the so-called "tribal insurrection strategy".[84] According to Kostiner, America's strategic ally, the KSA, in collaboration with YAR, encouraged Southern Yemeni exiles to gain access to the PDRY.[85] Due to the fact that the Soviets were behind the PDRY, the U.S. took measures to conceal their direct intervention to bring down the regime in Aden. The KSA provided logistical support while the U.S. was giving advisory services to Saudi.[86]

Under such circumstances, U.S. increased its aid to North Yemen, and it was the first time the U.S. provided military assistance. Similarly, the Soviet intelligence provided logistical support to South Yemen PDRY to defeat U.S. schemes. There was a kind of arms race between the North and South. The U.S. and Saudi Arabia were trying to verify that the military capabilities of North Yemen able to defeat South Yemen. For instance, in 1979, the American response to the second war between YAR and PDRY was unexpected. According to Stephen

Zunes, *"In response, Carter ordered the aircraft carrier Constellation and a flotilla of warships to move to the Arabian Sea as a show of force. Bypassing congressional approval, the administration rushed nearly $499 million worth of modern weaponry to North Yemen"*.[87] These modern weapons include the following: 70 armoured personnel carriers, 64 M-60 tanks, and 12 F-5E aircraft. As well as were an estimated 400 American advisers and 80 Taiwanese pilots for the training operations.

However, the U.S. military support to Yemen is still a sensitive issue because of the lack of confidence in the intentions of the regime in North Yemen in addition to Saudi Arabia's reservations. It created controversy within the U.S. Congress.[88] The sensitivity of this issue increased because during this competition North Yemen still held military relations with the USSR bloc. A sensitive American intelligence report indicated that the Soviets believed that it could support both North and South Yemen in a form that leads to put pressure on Saudi Arabia.[89] From the perspective of the U.S. Congress, lending the U.S. arms to Yemen was a means of protecting Saudi Arabia and American interests. Some members of the U.S. Congress wondered if the U.S. was shipping support to a friend or foe.[90] As for the KSA, they put a question of whether the U.S. arms support to YAR was more than enough to deter PDRY.

Doubtless U.S. relations with Yemen were influenced by the unstable external dynamics of the Cold War era. After the transformation of South Yemen to a Communist state, North Yemen-U.S. relations were positively affected. The implications of the Cold War saw a convergence of views on common issues, especially after Yemen was feared as being the subject of Communist extension in the region. However, Yemeni insistence on limiting the military presence of foreign forces in the region hindered the development of Yemen-U.S. relations. For instance, when the war between south and north Yemen ended, U.S. reduced its military support to North Yemen and withdrew its experts.

Such U.S. policy encouraged the YAR to change its policy in terms of the reorientation towards the Soviets for arms deals and to strengthen bilateral relations between the U.S. and Yemen. During the early 1980s, the deterioration of the YAR-U.S. relations was associated with improvements in the YAR-USSR relations. This deterioration of relations did not last long because the American oil companies discovered oil fields in commercial quantities in Yemen in 1986. This resulted in exchange of visits between the two countries' leaders, which was unprecedented.[91] This phase in Yemen-U.S. relations coincided with the end of the Cold War and represented a new era characterized by the dominance of other dynamics.

3.4 Democratization and the Human Rights Agenda

The collapse of the Soviet Union created a new international order which was characterized by American hegemony and the prevalence of liberal principles. The New International Order opened up new horizons in the Yemen-U.S. relations, especially after the U.S. pledged to spread the liberal values at a time when Yemen after the reunification of two parts, North and South, became the only Arab country to adopt such values in the region. Unlike during the Cold War, both countries now share ideological orientations. However, how can this factor advance their bilateral relations in the presence of many conflicting factors that are directly linked to other U.S. vital interests?

This section examines democratization and human rights as external dynamics affecting Yemen-U.S. relations. Even after the events of 9/11, promoting democracy and counter-terrorism became the twin policies of U.S. strategy, because U.S. leaders believed that international terrorism stemmed from the lack of democracy.[92] This section highlights the regional challenges faced by the American support for Yemen's democracy, and how these challenges led to a shift in U.S. policy to preserve the dictatorial states in the region from democracy and to withdraw support for Yemen. This is followed by an examination of the debates surrounding the U.S. foreign policy towards democracy in Yemen and how democratization could pose a threat to U.S. interests in the region by potentially strengthening terrorists.

In the post-Cold War period, Yemen-U.S. relations were not expected to improve because the dominant factor, such as the U.S.-USSR rivalry was no longer relevant. The U.S. was no longer committed to the policy of containment. The disintegration of the Communist bloc meant the end of America's fear of Soviet influence in the Arab Peninsula. But the rules of the game changed with the collapse of the Soviet Union and its Eastern camp, where U.S. began to lead the new international order. The promotion of democracy and human rights was supposed to be a key issue that governed the U.S. foreign policy in the post-Cold War world, especially during the 1990s. This policy coincided with Yemen's adopted democratic values early on and the changes in the international political system and power politics created favorable conditions for the reunification of North and South Yemen which was affected on May 22, 1991.

During Ali Saleh's visit to Washington in June 26, 1990, to discuss the unity of Yemen, U.S. welcomed and announced its support for the reunification of Yemen.[93] Despite the fact that U.S. formed an obstacle for the reunification of Yemen during the Cold War, its attitude completely changed from once being an antagonist to being a supporter. Despite the Saudi objection, U.S. support aimed to achieve the following objectives. It considered the reunification of Yemen as yet another proof of a symbolic victory for the West analogous to the fall of the Berlin Wall, not to mention

Signing the Yemeni Unity

the unity of Yemen as a factor of stability in the region. Moreover, the political parties adopted a democratic system, including the multiplicity of political parties, freedom of the press, human rights, a free market, and other principles promoted by the U.S. as part of the New World Order.[94] Furthermore, the establishment of Yemen's reunification took in account the observance of all human conventions.[95]

Moreover, the political parties adopted a democratic system, including the multiplicity of political parties, freedom of the press, human rights, a free market, and other principles promoted by the US as part of the New World Order.[96] Furthermore, the establishment of Yemen's reunification took in account the observance of all human conventions. During the Sana'a Summit held on December 22-26, 1989, an agreement was concluded between the two parts, paving the way for unity and emphasizing the following points:

- Studying the democratic experience, extracting its positives, and emphasizing them in Yemen unification.
- Preparing the draft election law.
- Preparing the draft constitution of the unified state and holding a popular referendum.
- Organizing the election period and procedures.
- Preparing the political organization's law.

The Constitution of Yemeni Unity, which was approved on May 16, 1991, through the first Yemeni popular referendum, Article No. 4 stipulates that "The people of Yemen are the possessor and the source of power, which they exercise directly through public referendums and elections, or indirectly through the legislative, executive and judicial authorities, as well as through elected local councils". Article No. 5 emphasizes *"The political system of the Republic of Yemen is based on political and partisan pluralism in order to achieve a peaceful transformation of power. The Law stipulates rules and procedures required for the formation of political organizations and parties, and the exercise of political activity*" " while Article No. 6 states that Yemen is committed to the Universal Declaration of Human Rights and all international laws in this regard.

According to the Yemenis, the values of democracy and human rights did not only mean intellectual harmony with the new international visions but also meant a notional political option. The continuation of the democratic choice in Yemen depends on the continuity of Yemen's unity, and vice versa.[97] Yemen's democratic transformation was unique compared to the dictatorial kingdoms in the Arab Peninsula. While the international press and democratic organizations expressed their admiration for the experience of Yemen, the developmental and economic environments in Yemen went from bad to worse. During the four years after the reunification, Yemeni leaders ignored economic and developmental issues and chose instead to focus on establishing democratic laws and institutions such as the constitution referendum in 1991, the enactment of laws and regulations of the democratic process, and the establishment of the parliament with the parliamentary elections of 1993.[98]

Accordingly, Yemen hoped to receive U.S. aid as part of its commitment to support democracy. But U.S. disappointed Yemen, as its assistance to Yemen was provided reluctantly and in rather symbolic amounts that did not commensurate with the democratic experience.[99] Regardless of the reality of U.S. policy toward democracy and human rights in Yemen, both the Republican and Democratic Parties in the U.S. committed themselves to sponsoring and promoting democracy and human rights throughout the world whether in their electoral programs or statements released in the media. The U.S. was involved in several wars and allocated huge budgets for the dissemination of liberal values.

Concerning the situation in Yemen, the failure of U.S. to support Yemen is incompatible with the above directions stated, but at the same time, this sheds light on other factors that might be more influential for U.S. foreign policy. At the time, any aid to Yemen would not have agreed with punitive policies following the rejection of Yemen to the U.S. war on Iraq and the foreign military presence on the Arabian Peninsula in 1991. Further, U.S. leaders were convinced that democratization in the Arabian Peninsula could be a threat to America's interests in the region. During the democratic process of Yemen, even under the global war on terrorism, U.S. supported the democratic experience in Yemen. But in general, its position on the democratic transition in the Arabian Peninsula is still vague and unclear.

There are considerable debates over the contradiction in the U.S. foreign policy concerning the Middle East. Scholars attempt to answer several questions, including "does democracy lead counter-terrorism since terrorism stems from tyranny, or rather does the implementation of democracy help fundamentalists to have access to the political power, as evident in the rise of *Hamas*?.[100] Ultimately, is there any incongruence between promoting democracy and other American interests?" [101] On the other side of the debate, some studies emphasized that the United States' long record of working with autocratic leaders in the region has spoiled the U.S. credibility in the Middle East.[102] Although the U.S. emphasizes that the spread of democracy is one of its priorities, studies argue that the U.S. support for emerging democracies was nothing but mere propaganda and was at the bottom of its list of priorities regarding its foreign policy.[103] While some researchers conclude that democracy and human rights are merely a means of exerting pressure to achieve the U.S. interests in the Middle East.[104]

On the other hand, Israel and some monarchical Gulf states, particularly Saudi Arabia, maintain a hostile stance toward the expansion of democracy in Arab countries, including Yemen. Israel has exerted considerable effort to persuade American decision-makers that democracy in Arab nations could lead to the rise of Islamists, posing a threat—a view that seems to resonate with neoconservatives. For the monarchical states, especially those on the Arabian Peninsula, the spread of democracy along their borders is perceived as a threat to the survival and continuity of their dictatorial regimes. These regimes typically fear the liberation of the people and their ability to think about their right to choose their rulers.

Through a careful reading of the U.S. dealings with the Yemeni democracy, all the above controversial assumptions are present in the U.S. behavior towards the Yemeni democratic experience. Consequently, the first U.S. ambassador to the Republic of Yemen stated that the U.S. was paying attention to Yemen's efforts to achieve internal unity, democracy, and economic and political freedom.[105] At the same time, the Assistant U.S. Secretary of State, David Mack, paradoxically pointed out that Yemen should not consider exporting its experience to neighboring countries.[106] Although there was a degree of U.S. aid, it was accompanied by a letter from the U.S. Ambassador, Arthur Hughes, who emphasized that the development of Yemen's relations with neighboring countries is more important than democracy and civil liberties.[107]

Either way, the democratic process in Yemen achieved a number of parliamentary elections in 1993, 1997, and 2003 as well as the presidential elections in 1999 and 2006, not to mention the election of local council elections. U.S., after every election, showed its admiration for democracy in Yemen accompanied by its evaluation. After the success of the 1997 election, a report of the U.S. embassy stressed that *"the support of the United States to democratic development, and the openness and enthusiasm of the Yemenis refutes the commonly known idea that the Arab world is not a suitable region for democracy"*.[108] Unfortunately, this statement did not change U.S. foreign policy towards democracy in other countries.

As observed from the implicit American objection to the exportation of the democratic experience of Yemen, the U.S. did not only deal with the authoritarian leaders in the region but, in fact, protected those states from democracy itself. Gulf countries considered Yemen's democracy as a threat to the survival of the current regimes and threatened the stability of the entire region, and thus conflicts with the vital interests of the U.S. leaders agreed with the premise that democracy does not suit the culture of Arab States.[109] The success of democracy in the more traditional Arab societies such as Yemen has enhanced the possibility of spreading democracy in the region. But U.S. remained content with accepting marginal reforms rather than putting its interests in those countries at risk.

Even after the events of 9/11, the U.S. sought to impose democracy in the framework of a comprehensive strategy known as a Greater Middle East project in addition to its efforts to amend curriculums and to discourage religious schools. In any case, the Gulf States, particularly Saudi Arabia, were excluded from this project due to their importance to the U.S. strategy and its unwillingness to risk its vital interests in this region. America's relationship with the region is a matter of balancing interests and principles endorsed by many of the supporters of democracy.[110]

Another dilemma facing the U.S. strategy of promoting democracy is the possibility of Islamic movements taking over in several Arab countries like Egypt, Jordan and Palestine.[111] In the case of Yemen, the Yemeni Reform Group (*Islah),* which is considered the only Islamic party in Yemen, was able to participate in a coalition government and won eight portfolios in 1993 to 1997. *Islah* later become part of the opposition and joined with the *Joint Meeting Parties* (JMP). Recently, *Islah* with *JMP* are leading the revolution in Yemen and are participating in the government that was formed in December 2011 jointly with the General People's Congress (GPC). It appears that the U.S. government has loosely accepted this party as they are yet to express any official concern.

At present, it appears that the Obama administration does not object to the arrival of Islamist parties to power, but also supports it, whether in Tunisia, Egypt or Yemen. However, the U.S. has its share or reservations in that it questions the position of the *Islah* party concerning human rights issues such as the Hijab, early marriage, and women's participation in the nation. Perhaps the lack of U.S. fear regarding this party is due to the fact that the *Islah* party has taken several steps to foster its global credibility including, the abandonment of its leaders suspected in U.S., as well as its quick take condemnation of any acts of terrorism both in the region and the world. In addition, *Islah* is marketing itself as a moderate party along the lines of the Justice and Development Party (AKP) in Turkey.

The U.S. embassy and American institutions played a major role in several different aspects to support democracy and human rights in Yemen.[112] The U.S. worked on encouraging a democratic dialogue among stakeholders in the entire political spectrum, encouraged the government to execute significant political and economic reforms, implemented various programs to support democratic principles and practices, and worked to strengthen a reform-oriented mentality for parliamentarians and political party members. In addition, The United States remains a significant contributor to anti-human and drug trafficking projects and the activation of civil society institutions, including journalists and domestic NGOs.

As noted in the impact of the external factors on the relations during the post-Cold War era, the common trends towards democracy and human rights values prompted the two countries to develop their relations. U.S. supported the Arab revolutions in the name of spreading democracy and freedom including the revolution in Yemen. However, that policy did not reach the Gulf States, and its attitude about Yemen's revolution was not echoed in the attempts for revolution in Bahrain or Saudi. After the success of Yemen's revolution, the U.S. policy to support liberal values is not yet clear because of its current focus on the war on terror in Yemen. It has yet to be determined if democracy and democratic institutions strengthen or weaken American perceptions of terror and terrorism.

3.5 The Global War on Terrorism

The 9/11 attacks have been one of the most important international events in modern history. Certainly, such a global event had an impact on the relations between Yemen and U.S. Due to the continuous and increase in terrorist activities, it is difficult to study the impact of the global war on terrorism (GWOT) as a dynamic on the relationships between Yemen and U.S. Two perspectives are however important for forming an evaluation of its impact.

As will be discussed in this section, the first perspective examines the influence of GWOT on the relationship by studying the changes that occurred in the international relations and the U.S. foreign policies after the 9/11 attacks. It also highlights the international treaties and conventions and the impact of the Arab response on Yemen's foreign policy. This section also highlights Yemen's role in these transformations. The second perspective neglects the external dimension to focus on the direct security and military cooperation between the two countries associated with counter-terrorism in Yemen. This forms the subject of discussion of the following chapter.

Concerning the implications of the 9/11 attacks on international relations, several main aspects reflected a shift in the international system. First, the main characteristic of the global war on terrorism era is the emergence of the non-state threats as an unconventional security issue, which gives a new dimension to national security.[113] International relations are no longer as they were in the Cold War era. The 9/11 attacks marked a change in the international system from once being competitive to now being cooperative. In essence, there is a new balance of terror between state and non-state actors. Bin Laden says, *"The towers of New York collapsed and their collapse precipitated an even greater debacle: the collapse of the myth of America, the great power"*.[114] Further, he adds, *"Just as they're Killing us, we have the right to kill them so that there will be a balance of terror... "*[115]

Second, the perspective of security dominated the nature of international relations. The U.S. policy has managed to affect the largest international coalition ever known in history. Following the events of 9/11, the response of Western countries, especially U.S. to the 9/11 attacks led to the securitization of the relations between states under the control of the international community through the United Nations and the UN Security Council. Old concepts and values have new connotations associated with the international security perspective such as individual liberty, free financial markets, democracy, freedom of belief, and social development. Hoffman says, *"Although the implications of these actions took some time to become clear, they have begun to force specialists and non-specialists alike, within several advanced Western armed forces, to re-think some basic models and assumptions."*[116] Moreover, Frederking, Artime, and Pagano express their view that, *"The post-cold war era is over and a new era dominated by the new U.S. grand strategy of pre-emption has begun".*[117]

The other side of the shifts in international relations is the lack of state independence, non-interference in internal Affairs, and sovereignty. From the first glance of the 9/11 attacks, nations were left with no option but to either join the coalition or risk being seen as the enemy. The U.S. declared that *"Every nation has to either be with us, or against us. Those who harbor terrorists, or who finance them, are going to pay a price".*[118] Some studies examine the nature of current international relations as a post-Westphalia. A recent dissertation concluded that *"the contemporary global political environment is distinctly post-Westphalian. The current era will be seen to be defined in direct opposition to the tenets of state-primacy, sovereignty, autonomy and territoriality that form the basis of the Westphalian era."*[119]

At the international level, there is no doubt that terrorism has become a global threat to both international and national security and has led to greater cooperation rather than competition between security agencies. Following the terrorist attacks on 9/11, the U.S. administration announced its leadership of the international coalition against terrorism, with the goal of bringing al-Qaeda and its leaders to justice and preventing the emergence of other terrorist organizations.[120] The U.S. strategy on its war on terrorism includes the war on countries that finance or act as safe havens for terrorist groups.[121]

Furthermore, the international community has constantly been perusing numerous short-term protective measures, as well as long-term proactive strategies, to counter terrorism. The international coalition is not limited as it includes procedures, plans, and alliances, in addition to social, political, economic, and military cooperation. Consequently, the foreign policies of nearly all nations have been rectified to inculcate the demands of the global war on terrorism. Doubtless, this includes Yemen's foreign policy. Although 12 of the current 16 international legal instruments about counter-terrorism are already promulgated by the international community, few countries have ratified it before the 9/11 events.[122] After the adoption of Security Council resolution 1373, 2001, the majority of UN member states have ratified the 16 legal instruments.[123] The role of UN has become more effectual to counter-terrorism.

Accordingly, Yemen-U.S. relations were affected by the shift in international relations, especially in light of the main aspects hitherto mentioned. The U.S. had appointed itself head of the global war while Yemen is popularly perceived as a haven for terrorists. Unexpectedly, U.S. found that its national security was linked to the security and stability of other weak countries such as Yemen. Similarly, Yemen found that its national security was linked to the military and security assistances from the U.S. and the international community, due to the potential weakness of Yemen in confronting international terrorism.[124] Therefore, both countries have become more interested in the development of bilateral relations according to their mutual vital interests.

In regards to the Yemen response, Yemen's leaders were aware of the international change in power politics and accordingly allied itself with the U.S. and the international community. Furthermore, nevertheless, Yemen feared that if it abstained from an alliance with the international community, it would become the target of U.S. retaliatory or pre-emptive strikes.[125] Some perceive that Yemen's role in the war on terrorism reflects internal needs rather than the subjugation of external pressures.[126] At any rate, Yemen understood its dire situation and quickly moved to condemn terrorist acts. President Saleh confirmed Yemen's position against terrorism and the importance of concerted global efforts to fight it.[127] But President Saleh during his speeches did not overlook the terrorism of Israel against the Palestinian people and the importance of identifying an agreeable definition of terrorism in addition to the Arabs to take a definitive position on terrorism through the Arab League.

Accordingly, Yemen increased and systematized its cooperation with the international community and the U.S. according to the international conventions and agreements for combating terrorism. The ensuing bilateral or international agreements opened a wide range of unprecedented platforms for cooperation between Yemen and U.S. Yemen agreed to provide financial information and intelligence in suspects and participated in combat operations in Yemen. Yemen's commitment to the war on terrorism including UN resolution 1373 on September 23, 2001, helped improve relations with U.S. and the international community. Simply, Yemen cooperation with the international community to eliminate terrorism is the same goal of U.S. security and military cooperation with Yemen. Furthermore, U.S. foreign policy usually seeks to push the international community to cooperate in carrying the burden of aid to Yemen.

In the framework of regional politics, the Yemen-U.S. cooperation affected adverse public opinion regarding the vague U.S. behavior towards its war on terrorism. The popular impression among Arabs including Yemenis was that the American counter-terrorism strategy is not just a reaction to the intimidation of terrorism, but a mirror image of the component of the domestic political processing.[128] Government institutions, the media, American elites, and the Zionist lobby were seen as playing a structural part in forming U.S. behavior in the context of the war on terrorism, and as such the initial aims of the war were seen as having been subjected to the personal interests of certain groups within the U.S. rather than a commitment to world peace and stability.[129]

Due to such factors, the American counter-terrorism policy changed from the concentration on counter-terrorism to the reformulation of the American interests in the Arab region. For example, the U.S. invaded Iraq under the fabricated justifications of Iraq's relationship with al-Qaeda, in addition to the classification of the resistance factions of the Zionist occupation of Palestine as terrorist organizations.[130] Moreover, the White House perspective of counter-terrorism became the only lens to interpret and manage regional issues. It persistently offered a unilateral definition of terrorism. In general, the U.S. policy to address the causes of terrorism was based on the use of pressure on Arab societies in order to bring about change quickly, which in turn might lead to instability.[131]

As a result, Yemeni politics preferred to push the Arab League to counter this trend, rather than Yemen's involvement in a direct dispute with U.S. In 2001, former Yemeni President Saleh took the initiative to invite Arab leaders to hold an emergency Arab summit to identify a unified Arab position. In a similar development, the Foreign Minister of Yemen al-Qirbi asked the United Nations to convene a conference to determine the definition of terrorism.[132]

In spite of the comprehensive cooperation between the two countries in the GWOT, there were many points of dispute between Yemen and U.S. within the Arabian dispute. The difference between the concept of terrorism and resistance was one of such point of contention. The legitimacy of *Hamas* and the Palestinian resistance is an example of the implications of this debate. In addition to banning religious schools, curriculum was modification and terrorism was unjustly limited to Islamic extremism.

Regardless of the previous points of contention, a factor which had a more important impact than the events of 9/11 on Yemen-U.S. relations is the transformation of security issues from being a marginal part of Yemen-U.S. relations to being a central issue of unprecedented importance. U.S. decision-makers understood the importance of Yemen as a strategic partner in the GWOT due to several internal factors in addition to the geo-strategic importance of Yemen.

3.6 Conclusion

A variety of external dynamics help explain the pattern of Yemen-U.S. relations, which is characterized by uncertainty. Some factors that shape the relationship may lead the two countries to strengthen their relations while others have hindered it. Regionally, Yemen is characterized by its important geographical location and its proximity to important maritime routes, straits, and natural resources. The geographical location of Yemen, in turn, increased the importance of maintaining good relations from the U.S. perspective. Meanwhile, the importance of the region caused U.S. to adopt a policy aimed at maintaining the stability of the region, which is consistent with the policy of Yemen.

On the other hand, the Yemen-U.S. contradictory policies in the region are a negative factor that has led to tension between the two countries. In this regard both countries differ over a number of issues among the more important are the U.S. military presence, in other words, regional security, the Saudi Arabia policy towards Yemen and the Arab-Israeli conflict and normalization.

The Yemen-U.S. relations appear closer in the light of the Cold War. Before South Yemen became a communist state, North Yemen succeeded to some extent to play the Eastern bloc against the Western bloc in order to secure its national interests and advanced its military capability. After PDRY became a communist state, U.S. orientations in the region prioritized its international hegemony followed by regional and U.S. interests in Yemen. In the wake of its containment policy, U.S. resumed and developed relations with North Yemen and engaged in the disputes of North and South Yemen. America's relationship to Yemen largely remained responsive to the degree of Yemen's involvement with the USSR.

The rules of the game that governed the relations between Yemen and the U.S. changed in the post-Cold War era. Although democracy is one of the factors that prompted the importance of bilateral relations between the two countries in the 1990s, U.S. aid to Yemen was less than expected, particularly with reference to the American approach to the full support of emerging democracies. The special status of the region played a negative role, which caused American leaders to believe that exporting the democratic experience of Yemen constitutes a threat to U.S. interests in the region. Yemen's democracy threatened to destabilise the non-democratic states in the region. However, at the same time, U.S. decision-maker believes that democracy is an important factor for the stability of Yemen and its unity, and thus it is considered as a stabilizing factor for the region. Ironically, U.S. policy helps to protect the dictatorial states from democracy itself. In any case and under such blatant contradiction, the events of 9/11 enhanced the democratic trend in America's strategy in the region. This strengthened the importance of Yemen's democracy as an early experiment. This does not mean, in any way, that the democratic principles in the U.S. strategy are prioritised over its security and economic interests in the region.

On the other side, the influence of the global war on terrorism is represented as another factor that drove the decision-makers in both countries to develop bilateral relations. The events of 9/11 and the subsequent international coalition to counter-terrorism have impacted on international relations. As such, Yemen-U.S. relations also underwent a degree of reconfiguration. The U.S. vision of threats to national security became highly sensitive and affected change on the global level through the enactment of international laws and international conventions. Accordingly, international conventions and bilateral agreements secure the Yemen-U.S. relations. These covenants are frameworks that define the obligations of both countries as well as provide a platform for cooperation in various fields. Yemen however became aware of the double standards of U.S. policy towards terrorism issues in the region as evident in public dissatisfaction with such policies. In Addition, the lack of differentiation between the U.S. policies to combat terrorism and America's interest in the region have adversely affected Yemeni cooperation.

[1] Mansour Al-Zandani. "The Principles of Yemen Foreign Policy" (class lecture, The Yemeni Foreign Policy, University of Sana'a, Sana'a, September, 2002).

[2] Those terms are often linked to foreign projects such as the New Middle East and the Greater Middle East, while Arabic literature considers that stems from the hostile schemes of Arab nationalism. Apart from that, the term of Middle East spread after used by Captain Mahan in his article in 1902. See; Clayton R. Koppes. "Captain Mahan, General Gordon, and the Origins of the Term 'Middle East'." *Middle Eastern Studies* 12, no. 1 (1976), pp. 95-98.

[3] The countries bordering the Red Sea are Somalia, Djibouti, Eritrea, Sudan, Egypt, Jordan, Israel and Saudi Arabia in addition to Yemen which has 450 kilometres.

[4] The (IOR-ARC) is an International/Diplomatic Organization. It defines a distinctive area in international politics consisting of coastal states bordering the Indian Ocean. For more reading see, "Background." *Indian Ocean Rim Association for Regional Cooperation* (2012), accessed 5/1/2012, http://www.iorarc.org/about-us/background.aspx

[5] The GCC member states are Kuwait, Saudi Arabia, Qatar, Bahrain, Oman and the United Arab Emirates.

[6] President Ali Saleh sought to establish Alliance of Sana'a in order to raise the level of cooperation among member states, and another analysis is seen it as Yemen response to unaccepted Yemen in the GCC, or that the alliance is aimed at trapping Eritrea that share the bad relations with member states.

[7] See Appendix A: Map of Bab el Mandeb in the Red Sea.

[8] Ali Al-Ghifari. *Al-Deplumasia Al-Yemenia 1900-2000*, p. 16.

[9] See Appendix B: Map of Trade Routes between the Indian Ocean, Red Sea and Mediterranean.

[10] US Department of State. *US Policy toward Yemen; Policy Statement Prepared in the Department of State,*p. 1192.

[11] US Department of State. *Telegram from Secretary of State Rogers to the Department of State* (Washington DC: Office of the Historian, July 3, 1972), accessed 3/9/2010, http://history.st-ate.gov/historicaldocuments/frus1969-76v24/d193

[12] According to statistics of 2011 for production and calculating the Libyan production for the year 2010, while the oil reserves according to the statistics of 2012. See, BP Organization. "Bp Statistical Review of World Energy." (London: BP Amoco, 2012), accessed 20/7/2012, http://www.bp.co-m/assets/bp...review_of_world_energy_full_report_2012.pdf, pp. 6-7.

[13] Appendix C: Figure of the World Oil Reserve 2011.

[14] "The Oil and Gas Producing Countries of North Africa and the Middle East." *IFP Energies Nouvelles* (2012), accessed 21/6/2012, http://www.ifpenergiesnouvelles.com/publications/notes-de-synthese-panorama/panorama-2012

[15] US Agency for International Development. *2010-2012 Yemen Country Strategy* (Washington DC: USAID, 2010), accessed 4/5/2012, http://pdf.usaid.gov/pdf_docs/PDACP572.pdf, p. 1.

[16] Subhash Kapila. "Middle East Changing Dynamics: Strategic Perspectives on Power Play of United States, Russia and China." *South Asia Analysis Group* 4336 (February, 2011), accessed 6/5/2011, http://www.southasiaanalysis.org/%5Cpapers44%5Cpaper4336.html

[17] Galal Fak'yrah. "Ta'abea't Almoared Fi Alsyasah Alk'regayah Alyemenyah." *Awarak Bah'thyah* (2009), accessed 3/2/2012, http://www.shebacss.com/ar/publications.php?action=viewPub&id=35, pp. 7-12.

[18] See Appendix H: Table of Yemen's Vote on the UN Resolutions Concerning Iraq.

[19] Nizar Alk'ader. "Alalakat Alyemeniah Alemrekiah Fi D'oa Althwapet Alwataniah." *26 September* (12/12/2002), accessed 5/9/2010, http://www.26sep.net/newsweekarticle.php?lng=arabic&sid=2253

[20] Kaled Ahmed Alramah. "Alkarsanah Alsomaliah Ka Tahdid Lelamn Alkomai Alyeamni." In *Alkarsanah Albahryah Fi Kalyg Aden and Almoh'iet' Alhandi,* (ed.) Mohammed Saif. (Sana'a: Wkalat Alanba Alyemaniah Saba, 2009), p. 100.

[21] Through my work in the Office of President of Yemen, Department of the Americas and Europe, in 2008, the Yemeni political leadership has sought to involve many great countries to protection of the Gulf of Aden from Somalia pirates because of the fear that America was seeking to control the territorial waters of Yemen.

[22] Salwa A. Dammag. "A Study Yemen-United States Relations 1990-2002.", p. 76.

[23] Mansour al-Zandani. "Almasaleh Alamericieah Kabl Almbadea." (paper presented at the Had'er wa Mostak'bal Alalakat Al-Yemeniah Al-Americiah, Sana'a, 2002), p. 53.

[24] Joseph was Assistance Secretary of State for Near East and South Asian Affairs (1969-1974). See, Foa'ad Shehab. *Tad'awer Alestrategiah Alamerikeyah Fi Alk'alig Alarabi* (Bahrain: Fak'rawi, 1994) p.35.

[25] Bakeel A. aL-Zandani. "US-Yemen Relations in a Changing World: A Study of Four Major Events in US-Yemen Relations.", p. 24.

[26] Michael Horton. "The Unseen Hand: Saudi Arabian Involvement in Yemen." *Terrorism Monitor* IX, no. 12, (2011), accessed 8/3/2012, http://global-security-news.com/tag/saudi-arabia-and-yemen/, p. 6.

[27] Many of the elites of Yemen are rejecting the Treaty of Jeddah, including the *Southern* movement, *Houthia*, the party of al-Nasserist and the spectra of young revolutionaries.

[28] Subhash Kapila. "Middle East Changing Dynamics: Strategic Perspectives on Power Play of United States, Russia and China." *South Asia Analysis Group* 4336, (February, 2011), accessed 6/5/2011, http://www.southasiaanalysis.org/%5Cpapers44%5-Cpaper4336.html

[29] David Frum. "America's Ally in the Middle East." *Foreign and Defense Policy* (May 03, 2008), accessed 4/6/2011, http://www.aei.org/article/27930

[30] Fayz Rash'ied. "America, Israel Man Yah'kom Man." *Al-Tajreed Al-Arabi* (November, 2010), accessed 2/1/2011, http://www.arabrenewal.info/2010-06-11-14-11-19/4255

[31] Ahmed Hamdan. "Lemath'a Tada'am Alwelayat Almotahedah Israel." *26 September News* (25/2/2012), p. 12.

[32] Ali Al-Ghifari. *Al-Deplumasia Al-Yemenia 1900-2000,* p. 188.

[33] Bakeel A. aL-Zandani. "US-Yemen Relations in a Changing World: A Study of Four Major Events in US-Yemen Relations", p. 23.

[34] Moath A. Alrefaei. "Hatheh Alh'rb Alea'alamiah Wa Aba'adaha." *26 September* (3/6/2004), accessed 8/7/2011, http://www.26sep.net/newsweekarticle.php?lng=arabic&sid=10164

[35] Director of Intelligence Central. *South Yemen-USSR: Outlook for the Relationship* (Washington DC: National Intelligence Estimate, 30 March 1984), accessed 19/9/2010, www.foia.cia.gov/do-cs/DOC_0000681975/DOC_0000681975.pdf, pp. 17-19.

[36] Roger R. Trask. "United States Relations with the Middle East in the Twentieth Century: A Developing Area in Historical Literature.", p. 293.

[37] US Department of State. *US Policy toward Yemen; Policy Statement Prepared in the Department of State,* pp. 1192-1198.

[38] In 8 March, 1956 the trade agreement between the Soviet Union and the Kingdom of Yemen was signed in Cairo. The Agreement was signed by the representative of the Foreign Trade Ministry Mr I.P.Krotov and on behalf of the King of Yemen by the State Minister, Mr Samad Abu Taleb. For more reading; "History of Embassy." *Embassy of the Russian Federation in the Republic of Yemen* (2011), accessed 7/7/2012, http://www.rusemb-ye.org/oldsite/content/view/38/lang,en/

[39] US Department of State. *Memorandum from the Director of the Office of near Eastern Affairs (Rockwell) to the Assistant Secretary of State for near Eastern, South Asian, and African Affairs (Rountree)*(Washington DC: Office of the Historian, February 21, 1958), accessed 3/6/2011, http://history.state.gov/historicaldocuments/frus1958-60v12/d360

[40] Bakeel A. aL-Zandani. "US-Yemen Relations in a Changing World: A Study of Four Major Events in US-Yemen Relations.", pp. 12-15.

[41] US Department of State. *Memorandum from the Director of the Office of near Eastern Affairs (Wilkins) to the Assistant Secretary of State for near Eastern, South Asian, and African Affairs* (Washington DC: Office of the Historian, January 2, 1957), accessed 5/2/2011, http://history.state.go-v/historicaldocuments/frus1955-57v13/d425

[42] Manfred W. Wenner. *Modern Yemen : 1918-1966* (Baltimore: Johns Hopkins Press, 1986), p. 181.

[43] Bakeel A. al-Zandani. "The Bush Doctrine, the War on Terror, and American Promotion of Democracy in the Middle East: The Cases of Egypt and Yemen." (PhD Thesis, University of Nebraska, 2010), p. 188.

[44] US Department of State. *Telegram from the Department of State to the Embassy in Egypt, Embassy Requested Convey Following Message Abu Taleb for Imam from Usg* (Washington DC: Office of the Historian, March 29, 1956).

[45] The rebels, known as Republicans, succeeded in killing Imam Ahmad, controlled urban areas, and sought to acquire international recognition. In the aftermath of the revolution, Crown Prince Bader fled to the northern regions bordering Saudi Arabia. He regrouped his tribal supporters, who were known as Royalists, and then started seeking external support.

[46] An editorial of the New York Times on November 23, 1962 urged the US to recognize the revolutionaries' government of Yemen. It indicated that the new system represents a nucleus for the dissemination of the progressive ideas of democracy in other parts of the Arabian Peninsula. See, Ahmad Mohamed AbdulGhani. "Wark'a K'odemat Ela Nidowit Al-Alak'at Al-Yemeni Al-Americiah." (paper presented at the Althadiat Alrahenh Amam al-Alak'at al-Yemeni al-Americiah, Sana'a, 2001), p. 8.

[47] Mansoor al-Zandani. "Al-Alakit Al-Yemeni Maa Al-Qwatine Al-Odhmaiene, 1962-1988." (PhD Thesis, Jaimat al-Qahera, 1988), p. 33.

[48] The United Arab Republic was a nation that established a union between Egypt and Syria. The union began in 1958 and existed until 1961, when Syria has been seceded from the union. But Egypt continued to be known officially as the "United Arab Republic" until early a1970s.

[49] Mohammed Ahmad Zabarah. *Yemen, Traditionalism Vs. Modernity* (New York : Praeger, 1982), pp.78-79.

[50] Ibid. p.78.

[51] Jabārāt, *Alaqat Al-Yamaniyah Al-Amrikiyah 1904-1948, 'Ahd Al-Imam Yaḥyá Ḥamid Al-Din*, pp.30-31.

52 Simon C. Smith. "Conflict and Co-Operation - Anglo-American Relations in the Gulf from the Nationalization of Anglo-Iranian Oil to the Yemeni Revolution." In *Britain's Revival and Fall in the Gulf: Kuwait, Bahrain, Qatar, and the Trucial States, 1950-71* (London: Routledge, 2004), p. 4.

53 US Department of State. *Memorandum from the Department of State Executive Secretary (Brubeck) to the President's Special Assistant for National Security Affairs* (Washington DC: Office of the Historian, December 6, 1962), accessed 5/6/2011, http://history.state.gov/historicaldocuments/frus1961-63v18/d112

54 Jholo Fsakia Elinak. *Political Tensions in the Arab Republic of Yemen 1962-1985* (Sana'a: al-Markaz al- Yemeni lel Derasat wa al-Buhoth, 1994), p. 38.

55 Memorandum From Robert W. Komer of the National Security Council Staff to President Kennedy on November 28, 1962 emphasized that *"After a bit of arm-twisting, we've gotten a very responsive reply from Cairo to our Yemen disengagement/recognition package.... We now have to get a satisfactory YAR declaration. They will probably balk at the reference to Aden and the new Federation which we seek at UK request. Our fall-back position is to propose instead that Yemen announce willingness to adhere to the 1934 treaty with UK which binds them to respect Aden's sovereignty. Our recognition statement will then interpret this to mean precisely that. We are keeping the British fully informed".*

56 US Department of State. *Memorandum from Robert W. Komer of the National Security Council Staff to President Kennedy* (Washington DC: Office of the Historian, November 28, 1962), accessed 3/5/2011, http://history.state.gov/historicaldocuments/frus1961-63v18/d104

57 "History of Embassy." *Embassy of the Russian Federation in the Republic of Yemen* (2011), accessed 7/7/2012, http://www.rusemb-ye.org/oldsite/content/view/38/lang,en/

58 Albahr. *Tareekh Al-Yemen Almoaser*, pp. 96-98.

59 Bakeel A. aL-Zandani. "US-Yemen Relations in a Changing World: A Study of Four Major Events in US-Yemen Relations", pp. 11-12.

60 Manfred W. Wenner. *Modern Yemen: 1918-1966*, p. 180.

61 Mojeeb Alrahman. *Al-Yemen Wa Al-Dwoal Al-Kobra', Derasah Tah'liliah Tawthekiah*, p. 26.

62 Washington recognized YAR on condition that "In view of confusing and contradictory statement which has cast doubt upon the intentions of the new regime in Yemen, the United States government welcomes the reaffirmation by YAR of its intentions to honour its international obligations, of its desire for normalization and establishment of friendly relations with its neighbors, and its intention to concentrate on internal affairs to raise the living standards of the Yemeni people."

63 Almadhagi. *Yemen and the United States: The Study of a Smallpower and Super-State Relationship 1962–1994* p. 46.

64 Jesse Ferris. "Egypt, the Cold War, and the Civil War in Yemen, 1962 -1966.", pp. 93-123.

65 Mohammed Ahmad Zabarah. *Yemen, Traditionalism Vs. Modernity*, p. 80.

66 After the independence of Southern Yemen, America was quick to recognise People's Democratic Republic of Yemen PDRY and did so on December 7, 1967. US recognition came a few days after South Yemen gained independence from Britain on November 31, 1967. See, Ali Al-Ghifari. *Al-Deplumasia Al-Yemenia 1900-2000*, p. 189.

[67] Telegram from the Department of State to the Embassy in Iran on December 13, 1967, indicated that "the Soviets may have moved in a phase of heightened direct involvement and greater risks to establish a dominant position in the Southwest Arabian Peninsula. In fact the character and scope of their activities suggest intent to carry out an armed intrusion that would exacerbate the inherently unstable conditions in this troubled area".

[68] Mohamed Aglan Ga'id. "Al-Alaqat Al-Yemenia Al-Ameicia 1990-1998.", p. 25.

[69] Khadeejah AL-Haysami. *Al-Alaqat Al-Yemenia Al-Saudia: 1962-1982* (Cairo: Dar al-Fath lel Nashr, 1983), p. 140.

[70] Fred Halliday. *Revolution and Foreign Policy the Case of South Yemen 1967-1987*, p.145.

[71] Faisal Jellol. *Al-Thawratien, Al-Gumhureityn Wa Al-Wehda 1962-1994* (Beirut: Dar al-Jadedd, 2000), p. 44.

[72] Mike Shuster. "The Middle East and the West: The US Role Grows." *NPR: National Public Radio* (August, 2004), accessed 29/9/2010, http://www.npr.org/templates/story/story.php?storyId=3865983

[73] John Peterson. "The United States and Yemen: A Historical of Unfulfilled Expectations." In *Handbook of US-Middle East Relations, Formative Factors and Regional Perspectives*, (ed.) Robert E. Looney. (London, New York: Routledge, 2009), p. 503.

[74] Robin Leonard Bidwell. *The Two Yemens*, p. 235.

[75] US Department of State. *Telegram from Secretary of State Rogers to the Department of State.*

[76] Fred Halliday. *The Society and Politic in the Arabian Peninsula*, trans. by Mohamed Al-Rumaihi. (Beirut: Dar Al-Nahar for Publication, 2000), p. 40.

[77] Muhsin Al-Aini. *Khamson Aamn Fi Al-Remal Al-Moth'rekah: Qasaty Maa Benaa Al-Dawlah Al-Yemeni Al-Hadetha* (Cairo: Dar al-Sharwak, 1999), pp. 170-200.

[78] Bowman L. Bradley. "Realism and Idealism: US Policy toward Saudi Arabia, from the Cold War to Today." *Parameters* 35, no. 4 (2005–2006), pp. 91-105.

[79] Foa'ad Shehab. *Tad'awer Alestrategiah Alamerikeyah Fi Alk'alig Alarabi*, p. 33.

[80] Yahiya Halmy Rajab. *Alk'alyg Alarabi Wa Alsera'a Aldoali Almoa'aser* (Kuwait: Dar Ala'arobah LeLnasher wa Altawziea'a, 1989), p. 2.

[81] Ethiopia was among the countries bordering the Red Sea until 24 May1991, when Eritrea declared its independence.

[82] Rajab. *Alk'alyg Alarabi Wa Alsera'a Aldoali Almoa'aser*, pp. 39-40.

[83] The roots of this war could be traced to the end of February 1972, when the PDRY intelligence killed more than sixty people and leaders of YAR's tribes. This development was followed by Aden's announcement that an invading force of 2,000 mercenaries, trained by American instructors, has been defeated and suffered heavy. On the contrary, Sana'a stated that Southern Yemenis invited the tribal leaders to a banquet where they were killed. YAR's leaders thought that these tribes were not satisfied with the reconciliation between Republicans and Royalists, either inside YAR or with Saudi Arabia, and were seeking to establish relations with the PDRY to create chaos in YAR.

[84] The KSA have encouraged some of exiles' groups in establishing the National Unity Front UNF, with headquarters in YAR. See, CIA and the intelligence organizations of the Departments of State and Defense. *Special National Intelligence Estimate* (Washington DC: Office of the Historian February, 1971), accessed 9/4/2011, http://history.state.gov/historicaldocuments/frus1969-76v24/d182#fn1

[85] Joseph Kostiner. *Yemen: The Tortuous Quest for Unity, 1990-94* (London: Royal Institute of International Affairs, 1996), p. 14.

[86] CIA and the Intelligence Organizations of the Departments of State and Defense. *Special National Intelligence Estimate* (Washington DC: Office of the Historian February, 1971), accessed 3/9/2011, http://history.state.g-ov/historicaldocuments/frus1969-76v24/d182#fn1

[87] Stephen Zunes. "Yemen: Latest US Battleground." *Foreign Policy in Focus* (January, 2010), accessed 9/9/2011, http://www.fpif.org/articles/yemen_latest_us_battleground

[88] Almadhagi. *Yemen and the United States: The Study of a Smallpower and Super-State Relationship 1962–1994,* pp. 107-110.

[89] Director of Intelligence Central. *South Yemen-USSR: Outlook for the Relationship,* p. 17.

[90] US House of Represetative Committe on Foreign Affairs. *Proposed Arms Transfers to the Yemen Arab Republic: Hearing March 12,1979* (Washington DC: US Govt. Print, 1979).

[91] Abd Alrahman Alromish. "Takrir Eh's'ai an Keta'a Alnafit' Wa Alma'aden Fi Al-Yemen." (Sana'a: Almarkaz Alwatany Lelma'alomat, 2003), pp. 7-8.

[92] F. Gregory Gause. "Democracy, Terrorism and American Policy in the Arab World." *Assessing Middle East Security Prospects* (April, 2005), accessed 12/1/2011, http://www.dtic.mil/cgibin/GetTR-Doc?Location=U2&doc=GetTRDoc.pdf&AD=ADA435048

[93] Abu Bakr Al-Qirbi. "US Wa Masirat' Aldomkra'tiah in Yemen." (paper presented at the Had'er wa Mostak'bal Alalakat Al-Yemeniah Al-Americiah, Sana'a, 2002), p. 11.

[94] Abdullah M. Al-faqih. "The Struggle for Liberalization and Democratization in Egypt, Jordan and Yemen." (PhD Thesis, Northeastern University, 2003), p. 191.

[95] See Appendix D: Table of Humanitarian Conventions Ratified by Yemen.

[96] Al-faqih., "The Struggle for Liberalization and Democratization in Egypt, Jordan and Yemen," 191.

[97] Hamod Monaser. "Almasar Altat'biky Ll-Tagrobah Aldemokrateiah Fi Al-Yemen Wa Mo'asherat Al-Mostak'bal." In *Aldemok'ratiah Wa Al-A'hzab Fi Al-Yemen*, (ed.) Fares al-Sakaf. (Sana'a: Dar al-Majed Lel-Teba'ah wa al-Nasher, 1998), p. 43.

[98] Ministry of Planning and Development and UNDP. "Yemen Human Development Report 2000_2001." (Sana'a: The Human Development Report CD-ROM, 2001), p. 3.

[99] During 7 years since began the democracy in Yemen. US established the National Democratic Institute NDIand has pledged the amount of USD 500,000, which mostly went to finance American observers and some equipment of the electoral process in 1997. It importance to note there are no inventory of US. aid in this aspect. But it is below the level expected.

[100] *Hamas* is an Islamist party in Palestine. It has been able to success in the parliamentary elections to be the governor of Gaza City, but the US considers it as a terrorist group.

[101] For further reading see: Fatma Izri Folensbee. "Spreading Democracy, Supporting Dictators: Pragmatism and Ideology in US Foreign Policy in the Global War on Terror." (Master Thesis, Georgetown University, 2009). And see also, Eric Richard Nitz. "Does Democracy Influence the Export of Terrorism?." (Master Thesis, Georgetown University, 2010).

[102] Council on Foreign relations. "In Support of Arab Democracy: Why and How." by Madeleine K. Albright and Vin Weber Co-Chairs. (New York, 2005), accessed 31/8/2012, http://www.cfr.org/con-tent/publications/attachments/Arab_Democracy_TF.pdf, p. 43.

[103] Al-Shameri. "Alsiasah Alk'argiah Tegah Altagrabah Aldemok'ratiah Alyemeniah 1990-2006.", pp. 164-174.

[104] Dammag. "A Study Yemen-United States Relations 1990-2002.", p. 78. And also see, Al-Shameri. "Alsiasah Alk'argiah Tegah Altagrabah Aldemok'ratiah Alyemeniah 1990-2006.", pp. 106-124.

[105] Almadhagi. *Yemen and the United States: The Study of a Smallpower and Super-State Relationship 1962–1994*, p. 151.

[106] Abu Bakr Al-Qirbi. "US Wa Masirat' Aldomkra'tiah in Yemen.", p. 16. And see, Eric Watkins. *Financial Times* (April, 1993).

[107] Abd Allah Al-Faqiah. "Al-A'lak'at Al-Yemeniah Al-Americiah Bein Alastemrar Wa Altaghieer." *Alwasa't News* (24/5/2006).

[108] Abu Bakr Al-Qirbi. "US Wa Masirat' Aldomkra'tiah in Yemen.", p. 17.

[109] Saliba Sarsar. "Can Democracy Prevail?." *Middle East Quarterly* VII, no. 1(March 2000), accessed 12/4//2010, http://www.meforum.org/40/can-democracy-prevail, pp. 39-48.

[110] Francis Fukuyama and Michael McFaul. "Should Democracy Be Promoted or Demoted?." *The Washington Quarterly* (WINTER, 2007-08), accessed 15/6/2011, http://www.twq.com/08win-ter/docs/08winter_fukuyama.pdf, pp. 36-37.

[111] Congressional Research Service. "US Democracy Promotion Policy in the Middle East: The Islamist Dilemma," by Jeremy M. Sharp. (Washington DC: CRS, June 15, 2006), pp. 17-24.

[112] US Department of states. "Advancing Freedom and Democracy Reports." (Washington DC: The Bureau of Democracy and Labor, May 23, 2008), accessed 9/12/2010, http://photos.state.go-v/libraries/yemen/231771/PDFs/advancing-freedom-and-democracy-reports--2008.pdf, pp. 1-3.

[113] For further more reading about emergence of the non-state actors in the international relations, Peter Hough. *Understanding Global Security*, pp. 65-91.

[114] Stefanie Tetenburg. "Diplomacy in the Post 9/11 Era; an Examination of the Role of Diplomacy in Containing the Terrorist Threat." (Dissertation, King's College London, 2009), p. 2.

[115] Sarah Sullivan. "Courting Al-Jazeera, the Sequel: Estrangement and Signs of Reconciliation." (2002), accessed 10/6/2011, http://www.tbsjournal.com/Archives/Fall01/Jazeera_special.htm

[116] Hoffman. "Complex Irregular Warfare: The Face of Contemporary Conflict." *The Military Balance* 105, no. 1 (2006), p. 411.

[117] Frederking, Artime and Pagano. "Interpreting September 11." *International Politics* 42, no. I (2005), p. 135.

[118] On September 13, 2001, Hillary Clinton exclaimed that phrase and also President Bush said *"Either you are with us, or you are with the terrorists."* See, "USA: You're Either with us or against us Al-Qaeda: Yes, We're with You.", accessed 31/5/2012, http://multipletext.com/2012/2you_are_eit-her_with_us_or_against_us.html

[119] For further reading see, James E.R. Unsworth J.P. "The Global Political System: The Demise of the Westphalian Era Post- 9/11." (PhD Thesis, International Islamic University, 2008).

[120] Todd A. Heussner. "Deterrence as a Means of Maintaining American Pre-Eminence." (Strategy Research Project, US Army War College, 2010), p. 15.

[121] Department of Defense. "National Military Strategic Plan for the War on Terrorism." (Washington, DC: Council on Foreign Relations, February 1, 2006), pp. 4-19.

[122] See Appendix E: Table of the 16 International Legal Instruments.

[123] "International Laws." *Security Council, Counter-Terrorism Commitiee* (21/1/2011), accessed 12/7/2012, http://www.un.org/en/sc/ctc/laws.html

[124] For more reading see; The Senlis Council. "Chronic Failures in the War on Terror: From Afghanistan to Somalia." (London: MF Publishing Ltd, May, 2008), accessed 19/4/2011, http://www.icosgroup.n-et/static/reports/chronic_failures_war_terror.pdf, pp. 6-12.

[125] Shaul Shay. "Terror Abductions in Yemen." accessed 24/6/2010, https://www.10million.org/en/Ter-ror%20abductions%20in%20Yemen

[126] Mohammed A. Mashrah. *Alsiash Alk'argiah Alyameniah Tegah Mokafah'at Alerhab Aldoally* (Sana'a: Mtabe'a Wkala't Alanba'a Alyamaniah Saba'a, 2008), p. 21.

[127] Check out the president Saleh statements in the official newspaper "*26 September"* published on September 13, 20, 26 and 27, 2001.

[128] Martha Crenshaw. "Counterterrorism Policy and the Political Process." *Studies in Conflict and Terrorism* 24, no. 5 (September/October 2001), pp. 329-335.

[129] For further reading see; Janice J. Terry. *US Foreign Policy in the Middle East; the Role of Lobbies and Special Interest Groups* (London: Pluto Press, 2005).

[130] Thomas Powers. "The Vanishing Case for War." *The Long Term View* 6, no. 2 (2004), pp. 106-114.

[131] Nasife Hati. "Alnad'am Alarabi Ba'd 11 September: Altahdieat Wa Alfras." *Alshoa'awn Alarabiah*, no. 109 (Rabia'a 2002), pp. 18-19.

[132] Nabiel al-Razaqi. *Ath'er D'aherat Al-Erhab A'la Al-A'mn Al-Q'aomy Alyemeni*, pp. 347-350.

CHAPTER FOUR:
INTERNAL DYNAMICS INFLUENCING THE
RELATIONSHIP

4.1 Introduction

Although the internal dynamics that govern Yemen relations with U.S. were initially considered to be of marginal influence, the overall vision of the importance of the relationship with each other changed after September 11, 2001. Yemeni internal issues have become a dominating dynamic that has shaped Yemen-U.S. relations until what so call Arab Spring. U.S. could no longer afford to solely consider international politics but was forced to take an interest in Yemen's internal dynamics as part of its interests. According to Wirt and Russell, *"The major impact of 9/11 was upon how the global citizens, particularly those within the US, view the prospective threats to their security: a shift in the long held mind frame of state-to-state interactions has occurred."*[1]

In 2001-2012, the major internal challenges facing the Yemen government were directly linked to the security of Yemeni citizens and Americans alike. Accordingly, a real partnership between the two governments was struck to address issues pertaining to security, politics and economics. Yemen was forced to address terrorism and improve its ability to respond to terrorist threats. In a like fashion, U.S. had no option but to establish a serious and meaningful relationship with Yemen to counter terrorism and to ensure that Yemen did not turn into a failed state. These arguments are examined in this chapter, along with the internal key turning points in the Yemen-U.S. relations.

The chapter aims to examine the influence of the main internal dynamics shaping Yemen-U.S. relations. It also explains the major changes in the relationship after the 9/11 attacks. Overall, four internal factors help to understand the relationship between the two countries and the shift after 9/11. Two of these factors are related to the security cooperation between the two countries while the other factors address Yemen's economic and developmental challenges, on the one hand, and political challenges on the other. The chapter also describes how security concerns act as a dominant internal dynamic that shaped the relationship during the global war on terrorism era.

4.2 The Rise of Jihadist Groups in Yemen

The activity of Jihadist groups in Yemen is one of the early internal dynamics that shaped the bilateral security cooperation between Yemen and U.S. in the 70s-90s. When tracking the sequence of rise of jihadist groups in Yemen, three confirmed cases have influenced the mutual relations between Yemen and U.S. The first case is when there was a tripartite security cooperation between the United States, Saudi Arabia and Yemen to create aggressive fundamentalist thought within Arab societies. The second case of influence on the relationship was when the Yemeni Jihadists returned from Afghanistan to counter the U.S. influence in Yemen. The third case began in the second half of the 90s, when the Yemen-U.S. security cooperation revival regarding counter-terrorism activities started.

This section attempts to illustrate the links between the presence of Yemeni Jihadist Groups and the development of the security cooperation between Yemen and U.S. It also highlights how Yemen's government relations with these jihadist groups shifted from cooperation to competition, in addition to the verification of the dual effect of such shifts on the bilateral relations between Yemen and U.S.

The emergence of the phenomenon of terrorism

During the 1970s, the CIA and Saudi Arabia contributed to the establishment of thousands of religious schools in Yemen. The purpose of this was to nurture a new generation of youths who were susceptible to recruitment or orientation.[2] In spite of Saudi's role as an intermediate state, U.S. formed a security collaboration with

North Yemen to contain the communist influence in the Arabian Peninsula for the first time. North Yemen was selected as an ideological battleground between the Islamists and the communists due to Yemen's unique strategic location, distinctive culture, and the South was the only communist country in the Arabian Peninsula.

The relationship of jihadist groups with Yemen underwent a new development in the 80s under the direction of Reagan-Bush administrations which began a covert project to create groups of jihadists in the battle to defeat Soviet Communism. U.S. provided funding, arming, and training at the estimated cost of $40 billion. Saudi leaders and wealthy Saudi families were involved in paying the bills.[3] These groups included Osama bin Laden and hundreds of Yemeni mujahedeen, who believed that they were in a sacred task for the liberation of Afghanistan. Moreover, some senior military leaders and the ruling class in Yemen were involved in the recruitment of the Mujahedeen.[4] The project formed a platform for the construction of fundamentalist ideology, members, leaders, and supporters with an independent financial network.

At that time, North Yemen played an important role in maintaining U.S. interests in the region. Therefore, particularly in the areas of security and military cooperation, the bilateral relations between the two countries experienced significant growth, especially when North Yemen engaged in two wars with South Yemen, as explained in the previous chapter.

Unlike the first case, the relationship adversely affected the relationship in the second stage of the rise of jihadist groups in Yemen, in particular in the first half of the 1990s. The U.S. intelligence and the Arab leaders involved in this were not aware of the concept of reverse strike or what is known as "Blowback".[5] Terrorism in the 1990s is a clear example of Blowback. In late 1989, the jihadist groups returned to their homes after the Soviets withdrew from Afghanistan. Unlike other Arab countries, Yemen did not object to the return of Yemenis from Afghanistan. But when the *Mujahedeen* returned to Yemen seeking to continue the holy war by founding the Jihadist groups, according to Abo Mosa'ab al-Sory -who is one of the great thinkers of the jihadists and close to Osama bin Laden, Bin Laden's main agenda was to create a jihadist movement in South Yemen.[6]

Consequently, the first confrontation between the jihadist groups and the U.S. military presence in the region was in Yemen. On December 29, 1992, approximately 100 American Marines at two hotels in Aden - *Mövenpick*, and *Goldmohur* -as well as the *United States Navy Galaxy aircraft* near the Aden Airport were the target of terrorist's explosives and rockets.[7] *Mujahedeen* warned U.S. to stay out of Yemen, though U.S. Marines were on their way to Somalia to assist in the humanitarian effort.[8] Moreover, the operations of Islamic Jihad Movement (IJM) in Yemen continued with several minor terrorist operations targeting U.S. oil companies operating as well as the assassination of leaders of the Yemeni Socialist Party (YSP).

As a result of IJM operations in Yemen, Yemen-U.S. relations declined for two reasons. The first reason was the U.S. response to the early terrorist operation in Yemen. The U.S. decision was to withdraw its troops immediately on 31, December, and reduce the activities of their nationals in Yemen.[9] Moreover, there is no evidence of any U.S. Yemeni cooperation in the investigation. It was clear that relations between the two countries were tense. U.S. decision to withdraw meant that it was not interested in engaging in a prolonged battle and as such withdrew from Yemen. The U.S. and Yemeni governments did not address terrorism seriously. From the U.S. point of view, it did not merit comprehensive measures, cooperation, or partnerships.

The second reason was regarding Yemen's response to Jihadist groups activities. Although it could be claimed that Yemen might possibly agree with such groups regarding the U.S. military presence in the region, it nonetheless is adamant that action should not be taken on Yemen's soil.[10] Yemen moved to arrest more than 500 suspects, which ended in the murder and arrest of several members of IJM group.[11] But with the civil war in 1994, Yemen again sought to exploit the fundamentalist currents in politics.[12] The two main parties in the north of Yemen -

the General Popular Congress GPC and *ISLAH*- did not mind accepting the jihadist groups in the civil war against the Yemeni Socialist Party YSP, when leaders of the south announced their departure from the Yemeni unity.[13] After the war ended, the government of Yemen permitted these jihadist groups limited security powers to maintain security in the provinces of South Yemen.[14]

The year 1998 witnessed a growth of jihadist groups not only in Yemen but in the region, in terms of the implementation of specific terrorist operations, such as the bombing of U.S. embassies in Tanzania and Kenya. In Yemen, leaders of radical Islamic groups established the *Aden-Abyan Islamic Army (*AAIA) on July 14, 1998. The Yemeni government was quick to open a dialogue with them to assimilate them. Some of its leaders such as Khalid Abdul Nabi responded to the dialogue, while other leaders such as Abu Hassan al-Mihdhar refused any dialogue and chose confrontation with the government.[15] In December 1998, the AAIA kidnapped 16 foreign tourists forcing Yemeni to undergo a military intervention to free the hostages. That led to the deaths of four Britons and the arrest of al-Mihdhar who was executed after his trial in 1999.[16]

As a result of the growth of jihadist groups in Yemen, the U.S. has become more aware of the importance of security cooperation with Yemen. The third case of influence of Yemeni jihadist groups began in the second half of the 90s, Yemen-U.S. security cooperation regarding counter-terrorism activities started. It was first faced with the challenge of addressing the Afghani-Arab issue.[17] Such groups in Yemen have relations with terrorist groups outside Yemen. The U.S. began to realize the importance of Yemeni cooperation when terrorism began to assert itself globally by placing explosives in the World Trade Center in New York City in 1993 and attacking a joint training facility in Riyadh in 1995.[18] Such attacks encouraged U.S. intelligence to investigate the jihadist groups and their presence in Yemen.[19]

The beginning of Yemeni-American cooperation

In the beginning, the government of Yemen and the U.S. agreed that Yemen had to take the necessary measures of rehabilitation and integration of returnees from Afghanistan into Yemeni society and the deportation of foreigners.[20] In this context, Yemen deported 14000 Afghani-Arabs.[21] Moreover, the Yemen government sought to restore the rule of law in the south and to contain JIM leaders within the official institutions of the state.[22]

Accordingly, the subject of Jihadist groups and counter-terrorism was a key security topic between the two countries. The bilateral security cooperation witnessed a turning point at that time. The fifth and sixth American fleets routinely visited the port of Aden, which the Yemeni government described as mere commercial facilities.[23] The U.S. security delegation visited Sana'a and requested the establishment of specialized departments for counter-terrorism. The visit was in sync with the first collaborative program, which was announced in 1997. It included the training of hundreds of police in counter-terrorism, especially airport police, custom officers and air navigation.[24] The most prominent visit was that of the commander of U.S. naval forces in the Gulf, Thomas B. Fargo in March and Anthony Zinni, head of U.S. Central Command in May.[25] In addition, Carlton Fulford, head of U.S. marine forces in the Pacific visited in October and met with President Saleh to discuss such issues.[26]

Similarly, the security relations between Yemen and the U.S. grew in an unprecedented way. U.S. recognized the importance of Yemeni cooperation in the investigation of terrorist attempts. Yemen welcomed U.S. participation in the investigations on the cell of al-Mihdhar, in addition to the participation of Yemen in the U.S. investigations on the bombings in Tanzania and Kenya.[27] It seems that the security and military cooperation between the two countries reached its peak in 1998. This is manifest through the successive visits of U.S. military leaders and security experts to Yemen.

In all circumstances, it can be argued that Yemeni jihadist groups won the battle with the U.S. over Yemen since U.S. failed to establish any military bases in Yemen, while jihadist groups established a covert training camp in *Abyan*.[28] Jihadist groups caused the U.S. to withdraw its military after two days of U.S. receiving the Mujahedeen's warning. Until mid-1990s, terrorist operations did not lead to any security cooperation between the two countries. The above fact may be a reflection of U.S. belief that state-sponsored terrorism was the major threat of the time.[29] In addition, the U.S. felt that such terrorist operations could be countered without international alliance or bilateral security cooperation.[30] The Clinton administration received harsh criticism for its mild stance towards terrorist operations.[31] In the second half of the 1990s, however, increased terrorist operations led the U.S. to change it strategy regarding counter-terrorism and to forge greater security ties with Yemen. Early Yemeni terrorist activities revived the relationship between the two countries even if it did not lead to establishing a full-fledged partnership in the war on terrorism.

4.3 The Implications of Yemen's War against Al-Qaeda Since 2000

Dealing with Yemeni jihadist groups in the 90s differed from the management of Yemen's war against al-Qaeda since the *USS Cole* accident. Internally, Yemen announced its war against al-Qaeda, while U.S. declared its commitment to stand by Yemen and work side by side. Of course, the Yemen-U.S. partnership in the long war against al-Qaeda in Yemen represented a turning point in relations. Yemen succeeded in this war in the first five years, however, a kind of relapse has taken place in recent years. The outcomes of this war and its implications formed the major dynamic shaping Yemen-U.S. bilateral relations.

This section aims to examine the impact of the stages and outcomes of Yemen's war against al-Qaeda on the bilateral relations between the two countries. It takes into account the effect on the relationship and the increased threat after the formation of the 'al-Qaeda in the Arabian Peninsula (AQAP)' in Yemen. The section also highlights the consequences of internal events during Yemen's war against al-Qaeda on the Yemen-U.S. relations. This will be explained by exploring the two incidents of the *USS Cole* and 9/11 attacks as well as the creation of a new generation of al-Qaida in Yemen after 2006.

First of all, the *USS Cole* incident represents the starting point of Yemen's war against al-Qaeda. In the midst of that momentum from security and military cooperation in the late 1990s, the *USS Cole* incident occurred, effectively resetting the relationship to its starting point. A group of al-Qaeda suicide bombers with an explosives-laden motorboat managed to blow up the U.S. Navy destroyer *USS Cole* during a refueling stop in Aden on October 12, 2000. According to the 9/11 Commission Report, al-Qaeda may have been involved in the *USS Cole* attack.[32]

Although Yemen's leaders announced their cooperation in the investigation of *USS Cole* incident, the security cooperation with U.S. stopped after the U.S. investigation team departed to home in June 2001. U.S. aid stopped and its Consulate in Sana'a closed its doors.[33] The lack of understanding of each party to view the other formed part of the crisis in relations. From the standpoint of Yemen, it was thought that the CIA was behind the incident to obtain a foothold in Aden. Some reports referred to a U.S. plan to seize Aden, especially after the U.S. failed to establish a military base. When President Saleh asked by *Al-Jazeera* about such reports, he said as a message to the U.S., that Yemen is not Panama and has always been known as a cemetery for invaders.[34]

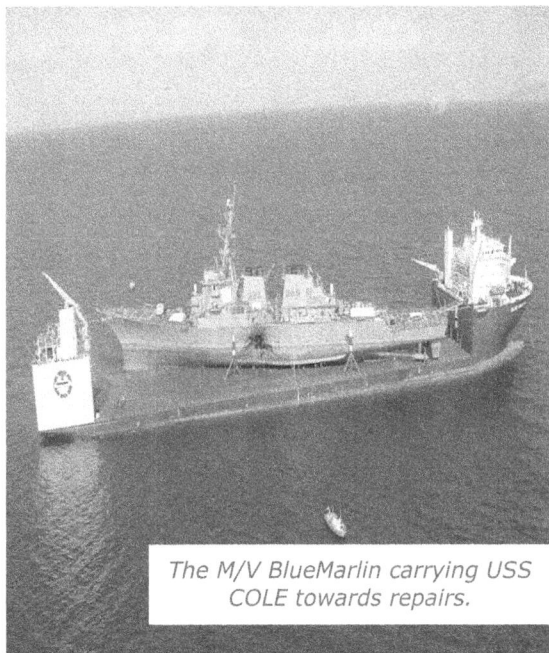

The M/V BlueMarlin carrying USS COLE towards repairs.

Yemen's government declared its commitment to the constitution to not hand over any Yemeni suspects to foreign authorities, and to maintain its sovereignty.[35] When Yemen rejected the deployment of two thousand U.S. Marines charged with defending 100 investigators, Yemen-U.S. relations suffered a formidable blow. Therefore, CNN reports noted Yemen's unresponsiveness to the demands of the United States, which implied that Yemen was supporting terrorists. An FBI team complained of the lack of Yemen cooperation, the difficulty of accessing suspects,[36] and Yemen's refusal to add prominent social and military leaders to the list of suspects.[37]

From the American perspective, the *Cole* incident differed with other attacks in terms of the debates created by U.S. media, political parties, and security leadership, especially in the presidential campaigns in U.S. In general, the debate was focused on three things. First, it criticized President Clinton's strategy in counter-terrorism. Mike Sheehan, the State Department's leading counter-terrorism official, asks surprisingly, *"Does al-Qaeda have to attack the Pentagon to get their attention?"*[38] Second was the issues discussed by congress as the mulled over *"how the U.S. responds and prevents further attacks"*.[39]

The debate on the diplomatic channels, which led to a split in the U.S. administration, was how to deal with Yemen. Eventually, that debate led to U.S. aggression towards Yemen which intensified tensions between both countries. The FBI urged the U.S. administration to take decisive action toward Yemen, while a contrary approach was adopted by the U.S. ambassador in Yemen, Barbara Bodine. She warned of the adverse results due to the aggressive actions by John O'Neill - the FBI team leader- toward Yemeni officials. Barbara prefers dealing with Yemen as a sovereign and independent state.[40] In the end, the FBI's more aggressive approach was adopted and Barbara Bodine was replaced as ambassador by Edmund Hall, a counter-terrorism expert.[41]

Repercussions of September 11th

With the unexpected attack on U.S. by al-Qaeda in 9/11, 2001, Yemen demanded U.S. and the international community to stand with Yemen in its fight against terrorism. Yemen's early warnings of the threat of al-Qaeda proved to be justified.[42] The Yemeni president hastened to visit U.S. and meet President Bush in the White House on November 28, 2001. On the subject of Yemen's national security, it was a highly successful visit and changed the U.S. policy towards Yemen. Saleh came back with U.S. aid estimated at 130-150 million dollars and a billion-dollar loan from the World Bank.[43]

US-YEMEN-BUSH-SALEH

During the period of 2001 to 2010, Yemen has engaged itself in a comprehensive and complex war against the al-Qaeda branch in Yemen despite it having been ill-prepared for this challenge. Yemen does not have specialized administrative restructuring, its soldiers are ill-prepared, and it has little to no advanced equipment. For example, Despite having a coastline of more than 2000 kilometers, Yemen does not have a Coast Guard. Yemen also suffers from poverty, a declining economy, and weak law enforcement. In addition, the social and geographical environments such as the difficult mountainous terrain, Yemeni tribal culture, and weapons proliferation help to lengthen the duration of the war on terror.[44]

Under the above circumstances, this internal war has forced Yemen to expand its intelligence, security, and military relations with other countries specifically the U.S. Therefore, Yemen has entered into a full partnership with U.S.

in its war against terrorists to develop its ability to defeat al-Qaeda. On the other hand, Bush committed to support Yemen in its counter-terrorism without intervening in Yemen's internal affairs.[45] The Yemen effort to defeat al-Qaeda in Yemen became an important issue in the agendas of both countries. Both recognized that ensuring its national security is directly linked to the success of the war on terrorism. In contrast, failure in such a war not only threatened Yemen's internal security but also posed a constant looming threat of international sanctions. U.S. leaders were aware of Yemen's importance as a partner in tracking terrorists, according to the bilateral security cooperation established in the 1990s.

Consequently, the development of relations between the two countries was not limited to security and military aspects but extended to other sectors, such as the social, developmental, and economic. For instance, the causes of terrorism such as redundancy, chronic poverty, poor economies, and social and political instability are long-term strategic targets. As will be discussed in the next sections, the United States and Yemen are working side by side to address Yemen's needs. U.S. is trying not to carry the burden of helping Yemen alone and thus seeks to engage the donor states.

Other forms of the Yemen-US partnership are linked to efforts to build and strengthen the capacity of the security institutions of Yemen to paralyze the movements of terrorists and take preventive measures as well as the implementation of pre-emptive strikes. With U.S. technical and training assistance, Yemen founded many government institutions and departments such as the National Security Bureau (NSB), the Anti-Terrorism Units, the Coast Guard, and other units and institutions.[46] In addition, Yemen has allowed U.S. to open intelligence offices in Yemen.[47] Despite Yemeni officials still denying it,[48] some maps showing the distribution of U.S. military bases around the world refer to a temporary U.S. military base in Yemen, at that time.[49]

Finally, Yemen and U.S. play a cooperative role in carrying out military operations against the leaders of terrorist organizations. Sometimes Yemen's government provides logistic support, while the U.S. aircraft target terrorists. An example of this is what transpired on November 3, 2002, in that missiles from U.S. drone aircraft targeted six suspects including Qaid al-Harithi, the leader of al-Qaeda in Yemen and the mastermind behind the attack on the *Cole*.[50] In general, most of the operations carried out against terrorist organizations were implemented by Yemeni forces specialized.[51]

Although Yemen's war on terrorism created this partnership, it also created some of the crises between the Yemeni and U.S. governments. The U.S. State Department reports on terrorism in Yemen criticized the Yemen government with the following points: Yemen sustained a surrender program with lenient requirements for terrorists notwithstanding American pressure,[52] the weakness of laws relating to fighting terrorism, the ineffectiveness of the judiciary and Yemen did not take action against al-Badawi and al-Zandani.[53]

On the other hand, Yemen however confirmed that Yemen was committed to the war on terrorism within the framework of its legal institutions, constitution, and international conventions. Furthermore, former Yemeni President Saleh emphasized that the partnership with the U.S. in the GWOT does not mean subordination.[54] Yemeni leaders tried to convince U.S. that they had their own ways and tactics of dealing with terrorism as expressed by Yemen's Minister of Interior.[55] However, it seems that U.S. was not convinced, especially since the position of Yemeni opposition parties fostered American mistrust.[56]

Accordingly, the above tension represented an opportunity to create a new generation of al-Qaeda militants.[57] Furthermore, both Yemen and the U.S. did not take into account the new orientation of al-Qaeda to make Yemen another base of battle after Iraq. Al-Qaeda's stated that Yemen will be the third frontline after Afghanistan and Iraq that depletes the NATO forces and U.S.[58] Gregory Johnsen stressed that, "*the lapsed vigilance by both the U.S. and Yemeni government allowed al-Qaeda to reorganize and rebuild itself; to essentially resurrect itself up from the ashes of its initial defeat*".[59] Moreover, the aggressive policy of the U.S.

somewhat helped to create a new generation, for example, the U.S. unjustly invaded Iraq and encouraged thousands of Yemeni *mujahedeen* to establish the so-called second generation of al-Qaeda.[60]

Furthermore, the new generation managed to pull off the so-called "Great Escape", when 23 prominent members of al-Qaeda escaped from the political security prison in Yemen.[61] Following this, the new generation accomplished several other operations such as an attack on a natural gas refinery in *Saffer* on September 2006, killing eight Spaniards tourists and two Yemenis in *Marib* in July 2007, killing two Belgian tourists in *Hadhramout* in January 2008, the highly accurate attack on the U.S. embassy in Sana'a in September 2008 to name a few. It reached a peak in 2009, after the announcement of the founding of al-Qaeda in the Arabian Peninsula (AQAP) in Yemen as their headquarters through the merger with the al-Qaeda branch in Saudi.[62]

The relationship between Yemen and U.S. has been affected by the development of the new generation of al-Qaeda in Yemen. Those events have come to confirm -to some extent- the failure of recent efforts by Yemen and the U.S. and enhance the importance of re-strengthening the Yemen-U.S. partnership. In response, Yemen and U.S. increased their level of partnership during 2006-2008 but did not advance to the level they reached in 2001.[63] However, after 2009 the AQAP was considered to be a greater threat than al-Qaeda in Afghanistan. According to the former U.S. ambassador Edmund Hall in Yemen, who served immediately following 9/11, *"terrorists in Yemen are the most pressing threat against the U.S. homeland and western interests in the area."*[64]

Accordingly, President Barack Obama decided to continue their partnership a few days after the Northwest Airlines attack. On January 2, 2010, President Obama confirmed that *"So, as President, I've made it a priority to strengthen our partnership with the Yemeni government-training and equipping their security forces, sharing intelligence and working with them to strike al-Qaeda terrorists."*[65] In Fact, U.S. and the international community realized the failure of the Yemen war and the reality of the threat. According to Brucee Hoffman, terrorism expert, the AQAP is now as much of a threat as al-Qaeda central.[66] This fact represented a shock to the competent authorities in the U.S. and the international community alike. The Senate Intelligence Committee report declared that CIA saw AQAP as a threat to U.S. targets in Yemen and not to U.S. itself.[67]

Consequently, U.S. strategy towards terrorism in Yemen completely changed, and its features are not yet clear. However, during the period of partnership in combating terrorism, the American strategy towards Yemen was characterized by three main aspects: Firstly, there was an increase in the volume of aid; secondly, the launch of an intensive strategy to support Yemen not only in the security and military fields of combating terrorism but also economically and in promoting political stability; and finally, there was oscillation and a lack of confidence in the political leadership in Yemen.

The change in American policy towards the war on terrorism in Yemen coincided with the emergence of the Arab Spring and the uprising in the Republic of Yemen in 2011. American policy supported the removal of President Saleh's regime, aiming to facilitate a peaceful and stable regime change to prevent extremist groups from exploiting the state's weaknesses and local conflicts. During this period, the US Air Force provided air support to the Ansar Allah (Houthi movement) in its conflict with al-Qaeda and ISIS in various Yemeni governorates. However, following the failure of the peaceful transition, the takeover of Sana'a by Ansar Allah, and the onset of a civil war with Gulf military intervention, American policy exhibited duplicity and ambiguity. While announcing American strikes against terrorist groups and supporting the Southern Movement against these groups, the US overlooked the expansion of extremist groups such as al-Qaeda and ISIS, as well as the policies of Saudi Arabia and the UAE in arming them to counter the Ansar Allah forces in northern Yemen.

The American lack of confidence in President Saleh's regime in the fight against terrorism likely contributed to this policy shift. Ali Abdullah Saleh was actively engaged in the war on terrorism, but his local, ideological, constitutional, and sovereign considerations often hindered the fulfilment of all American demands. These included changing educational curricula, positions on Palestinian resistance organizations, extradition of wanted Yemenis to America, and the establishment of permanent military bases.

Another instance illustrating this dynamic occurred during the author's tenure at the presidency of the Republic of Yemen. The author received a secret project funded by America, worth hundreds of millions of dollars, designed to fully secure Yemen's maritime borders. The project proposed establishing hundreds of surveillance points equipped with modern technology, including motion and sound sensors, and deploying dozens of vehicles with modern radars along the maritime border from Oman in the Arabian Sea to Saudi Arabia in the Red Sea. President Saleh approved the project but insisted that the Yemeni Coastal Forces manage the system and that its members be trained to use the modern equipment. However, America withdrew interest in the project after failing to respond to President Saleh's conditions.

Another reason for the American shift and loss of confidence in President Saleh's regime was the belief that the root causes of terrorism were social and economic factors. The U.S. viewed President Saleh's regime as incapable of addressing the deteriorating economic conditions and improving social aspects, topics we will explore in the following sections.

4.4 Yemen's Economic and Development Needs

Subsequent to the 9/11 attacks, the clarification of the internal dynamics shaping Yemen-U.S. relations, requires the study and analysis of non-security factors. In line with this, the economic and development challenges in Yemen represent another important factor in the Yemen-U.S. relations. At the start of this relationship, Yemen was considered one of the least developed countries (LDCs) that suffered from enormous economic and developmental challenges. There is no doubt that the economic and development imbalances had an effect on Yemen foreign policy, especially in terms of the priorities of its diplomatic goals towards donor states including U.S. Moreover, the traditional perspective towards such issues changed by means of a new security perspective adopted by the Yemen and U.S. governments.

In this context, this section attempts to study the role played by Yemen's economic and development needs in the formation of bilateral relations. It attempts to interpret how Yemen's needs shaped its foreign policy towards U.S. and how, in turn, the U.S. response to Yemen's needs represents an indicator for the development of bilateral relations. The section also highlights the change in this factor after the events of 9/11, especially since studies are arguing for the relationship between terrorism and the deterioration of economic and development in Yemen.

Yemen and U.S. Aid

Yemen's strategy depends on foreign aid to meet its internal economic challenges, particularly U.S. aid.[68] The economic needs of Yemen and the subsequent U.S. aid offered play a significant role in shaping Yemen's foreign policy and are evident at various stages of the relationship between the two countries. For instance, when Imam Yahya, the King of Yemen, sought U.S. aid and expertise in infrastructure and health, it served as one of the incentives for Yemen's request to establish official relations with the U.S. in 1945.[69] According to al-Ghifari, the King of Yemen was inspired by the enormous assistance U.S. provided to countries in Europe after World War II.[70] After seven years of civil war in the 1960s, Yemen was in urgent need of aid. In the memoirs of the Yemeni Prime Minister Al-Aini, at the time, he pointed out that the urgent need for U.S. aid encouraged Yemen to restore the relations with U.S. in 1972.[71]

On other hand, the good relations with Yemen made U.S. cooperate with Yemen in its economic and development issues to achieve the common interests between the two countries. Despite the fact that U.S. assistance since the Marshall Plan was based on U.S. interests,[72] the U.S. assistance to Yemen promoted its investment opportunities and was designed to maintain a good relationship between people and governments in the two countries. As earlier mentioned, U.S. assistance was provided by American merchants to strengthen the relationship with Yemen. In 1826, one of the American merchant fleet ships called *Ann* was carrying tons of food aid to Yemen during widespread famine.[73] Moreover, the development aid was offered by American millionaire Charles Cranein in 1927.[74]

During the 1990s, Yemen's economy was close to collapsing because Western donors to Yemen suspended aid as a response to Yemen's position in the second Gulf War. Similarly, the Gulf States suspended aid as well and expelled more than 850 thousand Yemeni immigrants from their countries.[75] With the establishment of unity between North and South of Yemen, the economic needs increased. Yemen's administrative system was formed on the basis of a merger between the two parts according to political satisfaction and was thus a fragile administrative system. In addition, Yemen was heavily indebted and had poor infrastructure, especially in the south.[76] In the civil war in 1994, Yemen was on the brink of failure as a state. In March 1995, The Yemeni government signed an agreement with the International Monetary Fund and the World Bank on a program called "Economic Stabilization and Structural Adjustment," through which Yemen commits to a comprehensive adjustment process consistent with the approaching Washington consensus in two phases (1995-2000) and (2000-2005).[77]

The dire circumstances made it necessary for Yemen to improve its relationship with U.S. in several aspects. In regards to development, Yemen adopted a package of political and economic reforms. Yemen's reform programs were designed to attract U.S. and international assistance and Yemen transformed itself to become compatible with U.S. liberal tendencies such as economic liberalization, modified trade laws, tax systems and customs, women's rights, freedom of press, the development of civil society and other such liberal notions. American economic experts believe that the success of Yemen in the field of economic reforms will enhance the interests of U.S. companies in Yemen.[78]

As a result, U.S. encouraged Yemen's reforms through the amount of aid awarded. During the 1990s, U.S. aid as a response to Yemen's needs rose from approximately 3 USD million per year to between USD 6-9 million during 1995-1997.[79] U.S. aid increased to USD 15 million in 1998, and doubled to 30 million in 1999. Approximately 177 tons of food was sent to Yemen as a donation with an estimated cost of USD 30 million as well as 4 million to support Yemeni education in 2000. The most important in bilateral economic relations was through a set of agreements between the two countries which exempt Yemen from 60 percent of their debt to U.S., and schedules the remaining debt estimated at USD 27 million to be paid back over thirty years.[80]

Economic and development deterioration

After the events of 9/11, Yemen's challenges to face its economic and development needs become more complex. Since the beginning of the third millennium, there are dozens of international reports that evaluate and review the alarming figures of the worst situation in Yemen. The Yemeni economy depends on foreign aid and remittances from expatriates. With the discovery of oil, the Yemeni economy became a yield economy.[81] Oil in Yemen accounts for 97 percent of exports and about 30 percent of national income. Oil accounted for an overall 76 percent of revenues in 2005.[82] Between 2005 and 2012, the Yemeni economy suffered a severe crisis because of the decline in Yemen's oil production which experts predict will dry up after ten years.

In general, in the first decade of this century, the situation in Yemen is characterized by a sharp deterioration in various aspects from year to year. According to the Economist Intelligence Unit EIU, the gross domestic product (GDP) for 2011–12 will drop in Yemen to less than 3 percent, while Yemen's annual population growth is 3.5 percent.[83] It ranked 151 out of 177 countries on the United Nations Development Program's Human Development Index (HDI) in 2007.[84] Yemen's ranking declined to 154 of 177 countries in HDI in 2011.[85] Furthermore, it is easy to claim that there is insufficient food or water security in Yemen.[86] The run out of water in Sana'a may range in time from 2017-2025.[87] Moreover, 43 percent of the population of nearly 24 million people lives below the poverty line, while it was 24 percent in 2006. Furthermore, 70 percent of them are illiterate and more than 15 percent of children do not go to school. Additionally, the decline in investment, the low standard of living education and health and tens of other indicators emphasize the critical situations in Yemen's economic and development needs.[88]

Figure 4.1: Decreased Oil Production in Yemen

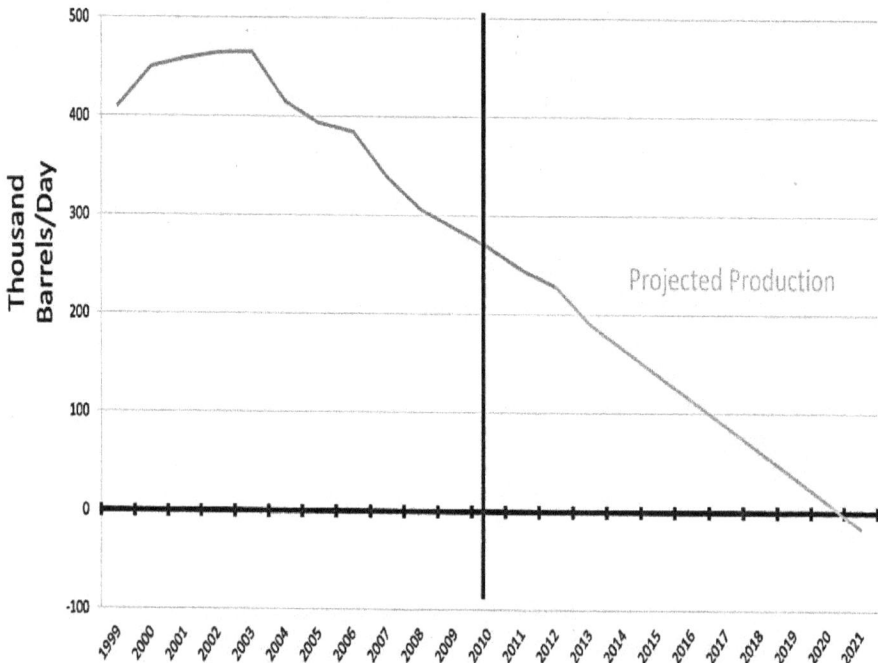

Source: USAID: Strategic Planning and Analysis Division. Yemen Gap Analysis (Washington DC: United States Agency, April 25, 2011), p. 22.

This critical situation creates a fertile environment for extremists. John Johnson argues that one of the reasons of extremism in Yemen is the tripling of the population during the past three decades, especially since half the population of Yemen is approaching old age, while the per capita income is low, unemployment is high and migration opportunities are poor.[89]

As such, this section highlights the security perspective of Yemen's economic needs during the global war on terrorism. The traditional influence of Yemen's needs and U.S. response 'USAID' on the bilateral relations changed.[90] Although the economic relations between the two countries are older than the security and military relations, its importance has become linked to security. Yemen has become a strategic partner of the United States in confronting such challenges, especially after U.S. response became a requirement to protect American security and not only to achieve common interests with Yemen. Howell and Lind emphasized that *"the global war on terror regime has contributed in diverse and complex ways to the increasing securitisation of development and aid policy"*.[91]

Consequently, U.S. aid has doubled and focuses on the military and security as well as the development aspects within the framework of the Yemen-U.S. partnership against terrorists. During 2002-2005 the rate of U.S. aid was approximately USD 27 million per year, 34 percent of which was for military aid.[92] In the following four years, there was a slight decline in U.S. aid to Yemen where aid totalled USD 22.6 million per year. During this period 2006-2009, the common perception was that terrorism in Yemen had been eliminated and that there was no longer a fear of al-Qaeda activity in Yemen.[93] This false perception explains the deterioration in U.S. interests and the way its military aid reduced from 34 percent of total aid during 2002-2005 to 24.8 percent during 2006- 2009.[94] Figure 4.1 shows the different scale of U.S. aid during 2006-2012.

Yemen's needs became prominent after the founding of al-Qaeda's branch in Yemen AQAP in 2009. It carried out terrorist operations inside U.S., such as the failed bomb attack against Northwest Airlines Flight 253 on Christmas Day, 2009, and the parcel bomb sent from Yemen.[95] Consequently, it witnessed that the size and objectives of U.S. aid to Yemen have changed substantially in 2010-2012. Yemen received USD 58.4 million in 2010 in addition to training and equipment for Yemen security estimated cost USD 150 million.[96] In 2011, the American plan to provide USD 106 million was effected by unrest during the Youth Revolution in Yemen so it did not receive any assistance from the Department of Defense (DOD). In 2011, the Obama Administration requested USD115.6 million for 2012 and USD 72.6 Million for 2013.[97]

Figure 4.2: U.S. Aid to Yemen 2006-2012

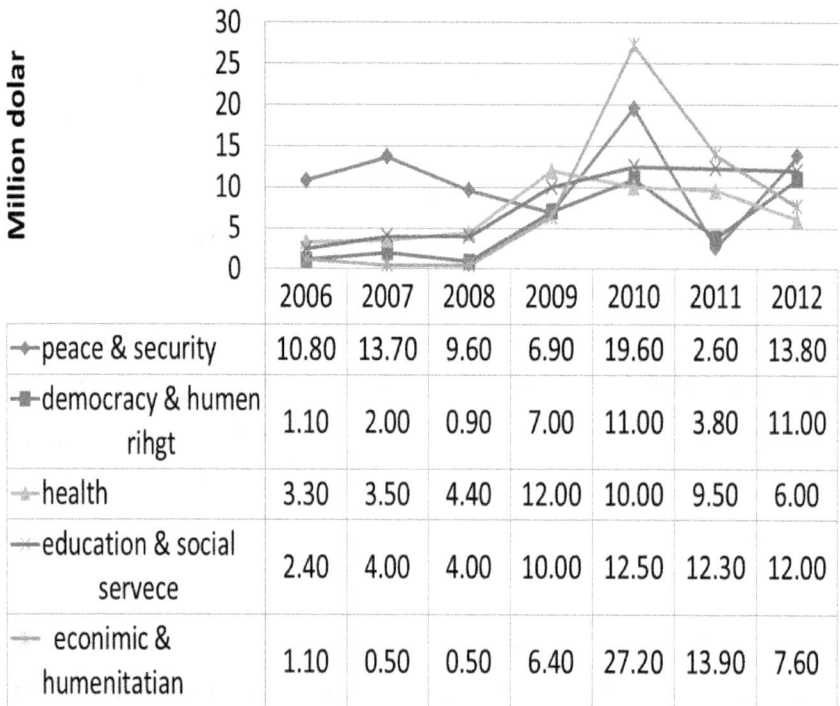

	2006	2007	2008	2009	2010	2011	2012
—peace & security	10.80	13.70	9.60	6.90	19.60	2.60	13.80
—democracy & humen rihgt	1.10	2.00	0.90	7.00	11.00	3.80	11.00
—health	3.30	3.50	4.40	12.00	10.00	9.50	6.00
—education & social servece	2.40	4.00	4.00	10.00	12.50	12.30	12.00
— econimic & humenitatian	1.10	0.50	0.50	6.40	27.20	13.90	7.60

Source: the figure and table designed by the author, according to statistics of State Department, Congressional Research Service.

Although the U.S. response to Yemen's needs increased and its aid doubled during the 2010-2012, dozens of experts are critical of the lack of U.S. response to Yemen's needs compared to the support of other countries such as Afghanistan USD 2.8 billion, Israel USD 2.8 billion, Egypt USD 1.55 billion, and USD 842 million to Jordan.[98] While this fact carries many questions about the potential reasons behind the insufficient American aid to Yemen, the justification of the U.S. Secretary of State was characterized by more vagueness. She said that American aid to Yemen depends on "expectations and conditions."[99] This fact casts a shadow on a set of other internal factors that also govern the relationship between the two countries, which are associated with Yemen's conflicts and the threat to becoming a failed state at that time.

4.5 Political Instability and the Fear of Becoming A Failed State

In the period 2001 to 2012, the potential failure of Yemen is another internal factor that shapes Yemen-U.S. relations. Many indicators point to Yemen turning into a failed state in the near future. The weakness of Yemen's government along with other internal crises such as the internal conflicts, political instability, and Yemen's war against al-Qaeda will eventually lead to the failure of Yemen. These internal issues are represented as a critical subject that governs the bilateral relations between Yemen and U.S. Both governments are fully aware of the consequences of Yemen becoming a failed state on the local and international level.

Before Yemen became a failed state following the so-called Arab Spring, it faced internal conflicts that significantly affected its relationship with the United States. This section aims to examine these conflicts and their impact. It explores the complex dilemma that arose due to Yemen's weak governance and the potential to become a failed state similar to Somalia, at that time. This analysis is drawn from a security perspective, considering the intricate link between Yemen's situation and American national security. Additionally, the section highlights the

U.S. conviction regarding the necessity of regime change in Yemen and its influence on bilateral relations between the two countries.

In that era, a very important question usually arises, is Yemen on the brink of becoming a failed state? This question was the focus of attention by those interested in Yemeni affairs, whether they were states, international and civil institutions, or institutions within Yemen. At the end of the 2010s, indicators of Yemen's potential failure had increased gradually. According to *Foreign Policy Statistics*, Yemen ranked was 18 in the failed states index in 2009 and became 13 in 2011.[100] Furthermore, there were dozens of international reports that highlight deteriorating economic and development environment in Yemen, which were referred to in the preceding section. Overall, those reports refer to the potential of Yemen to become a failed state.[101]

On the other hand, the spread of internal conflicts in Yemen was other indicator of the potential of becoming a failed state. Yemen was engaging in three wars at the same time. The first war is against al-Qaeda, the second against the *Houthi* movement in north Yemen, and the third was against the *Southern* movement insurgency in the south. Yemen's resources have been depleted because of these conflicts, which would have otherwise been exploited for economic development. According to a report by the Yemeni government delivered to the Yemeni parliament in December 2002, the Yemeni government bore the financial burden of such wars which would have otherwise been used to develop remote areas.[102]

Accordingly, the internal conflicts along with political instability in Yemen have created other factors that may lead to the collapse of Yemen at that time. It threatened the economic development of Yemen because of the lack of security, foreign investment, and migration capital of Yemen. For example, Yemen lost around USD 480 million after the *USS Cole* attack in 2000 and lost approximately USD 15 million monthly after the French ship *Limburg* was attacked in 2002.[103] According to Yousif Saeed's study,[104] *"Yemen's tourism sector suffered huge losses amounting to roughly 10 billion dollars, during the last ten years, in addition the bankruptcy of tens of tourism agencies, resulting in the loss of hundreds of thousands (700,000) of jobs across the country. Business for several hotels and transportation companies witnessed profits decrease by 50 percent.* "[105] Moreover, Yemen lost billions of dollars when the investments froze in addition to the migration of foreign and local capital.[106]

Map 4.1: The Internal Conflicts in Yemen 2012

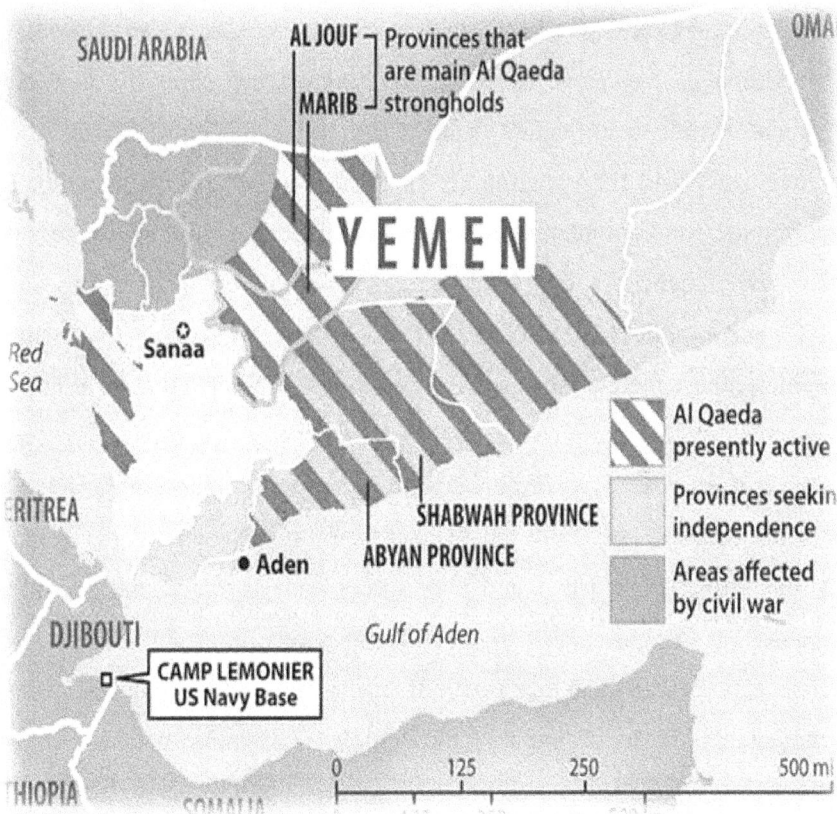

Source: "Yemen: Maps of Conflict/Crisis." The Project on Middle East Democracy (POMED), accessed 8/9/2012, http://pomed.org/blog/2011/04/yemen-maps-of-..html/#.

During the Arab Spring period in Yemen, the *Houthi* movement was engaged at war with the *Wahhabi Mujahedeen* in north Yemen.[107] Approximately 400 mujahidin came from several countries and there are hundreds of dead between the two parties. This war was not covered by the media and there was perhaps international support from Saudi Arabia and Iran.[108] The U.S. position as well as the position of the Yemeni government were vague. However, the U.S. has expressed concern about Iran's quest to exploit Yemen's instability, while the new President of Yemen Abd Rabbuh Hadi warned Iran to stay away from Yemen internal affairs. The declaration came after Yemen arrested Iranian cell intelligence in Sana'a.[109]

Although concerted international efforts in support of Yemen's government continued to decline, it highlights yet another problem namely the poor governance and the vulnerability of its leaders. The most complex factor threatening the common interest of Yemen and the U.S. was the weakness of the Yemeni government. As this book argues, poor governance creates internal conflicts and political instability and assists in weakening its economy. Furthermore, these factors increased the possibility of Yemen's failure. To briefly demonstrate the above argument, poor governance is the cause of several of Yemen's critical crises. The Yemeni government cannot enforce authority over all parts of the country, especially those areas far from the center of the state. As a result, the influence of tribal and clan forces has increased and provided an opportunity for the emergence of several armed rebellions. Furthermore, some American experts argue that the growth of terrorism occurs in countries with weak governments.[110] Figure 4.3 explains the complex correlation between the above factors.

Rampant corruption in Yemen's institutions represents one of the attributes of poor governance. The main reason for the failure is poor development and economic reform programs. Since 2006, Yemen's rank declined in the Index of Economic Freedom (IEF), and Corruption Perceptions Index (CPI), where it ranked 121 in the 2010 IEF, and 164 in the 2011 CPI.[111] Other negative aspects of poor governance and rampant corruption are the lack of effective employment of foreign aid and the lack of international support. Although the five international conferences of the donor countries 'Yemen's friends' discussed the crisis of Yemen after the AQAP targeted Northwest Airlines on Christmas Day, 2009, Yemen did not receive any financial support.[112] Poor governance was the main reason that prevented the international community from providing additional support and was the same reason behind the decrease of U.S. aid.[113] Therefore, several studies have critiqued U.S. aid to Yemen, arguing that it is inconsistent with the principles of America's commitment, which include selectivity, effectiveness, and predictability.[114]

In the shadow of a series of crises afflicting Yemen during 2001-2012, the critical situation in Yemen changes the nature of the relations between the U.S. and Yemen. Yemen's situation was the U.S. foreign policy dilemma towards Yemen. Although Yemen's foreign policy attempts to exploit its relations with the U.S. to solve its internal dilemmas, the U.S. has found itself compelled to engage in Yemen's crises to prevent the country from becoming a failed state. Amid these successive crises, the priority of U.S. leaders was to answer three important questions, as expressed by Congressman Berman, Chairman of Yemen on the brink 'hearing'- *"This hearing provides an opportunity to ask some key questions: How important is Yemen's stability to U.S. interests and U.S. security? Is Yemen on the brink of becoming another "failed state"? And, what, if anything, can the United States do to tip the balance in the right direction?"*[115]

The previous chapter addresses the first question and derives its importance from the stability of Yemen. This factor serves as the common denominator between the two countries and encourages an improvement in bilateral relations. On the internal level, it can be argued that U.S. with the Yemeni government is seeking to strengthen the stability of Yemen, as expressed by many U.S. policy-makers.[116]

Figure 4.3: Yemen's Current Dilemma

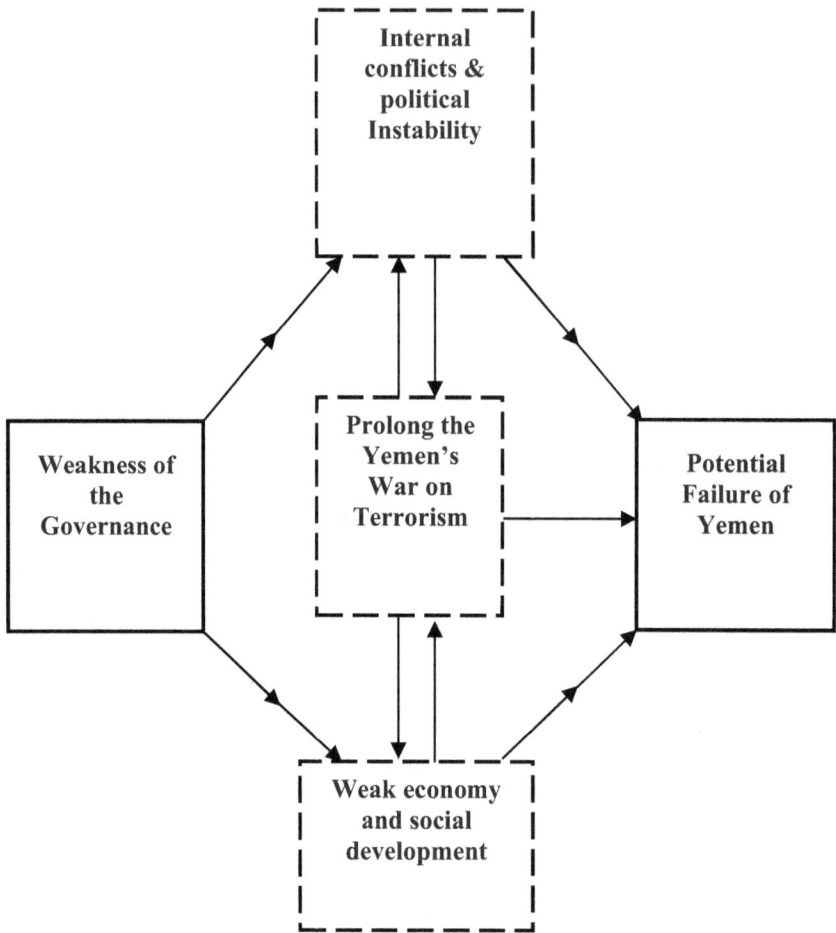

Note: the figure designed by the author.

Perhaps the U.S. did not have solutions for all of Yemen's crises, but it can assist in the survival of Yemen to maintain its security and interests. During the visit of U.S. Secretary of State, Hillary Clinton, to Yemen in January 2011, she said "*I do not pretend that the American Government or the American people have the answers to Yemen's complex challenges. I am well aware that Yemen faces many real and serious challenges. Some of them in my country we know more about than others. For example, we are aware of the immediate threat from violent*

*extremists, especially al-Qaida, posing to the stability of Yemen, the region, and
indeed the world."[117]*

Figure 4.4: The 2010-2012 USAID Strategic Goal in Yemen

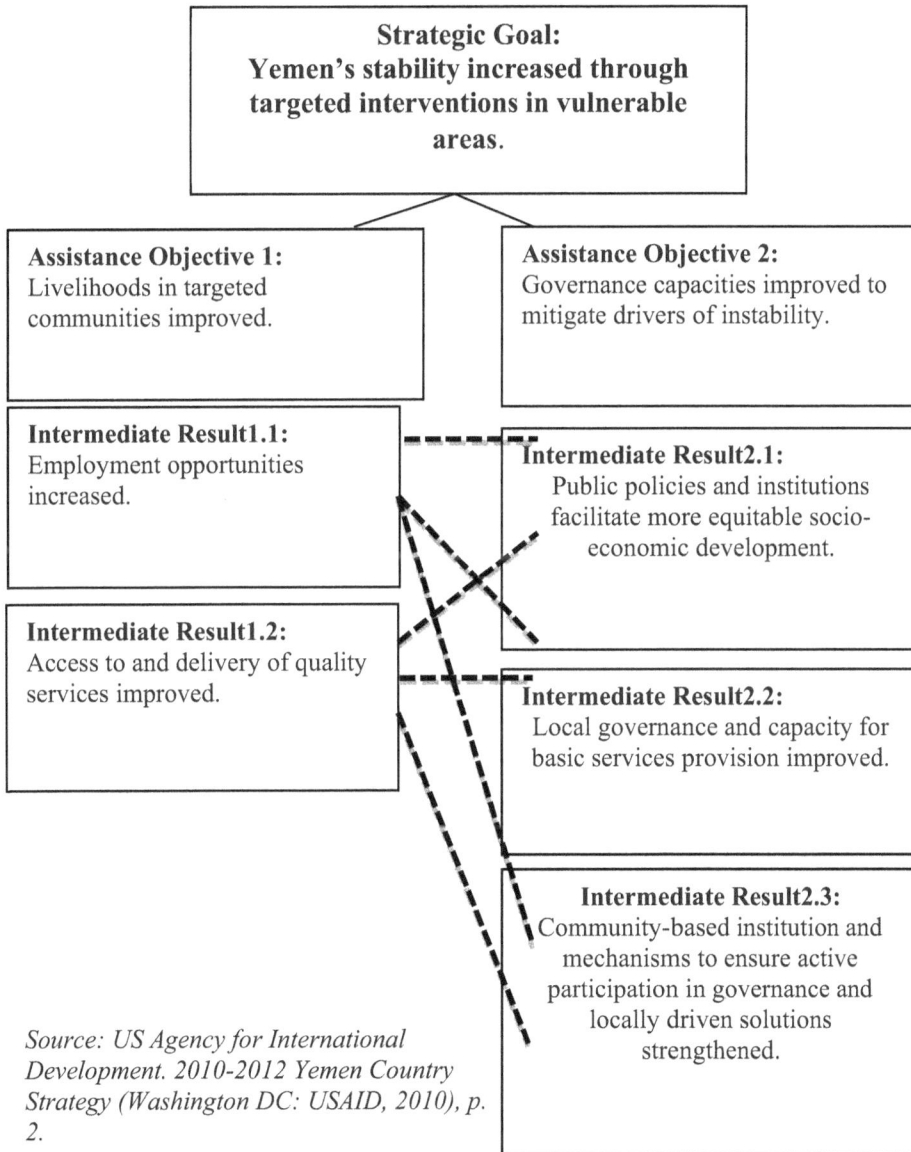

```
┌─────────────────────────────────────┐
│          Strategic Goal:            │
│  Yemen's stability increased through │
│  targeted interventions in vulnerable│
│                areas.               │
└─────────────────────────────────────┘
```

| Assistance Objective 1: Livelihoods in targeted communities improved. | Assistance Objective 2: Governance capacities improved to mitigate drivers of instability. |

Intermediate Result1.1: Employment opportunities increased.

Intermediate Result2.1: Public policies and institutions facilitate more equitable socio-economic development.

Intermediate Result1.2: Access to and delivery of quality services improved.

Intermediate Result2.2: Local governance and capacity for basic services provision improved.

Intermediate Result2.3: Community-based institution and mechanisms to ensure active participation in governance and locally driven solutions strengthened.

Source: US Agency for International Development. 2010-2012 Yemen Country Strategy (Washington DC: USAID, 2010), p. 2.

Accordingly, the U.S. foreign policy, backed by Congress, adopted a new strategy towards Yemen. This strategy was not limited to counter-terrorism but also aimed to meet the challenges of Yemen in the long term. The U.S. foreign policy was committed to a broad and comprehensive partnership with Yemen. As noted in the previous section, the comprehensive partnership goes beyond counter-terrorism to include other sectors such as the economic, social, and political sectors.[118] U.S. support doubled in the years 2010-2012 and focused on development issues such as livelihoods and governance capacity.[119] Figure 4.4 reflects the depth of U.S. involvement in Yemen's crises.

The second aspect of the comprehensive partnership is a partnership with the spectra of the Yemeni people. The U.S. foreign policy finds itself attempting to establish good relations with the Yemeni government, but also with the components of the Yemeni people such as civil society leaders, elites, and clan and tribal leaders. Hilary Clinton remarked, *"We are committed to a broad and comprehensive partnership not only with the Government of Yemen, but with the people of Yemen".*[120] The U.S. was able to create its wide influence within the institutions of civil society through the activities of its embassy in Sana'a. It worked to strengthen such institutions and to support its activities and to provide some kind of protection for its leadership through the various reports issued by U.S. institutions.[121] Moreover, the U.S. thought that civil society has a role to play in solving Yemen's crises. Hillary Clinton asserted, *"Civil society must be a key part of the solution. Empowering the Yemeni people to solve your own problems is the most effective tool any society has."*[122]

In this context, the U.S. developed its relations with the tribal and clan leaders in Yemen. Its goal was to impose peaceful solutions for disputes with the state. Many analysts pointed out that U.S. is afraid of an alliance between the tribes and al-Qaeda militants.[123] Furthermore, some tribes sympathize with al-Qaeda militants who portray themselves as Muslims weakened by American hegemony.[124] Moreover, both governments were working to contain the tribes through the allocation of large sums of money, just as Saudi Arabia was working to contain the tribal leaders by providing a monthly pension.[125] U.S. provided 3 million USD annually to the National Security Bureau NSB for this objective. In addition, a large project was carried out between the U.S., Saudi Arabia and Yemen to reduce the size of the weapons of the tribes by withdrawing arms from the markets in Yemen, especially medium-sized arms.

The third aspect of U.S. new strategy represents the involvement of the international community and regional countries in addressing the various crises in Yemen. The U.S. was aware that it is unable to bear all these burdens alone. Many analysts have recommended the U.S. Congress to encourage the countries in the region such as Saudi Arabia to contribute large sums.[126] Saudi Arabia assisted worth $ 2 billion.[127] The United States and the international community were beginning to realize the importance of adopting an integrated approach that addresses all the problems of Yemen and comprehensively addresses the long term and not limiting its vision to terrorism.[128] In fact, the U.S. played the main role in motivating the international community and the forming of its attitude. Hilary Clinton remarked, *"Now, we are not doing this alone; we are doing it in partnership with many of Yemen's friends and neighbors - the Gulf countries, Western donors, the World Bank, the IMF, the United Nations. We are working to help coordinate our efforts to create economic prosperity."*[129]

Finally, the U.S. has obvious benefits in supporting Yemen's government in its internal conflicts. This position enhanced the bilateral relations and led Yemen's foreign policy to maintain good relations with U.S. For example, U.S. stood with the unification of Yemen in 1990, while some Gulf countries sought to make it fail. In addition, in the civil war in 1994, U.S. supported the Yemeni government, while some Gulf countries militarily backed the separatist forces. After the events of 9/11, U.S. and Yemen's governments worked side by side to end the internal conflicts such as insurgencies in the north of Yemen, the *Houthi* movement, and in the south, the *Southern* movement.

Unfortunately, the broad partnerships between Yemen and the United States on the one hand, and the international community and the countries of the region on the other, failed to achieve its goals. After six wars against the *Houthis,* this movement has become stronger. This is also the case for the *Southern* movement. The movement has expanded its presence in South Yemen. The economic and developmental indicators have worsened. Yemen's war on terrorism may have succeeded in weakening al-Qaeda but has failed to eliminate al-Qaeda's presence in Yemen at that time. Currently, all of these factors have become much worse.

Consequently, it appears that both the United States and neighboring countries were convinced that the effective solution to the crisis in Yemen was regime change. Although this subject requires a thorough examination, it can be said that the U.S. has contributed early, at least, in the push for a Yemeni revolution. This revolution must depend on peaceful mechanisms and cannot threaten the stability of Yemen. Some evidence supports this argument such as documents leaked by *Wikileaks* that indicated that the U.S. has received numerous warnings by the Gulf countries about the danger of Saleh's weak government.[130] In addition, important document confirmed that a secret meeting in 2010 between U.S. Embassy in Sana'a and the leadership of the Islamic opposition addressed the possibility of a peaceful revolution with military divisions, including the defection of General Ali Mohsen who led the revolution against his relative Saleh in 2011.[131] Moreover, U.S. non-governmental organizations helped train hundreds of Yemeni young on the use of social networking sites such as *Twitter* and *Facebook*.[132]

However, the U.S. ambassador in Sana'a had strong relations and influence with all spectra of Yemeni society during the youth revolution in Yemen that began in February 2011. At the beginning of the Arab Spring phase in Yemen, the United States, and its partners namely the Gulf countries, European countries, and the UN succeeded in controlling the crisis in Yemen has thus far prevented the outbreak of civil war. In fact, the U.S. has succeeded in playing the role of the mediator between all conflicting parties and has thus given her the upper hand during the transitional phase and the period of dialogue between the political parties. U.S. pressure led the parties to adopt a political settlement based on the initiative of GCC as well as the UN Security Council Resolution no. 2014.[133] The Gulf initiative included presidential elections, the formation of a government divided equally between the opposition JMP and the ruling party GPC, and a new constitution through a dialogue between all spectra of Yemen.[134]

After the success of the presidential election and the rise of President Abdrabbuh Hadi in February 2012, Yemen-U.S. relations witnessed a new phase in their partnership. This phase is described by U.S. ambassador Gerald Firestein as being better than ever before.[135] The U.S. resumed its aid after being suspended since 2011 and international aid poured into Yemen after the Riyadh conference in May 2012.[136] Moreover, President Obama issued a decision to give America the right to take punitive measures against Yemeni people who may be involved in blocking a political settlement in Yemen.[137] The role of the U.S. Ambassador in Sana'a changed from mediator to play the role of observer in Yemen. After media criticism and demonstrations against the actions of the U.S. ambassador, Gerald Firestein said that he is not ruling Yemen but is a supervisor of the international resolutions regarding Yemeni affairs.[138]

The American role and that of regional countries failed to secure a successful transitional phase in Yemen when the Ansar Allah movement took control of Sanaa, prompting the Yemeni president to flee to Saudi Arabia in 2014. Subsequently, diplomatic missions, including the American mission, left Yemen. Following these events, three major movements emerged: Ansar Allah, the Southern Movement, and the Yemeni Sharia allied with the Islah Party. Each controlled significant territories but did not possess substantial military forces. In response, America and the regional countries, led by Saudi Arabia, formed an international coalition for military intervention. This coalition aimed to restore the Yemeni president to Sanaa and defeat the Ansar Allah movement, an effort supported by a green light and American military logistical aid starting in 2015. This phase continues to the present, and the complexities of the relationship between Yemen and America during this period warrant extensive study. Due to its breadth, the writer plans to devote a separate book to this topic.

4.6 Conclusion

There are a variety of dynamics that govern the bilateral relations between the U.S. and Yemen. Due to limited U.S. interests in Yemen such as investments or trade, the internal dynamics were marginal compared to factors emanating from the international and regional environment during the previous century. However, the influence of some internal factors dominated Yemen-U.S. relations after the 9/11 attacks. Therefore, relations took another course characterized by a broad partnership in various fields including the political, economic, and developmental and security. Despite the existence of such a partnership, the relationship was not always stable and has had its ups and downs.

The emergence of Yemeni jihadist groups was one of the factors that have had a dual influence on Yemen-U.S. relations. The negative impact of this factor on the relations appeared in the early 1990s. Yemeni *Mujahedeen* returned from Afghanistan to Yemen with a plan to establish Jihadist Groups to fight the U.S. presence in the Arabian Peninsula. Yemen witnessed the first operations against the U.S. military in 1991 in addition to the targeting of U.S. citizens and companies in Yemen. The relationship declined especially with the American decision to limit its activity in Yemen and its decision to avoid facing those groups due to several reasons. In the meanwhile, those groups have succeeded in improving the relationship of the ruling class in Yemen, which exploited the internal war in 1994. During the second half of the 1990s, the security cooperation between Yemen and U.S. reached its peak, at the time. The operations of Yemeni jihadists -IJM and AAIA- increased in the period that also witnessed an increase in attacks against U.S. interests in the region. Therefore, Yemen and U.S. raised the level of intelligence and security cooperation and formed joint investigations and exchanged information about these groups and their operations. However, at that time, the U.S. was not serious about forming an integrated strategy in the fight against these groups.

Another internal factor that changed the face of Yemen-U.S. relations is the implications of Yemen's war against al-Qaeda after the *USS Cole* incident. This war created a real partnership with the U.S. in order to eliminate al-Qaeda. The leadership of the two countries attempted to coordinate all possible efforts and avoid the mistrust that took place after the *Cole* incident. During the first five years of the war against terrorism, the relationship peaked. But the relations have witnessed a kind of decline due to the effort on the war on terrorism did not continue after the success of Yemen and the United States during 2001-2005. U.S. engaged in other interests, while al-Qaeda succeeded in rebuilding itself and became stronger in the 2006-2009 period.

The second generation of al-Qaeda caused Yemen-U.S. relations to return to the point wherein it first began the war on terrorism. Joint operations ensued due to al-Qaeda's activities inside the U.S., such as parcel bombs and an operation on Christmas 2009. The requirements of national security of the two countries have formed an imperative partnership in the global war on terrorism. Such terrorist operations cause the U.S. to believe that al-Qaeda's presence in Yemen not only threatens its global interests but also its national security. Therefore, U.S. has adopted a comprehensive strategy in Yemen which is not limited to the elimination of al-Qaeda, but also to the elimination of the causes of terrorism in Yemen. This strategy has enhanced the relations between the two countries in various aspects.

Yemen's economic and development needs are considered another internal dynamic in the foreign policies of both countries. It drove Yemen to maintain a good relationship with the U.S. because it depends on foreign aid to address its economic and developmental challenges. On the other hand, American aid response to the Yemeni needs contributed to strengthening of bilateral relations and served the common interests. The perspective of this factor completely changed after the events of September 11, in particular after U.S. adopted a comprehensive strategy towards Yemen during 2009-2012. U.S. considered Yemeni challenges as threats to their homeland security. Therefore, the U.S. response has dramatically increased. U.S. aid has become a tool to maintain the U.S. national security rather than a way to improve the relations between the two countries.

Finally, during 2001 -2012, the potential of the failure of Yemen was another factor in highlighting the most important aspects of the relations between the two countries. Yemen threatens to become a failed state like Somalia. Dozens of international reports include many of the indicators that Yemen is on the brink of failure. In addition, the Yemeni government engaged in three internal wars against the *Houthi* movement, the movement of the *Southern* and al-Qaeda. U.S. decision-makers were fully aware of the seriousness of the collapse of governance in Yemen and its reflection on the stability of the region and U.S. national security. Therefore, the United States and Yemen entered into a new partnership to address Yemen's crises. This partnership was characterized by a comprehensive approach in terms of all social and economic sectors and development in addition to the partnership between Yemen and U.S. on the one hand and civil society in Yemen and the donor countries (Yemen friends) on the other.

[1] James E.R. Unsworth J.P. "The Global Political System: The Demise of the Westphalian Era Post- 9/11.", p. 11. Also check out, Jim Wirtz and James Russell. "Viewpoint: US Policy on Preventive War and Premption." *The Nonproliferation Review* (2003), accessed 4/6/2011, www.comw.org/qdr/fullte-xt/03wirtz.pdf, pp. 119-120.

[2] The religious schools are often divided into two currents. The first is *Wahhabism*, which is a militant religious movement and its ideological affiliation and funding comes from Saudi Arabia. As for the other current, its ideological affiliation is attributed to the *global Muslim Brotherhood movement*, which contains two factions namely the political and the radical. For further reading check out, Moath A. Al-Refaei. "Eh'tmaliat Alsera'a Almath'habi Fi Alyemen." (Sana'a: Office of the Presidency of the Republic of Yemen, 2006), pp. 20-40.

[3] Douglas Kellner. "September 11, Terror War, and Blowback." *Columbia University* (2005), accessed 16/6/2011, http://www.gseis.ucla.edu/faculty/kellner/kellner.html , p. 16.

[4] Bakeel A. aL-Zandani. "US-Yemen Relations in a Changing World: A Study of Four Major Events in US-Yemen Relations.", p. 66.

[5] For further reading see; Chalmers A. Johnson. *Blowback: The Costs and Consequences of American Empire* (New York: Henry Holt, 2004).

[6] Abo Mosa'ab Alsory. "Masa'wliat Ahl Alyemen Tgah Mok'dasat Almoslmeen Wa Throatehm." (1999), accessed 8/7/2010, http://www.tawhed.ws/r?i=wksgfnyz

[7] The terrorist's operation killed one person and injured several others.

[8] Richard Rosthauser. "Terrorism Conflict: How the United States Responds to Al-Qaeda Violence and Expressed Grievances.", p. 68.

[9] "Middle East Overview." *Patterns of Global Terrorism* (1992), accessed 2/3/2010, http://www.fa-s.org/irp/threat/terror_92/mideast.html

[10] General, Ahmad Alrok'yhi. Chairman of the Department of Defense and Security in the Office of the Presidency, *Personal Interview*, 15/3/2012.

[11] At that time, Rashid al-Umayshi was its leader and followed by Tariq Nasir Abdullah al-Fadli, who became the leader in 1994. Currently, the group was dismantled its cells through governmental action in the second half of the nineties.

[12] Michael Knights. "Strengthening Yemeni Counterterrorism Forces: Challenges and Political Considerations." *Policy Watch* (2010), accessed 6/2/2010, http://files.embedit.in/embeditin/files/4P2g-mU5jiE/1/file.pdf, p. 2.

[13] According to the parliamentary elections of 1993, there were three most influence parties in Yemen; the *General People's Council* GPC, the *Yemeni Reform Group* ISLAH and *Yemeni Socialist Party* YSP.

[14] Saeed Obaid Algamh'y. "Almujahdeen Fi Alyemen." (paper presented at the Mostak'bal Ala'lakat bain Algama'at Aleslamiah wa Alhkomah Alyamniah, Sana'a, 2003).

[15] Nabiel al-Razaqi. *Ath'er D'aherat Al-Erhab A'la Al-A'mn Al-Q'aomy Alyemeni*, pp. 177-178.

[16] Jonathan Schanzer. "Yemen's War on Terror." *Pundicity, Information & Review* (Summer, 2004), accessed 6/7/2012, http://schanzer.pundicity.co-m/827/yemens-war-on-terror

[17] The Afghani-Arab term is referring to Arabs return from jihad in Afghanistan against USSR in 1980s.

[18] The attack on the World Trade Center was in February 26, 1993 and resulted in 6 killed and more than 1000injured. On the other side, the process of Riyadh has led to the deaths of five Americans in November 15, 1995.

[19] General, Ahmad Alrok'yhi. Chairman of the Department of Defense and Security in the Office of the Presidency, *Personal Interview*, 15/3/2012.

[20] Mohammed A. Mashrah. *Alsiash Alk'argiah Alyameniah Tegah Mokafah'at Alerhab Aldoally*, p. 216.

[21] Mohammed Alsabry. "Ala'ba'ad Alea'alamyah Fi Ala'alakat Alyemeniah Alemerciah." *Sha'awn Ala'aser*, no. 9 (2000), p. 21.

[22] Nabiel al-Razaqi. *Ath'er D'aherat Al-Erhab A'la Al-A'mn Al-Q'aomy Alyemeni*, p. 105.

[23] Maysa Shoga'a Aldein. "Ala'alakat Alyemeniah Alemerciah Wa Azmat Alta'awn." (2002), accessed 6/2/2011, http://www.onislam.net/arabic/newsanalysis/analysis-opinions/europe-north-americaaustrali-a/85815-2002-09-07%2000-00-00.html

[24] Noha Abdullah Al-Sadsy. "Ath'er Th'aherat Al-Erhab Aldoaly A'la Alsyasah Al-Yemeniah Ak'ab Ah'dath' Alhadie Ashar Men September.", p. 231.

[25] Almarkaz Ala'am Llelderast wa Albh'oth wa Alesdar. "Annual Strategic Report Yemen: 2000." by Abd Alaziz Alkomim *et al.* (Sana'a: Alkadasi Llteba'ah wa Alnasher, 2001), pp. 102-103.

[26] "Friends in Washington.", accessed 6/2/2012, http://www.al-bab.com/yemen/data/news99.htm

[27] Almarkaz Alyemeny Lelderasat wa Alabh'wth. "Yemen and the World, Strategic Report," (Sana'a, 2002), p. 208.

[28] Bruce Hoffman. "Al Qaeda,Trends in Terrorism and Future Potentialities: An Assessment." (paper presented at the The Middle East After Afghanistan and Iraq; 3rd Annual Conference, Geneva, 5 May 2003), accessed 3/4/2010, http://www.rand.org/pubs/papers/2005/P8078.pdf, p. 8.

[29] Richard Rosthauser. "Terrorism Conflict: How the United States Responds to Al-Qaeda Violence and Expressed Grievances.", p. 58.

[30] Nabiel al-Razaqi. *Ath'er D'aherat Al-Erhab A'la Al-A'mn Al-Q'aomy Alyemeni*, p. 253.

[31] Ian Shapiro. *Containment: Rebuilding a Strategy against Global Terror* (New Jersey: Princeton University Press, 2007), p. x.

[32] The attack killed 17 members of the ship's crew and 39 were injured. The three memorable suspects were AbdulRahim al-Nashiri, Walid Attash and al-Badawi. See, The National Commission on Terrorism Attack upon the US. *The 9/11 Commission Report* (New York: Regan Books, 2002), pp. 451-453.

[33] Nabiel al-Razaqi. *Ath'er D'aherat Al-Erhab A'la Al-A'mn Al-Q'aomy Alyemeni*, p. 362.

[34] "The Interview with President Saleh by Al-Jazeera TV, Weekly Program -without Borders-." *National Information Center in Yemen* (October, 2000), accessed 4/3/2011, http://www.yemen-nic.info/presidency/detail.php?ID=6800

[35] Article 44, Constitution of the Republic of Yemen, 1990.

[36] National Council on US-Arab Relations. "10th Anniversary of the Attack on the *USS Cole* in Yemen: A Retrospective." by John Duke Anthony. (Washington DC: October 12, 2010), accessed 8/2/2011, http://ncusar.org/publications/Publications/2010-10-12-Cole-Investigation-Retrospective.pdf, p. 5.

[37] Roger Hardy. "Kelaf Emraiki Yemeni H'aol Tahkikat Almodamerak Cool." *BBC Online Network* (2001), accessed 6/6/2011, http://news.bbc.co.uk/hi/arabic/news/newsid_1504000/1504744.stm

[38] Richard Clarke. *Against All Enemies: Inside America's War on Terror* (New York: Free Press, 2004), pp. 223-224.

[39] Congressional Research Service. "Terrorist Attack on *USS Cole*: Background and Issues for Congress." by Raphael Perl and Ronald O'Rourke. (Washington DC, January 30, 2001), p. 2.

[40] William A. Rugh. "Yemen and the United States: Conflicting Priorities." *The Fletcher Forum of World Affairs* 34, no. 2 (Summer, 2010), p. 112.

[41] Maysa Shoga'a Aldein. "Ala'alakat Alyemeniah Alemerciah Wa Azmat Alta'awn." (2002), accessed 6/2/2011, http://www.onislam.net/arabic/newsanalysis/analysis-opinions/europe-north-americaaustrali-a/85815-2002-09-07%2000-00-00.html

[42] Republic of Yemen. "Yemeni Experience in Counter-Terrorism." (paper presented at the International Conference on Counter-Terrorism, Riyadh, 2005).

[43] Almarkaz Alyemeny Lelderasat wa Albh'wth. "Yemen Strategic Report 2003." (Sana'a: Almarkaz AlYemeni, 2004), p. 150.

[44] There are approximately 17-60 million firearms among the people of Yemen. See, Graduate Institute of International and Development Studies. "Completing the Count Civilian Firearms." (Geneva, 2007), accessed 9/12/2011, http://www.smallarmssurvey.org/fileadmin/docs/A-Yearbook/2007/en/full/Small-Arms-Survey-2007-Chapter-02-EN.pdf, p. 45.

[45] Maickl Naits. "Alyemen Moltaka Alerhabeen Alalemeen." *Althawry News* (27/4/2006).

[46] Congressional Research Service. "Yemen: Background and US Relations 2009." by Jeremy M. Sharp (Washington DC: CRS, July 7, 2009), p. 21.

[47] Mohammed A. Mashrah. *Alsiash Alk'argiah Alyameniah Tegah Mokafah'at Alerhab Aldoally*, pp. 224-225.

[48] Ashraf al-Ashri. "No US Military Bases in Yemen." *Yemen News Agency SABA* (June,2010), accessed 14/6/2011, http://www.sabanews.net/en/news216543.htm

[49] See Appendix F: Map of US Military Bases around the World.

[50] Robert D. Burrowes. "Political Economy and the Effort against Terrorism." In *Battling Terrorism in the Horn of Africa*, (ed.) Robert I Rotberg. (Cambridge: World Peace Foundation, 2005), p. 160.

[51] Mohammed A. Mashrah. *Alsiash Alk'argiah Alyameniah Tegah Mokafah'at Alerhab Aldoally*, p. 224.

[52] The US State Department. "US State Department Report on Terrorism for 2008; Yemen." (2008), accessed 9/6/2011, http://photos.state.gov/libraries/yemen/231771/PDFs/2008.pdf

[53] The US State Department. "US State Department Report on Terrorism for 2007; Yemen." (2007), accessed 2/6/2011, http://photos.state.gov/libraries/yemen/231771/PDFs/2007.pdf

[54] Through my work in the Office of the Presidency of Yemen, in the Administration Yemeni-American relations, US has provided a comprehensive project in order to help Yemen to control all the borders of Yemen and communications. This project contains modern equipment, vehicles and aircraft, the US will bear the cost of aid to Yemen. President Saleh's rejection this project because of America did not accept the supervision of the Yemeni power on such advanced equipment.

[55] Jeremy M. Sharp. "Yemen: Background and US Relations 2009.", pp. 3-4.

[56] Nabiel al-Razaqi. *Ath'er D'aherat Al-Erhab A'la Al-A'mn Al-Q'aomy Alyemeni*, p. 366.

[57] There are two types of al-Qaeda operating at the local and regional levels. The first is al-Qaeda's organization that is associated with the central leadership in Afghanistan, the other type is intellectual and is not part of al-Qaeda's militant organization. Its members

often belong to the second generation of the Mujahedeen. Due to the negative US conducts in the region, they reject Western-styled culture and American hegemony.

[58] "Statement Adopting the Madrid Bombings by Ktae'b Abo H'afss Almasry." (2004), accessed 29/1/2010, http://www.paldf.net/forum/showthread.php?p=84314

[59] Committee On Foreign Relations United States Senate. *Yemen: Confronting Al-Qaeda, Preventing State Failure* (Washington DC: US Government Printing Office Washington, Jan 20, 2010), accessed 20/1/2011, http://www.gpo.gov/fdsys/pkg/CHRG-111shrg62357/html/CHRG-111shrg62357.htm

[60] Douglas Kellner. "September 11, Terror War, and Blowback." *Columbia University* (2005), accessed 16/6/2011, http://www.gseis.ucla.edu/faculty/kellner/kellner.html

[61] They escaped through a tunnel under the ground 5 meters in depth and length of 200 meters. Who escaped includes Nasser Wahayshi the current leader of AQAP, and Rimi the current field commander.

[62] Abd Alelah Haidar. "Tand'im Al Qaeda Fi Alyemen Men Almah'ly Ela Ala'klimy." *Markaz Aljazeera Lelderasat* (2010), accessed 17/1/2011, http://errorpage.aljazeera.net/AJA-error/index.htm

[63] Gregory D. Johnsen. "Hafwat Alyak'd'ah; Tareek Al Qaeda Ela Hjoom Lilat Alaaid." *Al-Madarat* no. 2 (January 2010), p. 95.

[64] See, "Understanding Modern Piracy: Terrorists and Their Maritime Campaign." (paper presented at the 10th Annual Maritime Homeland Security Summit 2012, Sheraton Norfolk Waterside, Norfolk, VA, 2012), p. 4.

[65] "Weekly Address: President Obama Outlines Steps Taken to Protect the Safety and Security of the American People." *The White House*, accessed 23/4/2012, http://www.whitehouse.gov/the-press-office/weekly-address-president-obama-outlines-steps-taken-protect-safety-and-security-ame

[66] Daniel E. Nowicki. "Assessing the Effectiveness of the US Counterterrorism Assistance Program to the Republic of Yemen." (Master Thesis, Georgetown University, 2011), p. iii.

[67] Senate Select Committee on Intelligence US Congress. *Attempted Terrorist Attack on Northwest Airlines Flight 253, 111th Cong., 2nd Sess., May 24, 2010* (Washington DC: GPO, 2010), accessed 20/1/2011, http://www.intelligence.senate.gov/pdfs/111199.pdf, p. 9.

[68] Mohamed Al-Hawri. Deputy Minister for Economic Studies and Forecasts Sector, Ministry of Planning and International Cooperation, *Personal Interview*, 18/1/2011.

[69] Mojeeb Alrahman. *Al-Yemen Wa Al-Dwoal Al-Kobra', Derasah Tah'liliah Tawthekiah*, p. 21.

[70] Ali Al-Ghifari. *Al-Deplumasia Al-Yemenia 1900-2000*, p. 182.

[71] Muhsin Al-Aini. *Khamson Aamn Fi Al-Remal Al-Moth'rekah: Qasaty Maa Benaa Al-Dawlah Al-Yemeni Al-Hadetha*, pp. 176-221.

[72] Yuval Levin. "American Aid to the Middle East: A Tragedy of Good Intentions." *Research Papers in Strategy* (2000), accessed 25/9/2010, http://www.iasps.org/strat11/strategic11.pdf, pp. 2-3.

[73] Eric Macro, *Yemen and the Western World, since 1571*, p. 26.

[74] Ali Al-Ghifari, *Al-Deplumasia Al-Yemenia 1900-2000*, p. 182.

[75] Congressional Research Service. "Yemen: Background and US Relations 2011." by Jeremy M. Sharp. (Washington DC:CRS, March , 2011), accessed 3/1/2012, www.fas.org/sgp/crs/mideast/RL34170.pdf, p.25

[76] Moath Alrefaei. "Altadweer Wa Altahdeth Aledary Fi Alyemen." (University Of Sana', a2006), p.43.

[77] Ministry of Planning and Development and UNDP. "Yemen Human Development Report 2003." (Sana'a: UNDP, 2003), p. 16.

[78] Hamod Monaser. "Almasar Altat'biky Ll-Tagrobah Aldemokrateiah Fi Al-Yemen Wa Mo'asherat Al-Mostak'bal.", p. 243.

[79] Mojeeb Alrahman. *Al-Yemen Wa Al-Dwoal Al-Kobra', Derasah Tah'liliah Tawthekiah*, p. 49.

[80] Ibid.

[81] Ministry of Planning and Development and UNDP. "Yemen Human Development Report 2003." (Sana'a: UNDP, 2003), p. 16.

[82] Kaled Kasem. "Economic Challenges." (paper presented at the Altah'dieat alYemeniah fi faterat al-Raeasah al-Gadidah, Sana'a, 2006), p. 11.

[83] Sarah Phillips. "Al-Qaeda and the Struggle for Yemen." *Survival* 53, no. 1 (February-March 2011), pp. 95-120.

[84] Congressional Research Service. "Yemen: Current Conditions and US Relations." by Alfred B. Prados and Jeremy M. Sharp. (Washingto DC: CRS, January 4, 2007), pp. 3-4.

[85] United Nations. "Yemen, Country Profile: Human Development Indicators." (2011), accessed 29/3/2012, http://hdrstats.undp.org/en/countries/profiles/YEM_print.html

[86] Mohamed Al-Hawri. Deputy Minister for Economic Studies and Forecasts Sector, Ministry of Planning and International Cooperation, *Personal interview*, 18/6/2011.

[87] USAID: Strategic Planning and Analysis Division. *Yemen Gap Analysis* (Washington DC: United States Agency, April 25, 2011), accessed 3/2/2012, http://www.usaid.gov/locations/europe_eur-asia/wp/mcp_gap_analyses-yemen_april_2011.pdf, p. 6.

[88] See appendix G: Yemen in Human Development Index: Trends 1995-2011.

[89] John Johnson. "Yemen, Which Is Unknown to American." *Al-Madarat*, no. 2 (January, 2010), pp. 48-51.

[90] Sarah Phillips. "Al-Qaeda and the Struggle for Yemen", p. 96.

[91] London School of Economics and Political Science. "Changing Donor Policy and Practice on Civil Society in the Post-9/11 Aid Context." by Jude Howell and Jeremy Lind. (London: July, 2008), accessed 9/1/2011, http://www2.lse.ac.uk/internationalDevelopment/research/NGPA/publications/WP25_Donors-_HowellLind_Web.pdf

[92] Ken Dilanian. "Yemen Hasn't Received as Much US Aid as Its Neighbors." *USA Today News* (2010), accessed 2/1/2011, http://www.usatoday.com/news/world/2010-01-05-yemen-aid_N.htm

[93] Gregory D. Johnsen. "Hafwat Alyak'd'ah; Tareek al-Qaeda Ela Hjoom Lilat Alaaid.", p. 95.

[94] Ken Dilanian. "Yemen Hasn't Received as Much US Aid as Its Neighbors." And see, Alfred B. Prados and Jeremy M. Sharp. "Yemen: Current Conditions and US Relations.", p. 6.

[95] "Al-Qaeda Claims Parcel Bomb Plot" *Al Jazeera English* (2010), accessed 12/9/2011, http://www.aljazeera.com/news/middleeast/2010/11/2010115204329353739.html

[96] Jeremy M. Sharp. "Yemen: Background and U.S. Relations 2011.", p. 25.

[97] Congressional Research Service. "Yemen: Background and US Relations 2012." by Jeremy M. Sharp. (Washington DC: CRS, April, 2012), accessed 2/5/2012, http://www.fas.org/sgp/crs/mideast/RL3417-0.pdf, p. 8.

[98] For further reading see, Ken Dilanian. "Yemen Hasn't Received as Much US Aid as Its Neighbors." See also, Congressional Research Service. "Yemen: Background and US Relations 2010." by Jeremy M. Sharp. (Washington DC: CRS, July 28, 2010), p. 25.

[99] Ken Dilanian. "Yemen Hasn't Received as Much US Aid as Its Neighbors." *USA Today News* (2010), accessed 2/1/2011, http://www.usatoday.com/news/world/2010-01-05-yemen-aid_N.htm

[100] See Appendix I: Identifying Yemen in the Failed States Index 2009- 2011.

[101] Moath A. Alrefaei. "Altk'arir Aldoalyeah Fi Alyemen." (Sana'a: Office of the Presidency of the Republic of Yemen, 2008), pp. 5-15.

[102] Ahmad Alhadrami. "Ena'akasat Alerhab Ala Algomhoriah Alyemeniah." In *Al-Yemen Wa Daherat Alerhab: Alah'dath Wa Alena'akasat* (Sana'a: Wkalat Alakba'a Alyemaniah Saba, 2008), pp. 147-154.

[103] Nabiel al-Razaqi. *Ath'er D'aherat Al-Erhab A'la Al-A'mn Al-Q'aomy Alyemeni*, pp. 221-224.

[104] Yousif Saeed is an associate professor at Aden University.

[105] "Yemeni Tourism Sector Loses USD 10 Billion." *Ministry Of Commerce People's Republic Of China*, accessed 6/21/2012, http://english.mofcom.gov.cn/aarticle/....port/201010/20101007195417.html

[106] Noha Abdullah Al-Sadsy. "Ath'er Th'aherat Al-Erhab Aldoaly A'la Alsyasah Al-Yemeniah Ak'ab Ah'dath' Alhadie Ashar Men September.", pp. 140-143.

[107] Yemen's *Houthia* Movement is one of the Shiite sects, while the Wahhabi is a fanatic Sunni sect.

[108] Abu Abdullah al-Zubaidi. A member of the *Mujahideen* in Yemen and participating in the current war against the *Houthia. Personal Interview*, 1/2/2012.

[109] "Yemen Warns Iran to Avoid Interference." *Aljazeera.Net* (2012), accessed 20/7/2012, http://www.aljazeera.net/news/pages/9303c95c-ca21-45a2-885c-fd510956ddd5?GoogleStatID=1

[110] William Rowe. "Yemen Fi Alehtmam Alemricay." *Wajhat Nad'ar* (2010), accessed 2/3/2011, http://www.alittihad.ae/wajhatdetails.php?id=50273

[111] The Heritage Foundation. "2012 Index of Economic Freedom (Yemen)." (2012), accessed 1/7/2012, http://www.heritage.org/index/country/yemen And see, Transparency Inernational. "Corruption Perceptions Index 2011 (Yemen)." (2012), accessed 1/7/2012, http://cpi.transparency.org/cpi2011/res-ults/#CountryResults

[112] Adel Amine. "Men Moa'tamer Landan Ela Riyadh" (January, 2010), accessed 8/4/2011, http://ww-w.alshibami.net/saqifa//showthread.php?t=79917

[113] Daniel E. Nowicki. "Assessing the Effectiveness of the US Counterterrorism Assistance Program to the Republic of Yemen.", pp. 242-244.

[114] For Further reading about the principles of America's commitment to aid see, Daniel R. Mahanty. "The Aid for Security Dilemma: The Distortive Impact of US National Security Interests on Development Assistance.", pp. 15-22.

[115] 111 Congress House Hearing. *Yemen on the Brink: Implications for US Policy* (Washington DC: US Government Printing Office, 2011), accessed 2/1/2012, http://www.gpo.gov/fdsys/pkg/CHRG-111hhrg54939/html/CHRG-111hhrg54939.htm, p. 2.

[116] Irene Gendzier. "Oil, Iraq and US Foreign Policy in the Middle East." *Situation Analysis*, no. 2 (March, 2003), p. 20.

[117] "Secretary Clinton's Town Hall in Sana'a, Yemen." *US Embassy in Sana'a* (January 11, 2011) accessed 3/4/2012, http://yemen.usembassy.gov/sth.html.

[118] Ibid.

[119] US Agency for International Development. *2010-2012 Yemen Country Strategy,* p. 2.

[120] "Secretary Clinton's Town Hall in Sana'a, Yemen." *US Embassy in Sana'a* (January 11, 2011) accessed 3/4/2012, http://yemen.usembassy.gov/sth.html

[121] Rahma Hujaira. Chairwoman at Media Woman Forum, *Personal Interview,* 24/4/2009.

[122] "Remarks with Yemeni President Ali Abdullah Saleh after Their Meeting." *US Embassy in Sana'a* (2011), accessed 5/6/2012, http://yemen.usembassy.gov/ryp.html

[123] Sarah Phillips. "What Comes Next in Yemen? Al-Qaeda, the Tribes, and State-Building." (March, 2010), accessed 1/8/2012, www.CarnegieEndowment.org/

[124] Major General Mohammad Rizk al-Sermy. Former Official of al-Qaeda File in the Yemeni Political Security Service (PSS), *Personal Interview,* 12/1/2012.

[125] Michael Horton. "The Unseen Hand: Saudi Arabian Involvement in Yemen.", p. 7.

[126] Senate Foreign Relations Committee. "Testimony of Gregory D. Johnsen." (Washington DC: US Congress, January 20, 2010), accessed 1/7/2011, http://www.foreign.senate.gov/imo/media/doc/Jo-hnsenTestimony-100120a1.pdf

[127] Daniel E. Nowicki. "Assessing the Effectiveness of the US Counterterrorism Assistance Program to the Republic of Yemen.", p. 36.

[128] Indeed, the above fact is a summary of the findings by Ahmed Saife's study, president of the Center of Studies and Research in Sana'a, through his participation with a series of conferences which discussed the situation of Yemen with many international institutions such as the Friends of Yemen (Group of justice and the rule of law), Royal Institute of International Affairs (Chatham House), as well as Center of Military analysis (Enigma) and the Carnegie Endowment for International Peace. See , Ahmad A. Saife. "Lenosa'aed Anfosena Awla." *Madarat,* no. 3 (Marc/June 2010), p. 8.

[129] "Secretary Clinton's Town Hall in Sana'a, Yemen." *US Embassy in Sana'a* (January 11, 2011) accessed 3/4/2012, http://yemen.usembassy.gov/sth.html.

[130] Those countries are Oman, Qatar, Kuwait and Saudia Arabiaone of, check out the following documents, "Wikileaks Cble: Oman's Ali Majid Warns Yemen on the Brink" *WIKILEAKS,* accessed 4/1/2012, http://www.washingtonpost.com/wp-srv/special/world/wikileaks-yemen/cablc8.html. And, "Wikileaks Cble: Discussion with Dr. Prince Turki, Saudi Ministry of Foreign Affairs." *WIKILEAKS* (2009), accessed 4/1/2012, http://www.washingtonpost.com/wp-srv/special/world/wikileaksyemen/cable6.html. And see, "Wikileaks Cble: Prime Minister: Qatar Deeply Concerned About Yemen." *WIKILEAKS,* accessed 4/1/2012, http://www.washingtonpost.com/wp-srv/special/world/wikileaks-yemen/cable10.html.

[131] Craig Whitlock. "US Was Told of Yemen Leader's Vulnerability." *The Washington Post with Foreign Policy* (April 8, 2011), accessed 2/3/2012, http://www.washingtonpost.com/world/us-was-told-of-plot-to-overthrow-yemen-leader/2011/04/07/AFBCY7xC_story.html.

[132] Mostafa Naser. Center Chairman of Studies and Economic Media Center. *Personal Interview,* 3/2/2012.

[133] See Appendix J: Security Council Resolution 2014, (2011).

[134] See Appendix K: The GCC Proposal to Solve Yemen's Political Crises.

[135] "Ambassador Gerald Firestein, Interview with Yemen News Agency (Saba)." *US Embassy in Sana'a* (Mach 7, 2011), accessed 10/2/2012, https://yemen2-ar.cms.getusinfo.com/fis.html.

[136] "Statement by US Assistant Secretary of State Jeffrey Feltman at the Friends of Yemen Conference." *US Embassy in Sana'a* (May 23, 2012), accessed 29/5/2012, http://yemen.usembassy.gov/ffyc.html

[137] See Appendix L: Executive Order 13611 of May 16, 2012, Blocking Property of Persons Threatening the Peace, Security, or Stability of Yemen.

[138] "Interview with US Ambassador in Sana'a Gerald Firestein by Middle East News." *Mareb Press*, accessed 8/6/2012, http://marebpress.net/articles.php?id=16346&lng=arabic.

CHAPTER FIVE:
CONCLUSION

It can be difficult to fathom the depth of Yemen-U.S. relations due to the instability and oscillation that characterizes the relationship. Moreover, the relationship is governed by a wide range of dynamics that have never been studied. These dynamics are characterized by plurality and overlapping as well as dual influence. Furthermore, the Yemen-U.S. relations are a good example of complex relations between great states like U.S., which led to the current international system, and a small state like Yemen that risks becoming a failed state.

The complex relationship also stems from changes in the regional and international regarding security environment. Moreover, it stems from the complexity of the internal environment of Yemen regarding politics, economics, and development. As a result, the nature of the Yemen-U.S. relations is malleable according to the incentives of any given period and environment. The relationship may converge on certain points, while on other points intersect. Consequently, this final chapter aims to bring out the study's overall conclusion and highlights how changes in factors have shaped Yemeni-American relations and their future.

This book aims to simplify the complexities characterizing the relationship between the two countries. According to its objectives, the book first analyzes and classifies the series of events, issues, and milestones in bilateral relations to understand and identify the dynamics that have shaped the pattern of this relationship. These events and issues are then restructured into a more streamlined template, focusing on the main dynamics—whether internal or external—that have influenced the relationship.

The behavior of both U.S. and Yemen towards each other represents a good example of the state's behavior according to the norms of neo-realism theory. Several issues and events are posited as turning points in the relationship between the two countries and effectively serve to support the assumptions of neo-realism theory. According to the bilateral relations between the two countries, they both aim to gain power and survive in a competitive environment.

The U.S. foreign policy towards Yemen during the Cold War era, the U.S.-USSR competition made American policy-makers enhance its relations with Yemen to prevent USSR from getting a foothold on such a strategic location. Hence, Yemen's importance increased in the balance between the two great powers due to the strategic location and regional factors that caused Yemen to affect U.S. goals and interests. The implication of the bipolar international political system constitutes the dominant factor in governing this relationship and led the U.S. to achieve five strategic goals in the Middle East and the Arabian Peninsula. Arranged according to its importance those five objectives are to protect its allies in particular Israel's security, control energy resources, the safe navigation of maritime oil lines and control the strategic straits, prevent the rise of competing influences whether regional and international, and finally, to protect the security and stability of the region against any threat internally or externally.

In this context, U.S. concern grew after North Yemen strengthened its military cooperation with USSR, while South Yemen remained under British colonial rule. The influence of the Soviet Union then became a real threat to U.S. vital interest in the Arabian Peninsula after the Soviets succeeded in bringing South Yemen to the Eastern bloc. Consequently, U.S. relations with North Yemen witnessed improvement and started the security and military cooperation for the first time and saw an increase in its development and economic aid.

Although the remarkable development in the relations between the two countries, the Yemen-U.S. cooperation did not reach the peak due to Yemen's behavior to get power and maintain survival under a competitive regional environment. Yemen exploited the rivalry between the two great powers to achieve its interests, such as getting arms deals, along with developmental and economic aid in addition to reducing the influence of some regional powers competing with Yemen, namely Britain in the south of Yemen and Saudi Arabia in the north.

After North Yemen realized the security risk of an ambitious South Yemen, North Yemen participated in security cooperation with some countries in the region and the U.S. against South Yemen. However, the U.S. and Saudi Arabia believed that the extensive arms to North Yemen could threaten their common interests. The U.S.-USSR conflict gave Yemen additional bargaining power to affect the U.S. and was prepared to find a balance between various and contradiction interests in the region. This explains why the U.S. policy towards Yemen was characterized by a kind of schizophrenia.

On the other hand, Yemen-U.S. relations are dependent on Yemen's conformity with U.S. interests in the region. The regional scale includes two influential directions. The first direction pushed both countries to improve their relations such as the strategic importance for the region that required stability. Yemen agreed with U.S. on the importance of maintaining stability in the region, but differed in regards to its military presence in the region. The other direction is an overall decline in relations due to such factors like U.S. contradiction of Yemen's policies on regional issues. The Yemeni foreign policy intersected with some U.S. goals in the region and this led to the erosion of relations to the lowest levels or completely severance of ties. The conflicting national interests of both countries in the region are the important factor shaped the relationship. For example, it led to the severance of relations in 1967 and a staggering decline after the reestablishment of relations to the lowest level in 1973 and 1991. On the other way, the advancement of Yemen-U.S. relations also led to improved relations with Israel and Saudi Arabia.

Even after the post-Cold War, neo-realism theory offers explanations about the behavior of the hegemonic power.[1] Over the past two decades, the U.S. alone has led the new international order. It championed the spread of democracy and liberal principles as well as counter-terrorism. This agenda is associated with the presence of dozens of U.S. bases and hundreds of thousands of soldiers in the Middle East. The Gulf War acted as a justification for the presence of such forces and the establishment of U.S. military bases. Yemen was one of the few countries that opposed so a new policy, by refusing to Yemen to UN resolutions to use military intervention against Iraq in 1991. Yemen paid a high price for this position that led to the deterioration in bilateral relations with U.S. after the Gulf War in 1991.

The U.S. position towards the Yemeni democratic experience, in the same period, is another example that further supports the assumptions of the neo-realists. Yemen adopted a pioneering experiment in the field of democracy, human rights, the free market and administrative and financial reforms that are consistent with liberal principles promoted by the U.S. Although the Yemeni democratic experience succeeded in attracting the attention of U.S. towards Yemen, the U.S. did not provide full support for such an experience that was unique in the region at that time. Ironically, U.S. warned the Yemeni leadership of any attempt to export their experience in the Arabian Peninsula. Therefore, the democratization and human rights agenda as an external dynamic did not have a strong influence on the conduct of relations between the two countries compared to the impact of the Cold War and the strategic location and regional factors.

After the events of 9/11, the Yemen-U.S. relations changed. The relationship has been completely reformed, especially when the concept of security expanded and the non-military threats led to the erosion of some norms in traditional IR. In fact, the U.S. security agenda to protect its national security differed and new international alliances were formed. The international community's engagement toward counter-terrorism also changed. Many international conventions prove that Yemen and U.S. were allies. These covenants were frameworks that define the obligations of both countries as well as open their structures and cooperation in various fields. In the regional response to the new U.S. policy, Yemen was affected by the impression of the Arabs against the U.S. double standards towards terrorists and religious schools in the region. In short, these factors did not have a strong influence on the conduct of the relationship compared to the internal factors that also completely changed after 9/11.

Internally, Yemen is a good sample for the assumptions of the securitization approach. The emergence of non-military threats by non-state actors changed and extended the security concept in addition to assisting the cooperation between the states rather than competition. The two countries, Yemen and U.S., found that their national security was linked to one another. The U.S. national security was threatened by a series of economic and developmental crises, internal conflicts and political instability in Yemen. In the same way, Yemen's national security was dependent on the military and security assistance by the U.S. and the international community as well as a comprehensive partnership to face its internal challenges.

Accordingly, it can be emphasized that the change of the security perspective in international relations renders the internal dynamics more influential in determining the course of Yemen-U.S. relations. The rise of jihadist groups in Yemen and the implications of Yemen's war against al-Qaeda are important factors. These two factors pushed Yemen and U.S. to strengthen their security and intelligence cooperation in order to avoid threats from non-state actors.

Other internal challenges extended the partnership between Yemen and U.S. from security to a comprehensive partnership. Yemen's economy, development, and political instability became important issues. The U.S. penetrated Yemen's internal conflicts through the *Houthi* movement, the *Southern* movement, and Yemen's war against al-Qaeda. It had a role in strengthening the military and security of Yemen's government, in addition to play the role of mediator in many cases. On the other hand, the U.S. provided hundreds of millions in social and economic aid. It urges the Yemeni government to implement financial and administrative reform programs and counter-corruption.

In short, the U.S. has not been unable to leave Yemen alone to face its critical challenges. It was concerned not only with its interests in Yemen and the Arabian Peninsula but also with the security of its citizens on U.S. soil. The U.S.

had found itself forced to extend its relations with all spectra of Yemen parties, groups, elites, tribes, and clans, especially with the current critical situation in Yemen that has accompanied the so-called Arab Spring. Moreover, Yemen's successes in addressing its internal challenges—such as raising the level of development, reducing poverty, countering corruption, strengthening governance, reforming institutions, and enhancing the democratic experience—will help strengthen the comprehensive partnership through effective exploitation of foreign aid.

Predicting the future of relationships

In light of the repercussions of the current Yemeni crisis, the future of Yemeni-American relations, based on the internal and external factors evaluated in this book, leads us to contradictory scenarios. America will seek to achieve its interests gradually according to priority, starting with its international interests, then regional, and finally local interests related to Yemen. Consequently, the eastern camp, extending from Russia to Iran, aims to control Yemen through Ansar Allah, in addition to securing sea lanes, the flow of Gulf oil, creating regional stability, and combating terrorist groups. These goals are encapsulated in one scenario, which involves resuming dialogue between all Yemeni parties to form a unified state and coalition government and end the current crisis. Although other scenarios are possible, this scenario is the most desirable, though difficult to achieve; failure to achieve it would lead to other scenarios.

The success of the United States in addressing the Palestinian issue and the current Egyptian measures will help restore American rapport with all Yemeni parties, reestablish stability in the region, and secure sea lanes. This paves the way for the return of dialogue between the Yemenis, led by Oman, the indirect negotiations between Ansar Allah and America. This sets the stage for the aforementioned scenario, an end to the Yemeni crisis in the future, and the full return of American-Yemeni relations in the long term. The probability of failure in this task leads to another form of relations between the two countries.

Another possibility is the American effort to maintain the Yemeni militias in the status quo, where they live in a temporary peace with unclear features, while seeking to improve the relationship with the legitimate leadership in Yemen and restore their influence over all factions except Ansar Allah. In this case, decision-makers in both countries are likely to opt for continuing their bilateral partnership, which appears to be the most plausible prospect. The relationship could strengthen further if the existing external and internal dynamics persist, particularly in supporting the legitimate government and its forces against Ansar Allah, who are backed by Iran and perceived as a regional threat from American and Israeli perspectives. The American endeavor to exclude the influence of the eastern camp in the Arabian Peninsula necessitates the continuation of the war against the Ansar Allah movement, but at the same time, it imposes a state of instability in the region and threatens vital interests such as sea laines and the flow of oil.

Similarly, movements opposing American policies in the region and Yemen as the presence of Shiite groups as well as al-Qaeda and ISIS, have also strengthened. For instance, AQAP has succeeded in controlling some cities such as the city of Jaar in Abyan province, in addition to its spread in many tribes in the south, central, and north of Yemen. Some indicators demonstrate that the current leadership in Yemen is determined to completely eradicate terrorism. However, the events of the current war on terrorism are marred by uncertainty, especially after the success of al-Qaeda in regaining some of their positions after the recent military campaign. Furthermore, al-Qaeda's strategy of targeting Yemeni tribal leaders may weaken public cooperation and prolong the duration of the war. From another perspective, in the post-civil war period, combating the local terrorist group will become a priority for the government. This focus may renew the strategic partnership with the United States in the war on terrorism.

From the American perspective, the growing power of extremist Islamic and Shiite groups requires America to either intervene militarily or attempt to contain one party against the other, for example, containing the *Houthis*, with the aim of confronting extremist groups in the future, or alternatively, direct American military intervention to limit both sides.

The U.S. may opt not to engage in war for many reasons, the most important being the complexity of the situation and the severe hardship suffered by Yemen. Moreover, the deteriorating economy has contributed to the emergence of a new generation of al-Qaeda in Yemen and has led to its resurgence in the Arabian Peninsula. Additionally, previous U.S. military interventions have not achieved success, whether in Afghanistan or Iraq, but instead led to the resurgence of jihadist organizations. This outcome is possible in Yemen, especially given the environment that includes widespread availability of weapons and the tribal nature of Yemeni society. Such factors may lead the U.S. to reconsider any decision to go to war in Yemen.

In summary, the near-term outlook for relations between the two countries is not promising. However, there is always the potential for improvement if a dominant factor emerges that compels both sides to engage positively. Future prospects will depend on how domestic issues in Yemen evolve over the coming years.

---

[1] Robert O. Keohane. *After Hegemony: Cooperation and Discord in the World Political Economy*, pp. 31-39.

BIBLIOGRAPHY

Books and Chapter in Books

A'bad'ah, Farok' O'thman. *Alh'okm Al-Ottmani F'i Al-Yemen 1872-1818* (Cairo: al-Haia'ah al-A'amah ll-Ketab, 1986).

Ahmed, Mojeeb Alrahman. *Al-Yemen Wa Al-Dwoal Al-Kobra', Derasah Tah'liliah Tawthekiah* (Sana'a: Wkalat Alanba'a Al-Yamniah Saba, 2003).

Al-Aini, Muhsin. *Khamson Aamn Fi Al-Remal Al-Moth'rekah: Qasaty Maa Benaa Al- Dawlah Al-Yemeni Al-Hadetha* (Cairo: Dar al-Sharwak, 1999).

Al-Azem, Nazeeh Mu'ayyed. *Rehlah Fi Al-Arabia Al-Saeda* (Beirut: al-Tanweer, 1986).

Albahr, Mohamed Ali. *Tareekh Al-Yemen Almoaser* (Cairo: Madbouly Maktabah, 1990).

Al-Ghifari, Ali. *Al-Deplumasia Al-Yemenia 1900-2000* (Sana'a: Dar al-Affaq lel- Tebaah we al-Nashr, 2000).

Alhadrami, Ahmad. *Al-Yemen Wa Daherat Alerhab: Alah'dath Wa Alena'akasat* (Sana'a: Wkalat Alakba'a Alyemaniah Saba, 2008).

AL-Haysami, Khadeejah. *Al-Alaqat Al-Yemenia Al-Saudia: 1962-1982* (Cairo: Dar al-Fath lel Nashr, 1983).

Almadhagi, Ahmed Noman Kassim. *Yemen and the United States: The Study of a Small Power and Super-State Relationship 1962–1994* (London, New York: I.B.Tauris Publishers, 1996).

Alramah, Kaled Ahmed.

"Alkarsanah Alsomaliah Ka Tahdid Lelamn Alkomai Alyeamni." In *Alkarsanah Albahryah Fi Kalyg Aden and Almoh'iet' Alhandi,* edited by Mohammed Saif. (Sana'a: Wkalat Alanba Alyemaniah Saba, 2009): 30-60.

Al-Razaqi, Nabiel. *Ath'er D'aherat Al-Erhab A'la Al-A'mn Al-Q'aomy Alyemeni* (Sana'a: Markaz Abady Llderast wa Alnasher, 2010).

Amri, Husayn Abd Allah. *The Yemen in the 18th and 19th Centuries: A Political and Intellectual History* (London: Centre for Middle Eastern, Islamic Studies, University of Durham by Ithaca Press, 1985).

Badeeb, Saeed M. *The Saudi-Egyptian Conflict over North Yemen, 1962-1970* (Boulder, Washington DC: Westview Press and American-Arab Affairs Council, 1986).

Bidwell, Robin Leonard. *The Two Yemens* (London: Longman, 1983).

Burrowes, Robert D. "Political Economy and the Effort against Terrorism." in *Battling Terrorism in the Horn of Africa,* edited by Robert I Rotberg. (Cambridge: World Peace Foundation, 2005): 1-22

_____. *The Yemen Arab Republic: The Political of Development 1967-1986,* (Boulder: Co, Westview Press, 1987).

Buzan, Barry. *People, States and Fear: The National Security Problem in International Relation* (Sussex: John Spiers, 1983).

Buzan, Barry, Ole Wæver, and Jaap De Wilde. *Security: A New Framework for Analysis* (Boulder, CO: Lynne Rienner Publishers, 1998).

Carruthers, Susan L. "International History, 1900-1945." in *The Globalization of World Politics; an Introduction to International Relations,* edited by John Baylis and Steve Smith. (New York: Oxford University Press, 2001): 51-73.

Clark, Joshua Reuben. *The Monroe Doctrine* (New York: Committee for the Monroe Doctrine, 1928).

Clark, Victoria. *Yemen: Dancing on the Heads of Snakes* (New Haven, Conn: Yale University Press, 2010).

Clarke, Richard. *Against All Enemies: Inside America's War on Terror* (New York: Free Press, 2004).

Darweesh, Madeehah. *Nashat Al-Americi Fi Al-Yemen Ma Bayn Al-Harbain Al- Alamytiene (1981-1939), Men Waqea Al-Ershief Al-Consulia Al-Americia Fi Aden* (Al-Qahera: al-Hayaa al-Aamma lel-Ketab, 2002).

Donnelly, Jack. "Realism." In *Theories of International Relations*, edited by Scott Burchill and Andrew Linklater. (Houndmills, Basingstoke: Palgrave, 2005): 29-54.

Dresch, Paul. *A History of Modern Yemen* (Cambridge: Cambridge University Press, 2000).

_____, *Tribes. Government, and History in Yemen* (New York: Oxford University Press, 1989).

Ehteshami, A. *Globalization and Geopolitics in the Middle East: Old Games, New Rules* (New York: Routledge, 2007).

Elinak, Jholo Fsakia. *Political Tensions in the Arab Republic of Yemen 1962-1985* (Sana'a: al-Markaz al-Yemeni lel Derasat wa al-Buhoth, 1994).

Feldman, Noah. *After Jihad: America and the Struggle for Islamic Democracy* (New York: Farrar, Straus and Giroux, 2004).

Halliday, Fred. *The Middle East in International Relations. Power, Politics and Ideology* (New York: Cambridge University Press, 2005).

_____. *Revolution and Foreign Policy the Case of South Yemen 1967-1987* (New York: Cambridge University Press, 1990).

_____. *The Society and Politic in the Arabian Peninsula*, trans. by Mohamed Al-Rumaihi. (Beirut: Dar Al-Nahar for Publication, 2000).

Hopf, Ted. *Peripheral Visions: Deterrence Theory and American Foreign Policy in the Third World, 1965-1990* (Ann Arbor: University of Michigan Press, 1994).

Hough, Peter. *Understanding Global Security* (London: Routledge, 2008).

Ingrams, Harold. *The Yemen: Imams, Rulers and Revolutions* (London: John Murray, 1963).

Iriye, Akira. *From Nationalism to Internationalism: U.S. Foreign Policy to 1914* (London: Boston Routledge and K. Paul, 1977).

Jabārāt, Maḥmūd Hamlān. *Alaqat Al-Yamaniyah Al-Amrikiyah 1904-1948, 'Ahd Al-Imam Yahiya Hamid Al-Din* (Amman: Moa'assat Alamam Zaied, 2008).

Jellol, Faisal. *Al-Thawratien, Al-Gumhureityn Wa Al-Wehda 1962-1994* (Beirut: Dar al-Jadedd, 2000).

Johnson, Chalmers A. *Blowback: The Costs and Consequences of American Empire* (New York: Henry Holt, 2004).

Jonas, Manfred. "Isolationism." In *Encyclopedia of American Foreign Policy*, edited by Richard Dean, Alexander DeConde, and Fredrik Logevall. (New York: Charles Scribner's Sons, 2002): 337-51.

Kegley, Charles W. *Controversies in International Relations Theory: Realism and the Neoliberal Challenge* (New York: St. Martin's Press, 1995).

Keohane, Robert O. *After Hegemony: Cooperation and Discord in the World Political Economy* (Princeton, NJ: Princeton University Press, 1984).

Keohane, Robert Owen. *Neorealism and Its Critics* (New York: Columbia University Press, 1986).

Kostiner, Joseph. *Yemen: The Tortuous Quest for Unity, 1990-94* (London: Royal Institute of International Affairs, 1996).

Lamy, Steven L. "Contemporary Mainstream Approaches: Neo-Realism and Neo-Liberalism." In *The Globalization of World Politics: An Introduction to International Relations,* edited by John Baylis, Steve Smith and Patricia Owens. (New York: Oxford University Press, 2008): 124-41.

Loomba, Ania. *Colonialism-Postcolonialism, The New Critical Idiom* (London, New York: Routledge, 1998).

Macro, Eric. *Yemen and the Western World, since 1571* (New York: Praeger, 1968).

Mashrah, Mohammed A. *Alsiash Alk'argiah Alyameniah Tegah Mokafah'at Alerhab Aldoally* (Sana'a: Mtabe'a Wkala't Alanba'a Alyamaniah Saba'a, 2008).

McMullen, Christopher J. *Resolution of the Yemen Crisis 1963 a Case Study in Mediation* (Washington DC: University Press of America, 1985).

Monaser, Hamod. "Almasar Altat'biky Ll-Tagrobah Aldemokrateiah Fi Al-Yemen Wa Mo'asherat Al-Mostak'bal." In *Aldemok'ratiah Wa Al-A'hzab Fi Al-Yemen*, edited by Fares al-Sakaf. (Sana'a: Dar al-Majed Lel-Teba'ah wa al-Nasher, 1998): 36-56.

Olsen, Wendy. "Triangulation in Social Research: Qualitative and Quantitative Methods Can Really Be Mixed." In *In Developments in Sociology*, edited by M. Holborn, and Haralambos. (Lancashire: Causeway Press, 2004): 103-21.

Page, Stephen. *The USSR and Arabia: The Development of Soviet Policies and Attitudes towards the Countries of the Arabian Peninsula*, 1955-1970 (London: Central Asian Research Centre in association with Canadian Institute of International Affairs, 1971).

Peterson, John. "The United States and Yemen: A Historical of Unfulfilled Expectations." In *Handbook of U.S.-Middle East Relations*, *Formative Factors and Regional Perspectives*, edited by Robert E. Looney. (London, New York: Routledge, 2009): 502-12

_____. *Yemen, the Search for a Modern State* (Baltimore: Johns Hopkins University Press, 1982).

Phillips, Sarah. *Yemen's Democracy Experiment in Regional Perspective: Patronage and Pluralized Authoritarianism* (New York: Palgrave Macmillan, 2008).

Rajab, Yahya Halmy. *Alk'alyg Alarabi Wa Alsera'a Aldoali Almoa'aser* (Kuwait: Dar Ala'arobah LeLnasher wa Altawziea'a, 1989).

Ribuffo, Leo P. "Religion." In *Encyclopedia of American Foreign Policy*, edited by Richard Dean and Fredrik Logevall Alexander Deconde. (New York: Facts on File, 2004): 371-93.

Salem, Sai'ed Most'afa. *Albah'r Alah'mar W'a Aljoz'er Al-Yamniah Tarik'h*

Wa K'ad'iah (Sana'a: Dar Almith'ak' LelNash'er Wa Altwzia'a, 2006).

Sanger, Richard H. *The Arabian Peninsula* (Ithaca: Cornell Univ. Press, 1954).

Schmidt, Dana Adams. *Yemen: The Unknown War* (London: Bodley Head, 1968).

Scott, Hugh. *In the High Yemen* (London: Murray, 1942).

Shapiro, Ian. *Containment; Rebuilding a Strategy against Global Terror* (New Jersey: Princeton University Press, 2007).

Shehab, Foa'ad. *Tad'awer Alestrategiah Alamerikeyah Fi Alk'alig Alarabi* (Bahrain: Fak'rawi, 1994).

Smith, Simon C. "Conflict and Co-Operation - Anglo-American Relations in the Gulf from the Nationalization of Anglo-Iranian Oil to the Yemeni Revolution." In *Britain's Revival and Fall in the Gulf: Kuwait, Bahrain, Qatar, and the Trucial States, 1950-71* (London, New York: Routledge, 2004): 109-28.

Stookey, Robert W. *Yemen: The Politics of the Yemen Arab Republic* (Boulder, Colo: Westview Press, 1978).

Tarseesi, Adnan. *Ardh Saba Wa Al-Hadharah Al-Arabia Al-Mub* (Beirut: Dar al-Fiker al-Muasir, 1985).

Terrill, W. Andrew. *The Conflicts in Yemen and U.S. National Security* (Washington DC: The Strategic Studies Institute SSI, 2011).

Terry, Janice J. *U.S. Foreign Policy in the Middle East; the Role of Lobbies and Special Interest Groups* (London: Pluto Press, 2005).

Trask, Roger R. "United States Relations with the Middle East in the Twentieth Century: A Developing Area in Historical Literature." In *American Foreign Relations, a Historiographical Review*, edited by Gerald K. Haines and Samuel Walker. (Westport, Conn: Greenwood Press, 1981): 293-309.

Vine, D. *Island of Shame: The Secret History of the U.S. Military Base on Diego Garcia* (New Jersey: Princeton University Press, 2009).

Waltz, Kenneth. *Man, the State, and War* (New York: Columbia University Press, 1959).

_____. *Theory of International Politics* (New York: Random House, 1979).

Wenner, Manfred W. *Modern Yemen: 1918-1966* (Baltimore: Johns Hopkins Press, 1986).

_____. *The Yemen Arab Republic: Development and Change in an Ancient Land* (Boulder: Westview Press, 1991).

Wright, Lawrence. *The Looming Tower: Al-Qaeda and the Road to 9/11* (New York: Alfred A. Knopf, 2006).

Yaqub, S. *Containing Arab Nationalism: The Eisenhower Doctrine and the Middle East* (Chapel Hill, N.C.: University of North Carolina Press, 2004).

Yetiv, Steven A. *Explaining Foreign Policy: U.S. Decision-Making in the Gulf Wars* (Baltimore: The Johns Hopkins University Press, 2011).

Zabarah, Mohammed Ahmad. *Yemen, Traditionalism Vs. Modernity* (New York: Praeger, 1982).

Articles in Journal

Al-Abdin, A. Z. "The Free Yemeni Movement (1940–48) and Its Ideas on Reform." *Middle Eastern Studies* 15, no. 1 (1979): 36 - 48.

Al-Faqiah, Abd Allah. "Men Eh'toa'a Al-Soai'ah Ela Eh'toa'a Al-Qa'edah." *Al-Madarat* 1, no. 1 (2009): 28-31.

Azhary, M.S.El. "Aspects of North Yemen's Relations with Saudi Arabia." *Asian Affairs* 15, no. 3 (1984): 277-86.

Badahdah, Abdallah, Najat Sayem, and Carrie E. Foote. "Development of a Yemeni Aids Stigma Scale." *AIDS Care: Psychological and Socio-medical Aspects of AIDS/HIV* 21, no. 6 (2009): 1-6.

Baldry, John. "Soviet Relations with Saudi Arabia and the Yemen 1917–1938." *Middle Eastern Studies* 20, no. 1 (1984): 53-80.

Bradley, Bowman L. "Realism and Idealism: U.S. Policy toward Saudi Arabia, from the Cold War to Today." *Parameters* 35, no. 4 (2005–2006): 91-105.

Crenshaw, Martha. "Counter-terrorism Policy and the Political Process." *Studies in Conflict and Terrorism* 24, no. 5 (September-October, 2001): 329-37.

Dalacoura, Katerina. "U.S. Democracy Promotion in the Arab Middle East since 11 September 2001: A Critique." *International Affairs* 81, no. 5 (October, 2005): 963-79.

Difo, Germain. "Yemen and U.S. Security: Assessing and Managing the Challenge of Al-Qaeda in the Arabian Peninsula (AQAP)." *Perspectives* (June, 2010): 1-15, accessed

29/10/2010, http://americansecurityproject.org/wpcontent/uploads/2010/11-/Yemen-and-U.S.-Security-Re-Release.pdf

East, Maurice A. "Foreign Policy-Making in Small States: Some Theoretic Observations Based on a Study of the Uganda Ministry of Foreign Affairs." *Policy Sciences* 4, no. 4 (1973): 491-508.

Erhan, Cagri. "Ottoman Official Attitudes towards American Missionaries." *Council on Middle East Studies* (CMES), (2007), accessed 5/4/2011, http://opus.macmilla-n.yale.edu/workpaper/pdfs/MESV5-11.pdf

Fak'yrah, Galal. "Ta'abea't Almoared Fi Alsyasah Alk'regayah Alyemenyah." *Awarak Bah'thyah* (2009), accessed 3/2/2012, http://www.shebacss.com/ar/publicatio-ns.php?action=viewPub&id=35

Frederking, Artime, and Pagano. "Interpreting September 11." *International Politics* 42, no. I (2005): 135-51.

Freeman, Jack. "The Al Houthia Insurgency in the North of Yemen: An Analysis of the Shabab Al Moumineen." *Studies in Conflict and Terrorism* 32, no. 11 (2009): 1008-1019.

Freitag, Ulrike. "A History of Modern Yemen." *International Journal of Middle East Studies* 34, no. 03 (2002): 575-77.

Frum, David. "America's Ally in the Middle East." *Foreign and Defense Policy* (May, 2008), accessed 4/6/2011, http://www.aei.org/article/27930

Fukuyama, Francis, and Michael McFaul. "Should Democracy Be

Promoted or Demoted?." *The Washington Quarterly* (WINTER, 2007-08), accessed 15/6/2011, http://www.twq.com/08winter/docs/08winter_fukuyama.pdf.

Gause, F. Gregory. "Democracy, Terrorism and American Policy in the Arab World." *Assessing Middle East Security Prospects* (April, 2005), accessed 12/1/2011, http://www.dtic.mil/cgi-bin/GetTRDoc?Location=U2&doc=GetTRDoc.pdf&AD=A-DA435048.

Gendzier, Irene. "Oil, Iraq and U.S. Foreign Policy in the Middle East." *Situation Analysis*, no. 2 (March, 2003): 18-28.

Guldescu, Stanko. "Yemen: The War and the Haradh Conference." *The Review of Politics* 28, no. 03 (1966): 319-31.

Haidar, Abd Alelah. "Tand'im Al-Qaeda Fi Alyemen Men Almah'ly Ela Ala'klimy." *Markaz Aljazeera Lelderasat* (2010), accessed 17/1/2011, http://error-page.aljazeera.net/AJA-error/index.htm

Haider, Mohammed Saif. "Men Osamah Ela Alwhaishy." *Al-Madarat*, no. 2 (January, 2010): 88-93.

Halliday, Fred. "The Third Inter-Yemeni War and Its Consequences." *Asian Affairs* 26, no. 2 (1995): 131-140.

Hati, Nasife. "Alnad'am Alarabi Ba'd 11 September: Altahdieat Wa Alfras." *Alshoa'awn Alarabiah*, no. 109 (Rabia'a, 2002): 16-36.

Hoffman. "Complex Irregular Warfare: The Face of Contemporary Conflict." *The Military Balance* 105, no. 1 (2006): 411-20.

Horton, Michael. "The Unseen Hand: Saudi Arabian Involvement in Yemen." *Terrorism Monitor* IX, no. 12, (2011), accessed 8/3/2012, http://global-security-news.com/tag/saudi-arabia-and-yemen/

Jiadong, Zhang. "Terrorist Activities in Yemen and the U.S. Counter-measures." *Middle Eastern and Islamic Studies in Asia* 4, no. 1 (2010): 101-15.

Johnsen, Gregory D. "Hafwat Alyak'd'ah; Tareek Al-Qaeda Ela Hjoom Lilat Alaaid." *Al-Madarat*, no. 2 (January, 2010): 94-97.

Johnson, John. "Yemen, Which Is Unknown to American." *Al-Madarat*, no. 2 (January, 2010): 49-51.

Jones, Andrew. "Comparatively Assess Neo-Realism and Neo-Liberalism. Whose Argument Do You Find the More Convincing and Why?." *E-IR Articles* (2007), accessed 3/6/2010, http://www.e-ir.info/

Kapila, Subhash. "Middle East Changing Dynamics: Strategic Perspectives on Power Play of United States, Russia and China." *South Asia Analysis Group,* 4336 (February, 2011), accessed 6/5/2011, http://www.southasiaanalysis.org/%5Cpapers44%5Cpape-r4336.html

Kemp, Geoffrey, and Robert Harkavy. "Strategic Geography and the Changing Middle East: Concepts, Definitions, and Parameters." *Strategic Geography and the Changing Middle East* (1997), accessed 3/8/2011, http://acc.teachmideast.org/texts.php?mo-dule_id=4&reading_id=120&print=1

Knights, Michael. "Strengthening Yemeni Counter-terrorism Forces: Challenges and Political Considerations." *Policy Watch* (2010), accessed 6/2/2010, http://files.emb-edit.in-/embeditin/files/4P2gmU5jiE/1/file.pdf

Koppes, Clayton R. "Captain Mahan, General Gordon, and the Origins of the Term 'Middle East." *Middle Eastern Studies* 12, no. 1 (1976): 95-98.

Kreutz, Andrej. "Russia and the Arabian Peninsula." *Journal of Military and Strategic Studies* 7, no. 2, (2004), accessed 30/12/2010, http://www.jmss.org/jmss/index.-php/jmss/article/download/184/201

Levin, Yuval. "American Aid to the Middle East: A Tragedy of Good Intentions." *Research Papers in Strategy* (2000), accessed 25/9/2010, http://www.iasp-s.org/strat11/strategic11.pdf

Mawby, Spencer. "The Clandestine Defence of Empire: British Special Operations in Yemen 1951–64." *Intelligence and National Security* 17, no. 3 (2002): 105-30.

McDonald, Matt. "Securitization and the Construction of Security." *European Journal of International Relations* 14, no. 4 (2008): 563-87.

Morgenthau, Hans J. "Another 'Great Debate': The National Interest of the United States." *The American Political Science Review* 46, no. 4 (1982): 961-988.

Phillips, Sarah. "Al-Qaeda and the Struggle for Yemen." *Survival* 53, no. 1 (February/March 2011): 95–120.

Powers, Thomas. "The Vanishing Case for War." *The Long Term View* 6, no. 2 (2004): 106-14.

Pram, Ulrik, and Karen Petersen. "Concepts of Politics in Securitization Studies." *Security Dialogue* 42, no. 4-5 (2011): 315-28.

Rowe, William. "Yemen Fi Alehtmam Alemricay." *Wajhat Nad'ar* (2010), accessed 2/3/2011, http://www.alittihad.ae/wajhatdetails.php?id=50273

Rugh, William A. "Yemen and the United States: Conflicting Priorities." *The Fletcher Forum of World Affairs* 34, no. 2 (Summer, 2010): 111-18.

Saife, Ahmad A. "Lenosa'aed Anfosena Awla." *Al-Madarat*, no. 3 (Marc/June 2010): 8-9.

Sarsar, Saliba. "Can Democracy Prevail?." *Middle East Quarterly* VII, no. 1(March, 2000), accessed 12/4//2010, http://www.meforum.org/40/can-democracy-prevail

Sidaway, J. D. "The (Geo) Politics of Regional Integration: The Example of the Southern African Development Community?." *Environment and Planning D: Society and Space* 16, no. 5 (1998): 549-76.

Smith, Simon C. "Revolution and Reaction: South Arabia in the Aftermath of the Yemeni Revolution." *The Journal of Imperial and Commonwealth History* 28, no. 3 (2000): 193-208.

Snyder, Robert S. "The U.S. and Third World Revolutionary States: Understanding the Breakdown in Relations." *International Studies Quarterly* 43, no. 2 (1999): 265-90.

Stone, Marianne. "Security According to Buzan: A Comprehensive Security Analysis." *Security Discussion Papers Series* (2009), accessed 6/9/2011, http://gee-st.msh-paris.fr/IMG/pdf/Security_for_Buzan.mp3.pdf

Whitlock, Craig. "U.S. Was Told of Yemen Leader's Vulnerability." *The Washington Post with Foreign Policy* (April, 2011), accessed 2/3/2012, http://www.washington-post.com/world/us-was-told-of-plot-to-overthrow-yemen-....AFBCY7xC_story.html

Wieland, Alexander R. "Anglo-American Relations and the Yemeni Revolution, 1962-1963." *Cold War Studies* (2009), accessed 18/2/2011, www2.lse.ac.uk/IDEAS/pub-lications/workingPapers/wieland.pdf

Wirtz, Jim, and James Russell. "Viewpoint: U.S. Policy on Preventive War and Premption." *The Nonproliferation Review* (2003), accessed 4/6/2011, www.com-w.org/qdr/fulltext/03wirtz.pdf

Zunes, Stephen. "Yemen: Latest U.S. Battleground." *Foreign Policy in Focus* (January, 2010), accessed 9/9/2011, http://www.fpif.org/articles/yemen_latest_us_battleground.

"International Committee's Action in the Yemen." *International Review of the Red Cross* 4, no. 40 (1964): 350-51, accessed

12/4/2011, http://journals.cambrid-ge.org/action/display-Abstract?fromPage=online&aid=5814872

"Mistrust Bedevils Yemen's Foreign Relations." *Strategic Comments* 16,

no. 2 (2010): 1-3, accessed
1/4/2011, http://www.informaworld.com/10.1080/13567888.2010.486-611

Government Documents and Publications

111 Congress House Hearing. *Yemen on the Brink: Implications for U.S. Policy* (Washington DC: U.S. Government Printing Office, 2011), accessed 2/1/2012, http://www.gp-o.gov/fdsys/pkg/CHRG-111hhrg54939/html/CHRG-111hhrg54939.htm

CIA and the Intelligence Organizations of the Departments of State and Defense. *Special National Intelligence Estimate* (Washington DC: Office of the Historian February, 1971), accessed 9/4/2011, http://history.state.gov/historicaldoc-umen-ts/frus1969-76v24/d182#fn1

Committee on Foreign Relations United States Senate. *Yemen: Confronting Al-Qaeda, Preventing State Failure* (Washington DC: U.S. Government Printing Office Washington, Jan 20, 2010), accessed

20/1/2011, http://www.gpo.gov/fdsys/pkg/C-HRG111shrg62357/-html/CHRG-111shrg62357.htm

Congressional Record. *Wilson's Fourteen Points an Address to a Joint Session of Congress* (Washington DC: Wikispaces, January 8, 1918) http://worldhistoryiis-pa.wikispaces.com-/file/view/14pts2.pdf

Director of Intelligence Central. *South Yemen-USSR: Outlook for the Relationship* (Washington DC: National Intelligence Estimate, 30 March 1984), accessed
19/9/2010, www.foia.cia.gov/docs/DOC_0000681975/DOC_0000681975.pdf

Federal Research Division. *Country Profile: Yemen* (Washington DC: Library of Congress, 2008), accessed 28/03/2011, http://memory.loc.gov/frd/cs/profiles/Yem-en.pdf

Royal Embassy of Saudi Arabia. *Saudi-U.S. Relations* (Washington DC: Royal Embassy, 2008), accessed 8/4/2011, http://www.saudiembassy.net/files/PDF/Brochu-res/DFS_us-saudi_relations.pdf

Senate Select Committee on Intelligence U.S. Congress. *Attempted Terrorist Attack on Northwest Airlines Flight 253, 111th Cong., 2nd Sess, May 24, 2010* (Washington: GPO, 2010), accessed 20/1/2011, http://www.intelligence.senate.gov/pdfs/111199.pdf

The National Commission on Terrorism Attack upon the U.S.. *The 9\11 Commission Report* (New York: Regan Books, 2002).

U.S. Agency for International Development. *2010-2012 Yemen Country Strategy* (Washington DC: USAID, 2010), accessed

4/5/2012, http://pdf.usaid.gov/p-df_docs/PDACP-572.pdf

U.S. Department of State. *Foreign Relations of the United States: Diplomatic Papers, 1945. The near East and Africa* (Washington DC: U.S. Government Printing Office, 1945), accessed 12/11/2010, http://digital.library.wisc.edu/1711.dl/FRUS.FRUS19-45v08

_____. *The Secretary of State's Dispatch to the Consul of Aden* (Washington: the U.S. Foreign Relations, 1927), accessed 12/3/2011,http://images.library.wisc.edu/FRUS/EFacs/1927v03/reference/frus.frus1927v03.i0032.pdf

_____. *Memorandum by the Acting Secretary of State to President Truman* (Washington DC: Office of the Historian, May 1, 1945), accessed 4/5/2011, http://images.library.wisc.edu/FRUS/EFacs/1945v08/reference/frus.frus1945v08.i0016.pdf

_____. *Memorandum by the Acting Secretary of State to President Truman* (Washington DC: Office of the Historian, November 16, 1945), accessed 4/5/2011, http://images.library.wisc.edu/FRUS/EFacs/1945v08/reference/frus.frus1-945v08.i0016.pdf

_____. *Memorandum from Robert W. Komer of the National Security Council Staff to President Kennedy* (Washington DC: Office of the Historian, November 28, 1962), accessed 3/5/2011, http://history.state.gov/historicaldocuments/frus1961-63v18/d104

_____. *Memorandum from the Department of State Executive Secretary (Brubeck) to the President's Special Assistant for National Security Affairs* (Washington DC: Office of the Historian, December 6, 1962), accessed 5/6/2011, http://history.state.go-v/historicaldocuments/frus1961-63v18/d112

_____. *Memorandum from the Director of the Office of near Eastern Affairs (Rockwell) to the Assistant Secretary of State for near Eastern, South Asian, and African Affairs 'Rountree'* (Washington DC: Office of the Historian, February 21, 1958), accessed 3/6/2011, http://history.state.gov/historicaldocuments/frus195860v1-2/d360

_____. *Memorandum from the Director of the Office of near Eastern Affairs (Wilkins) to the Assistant Secretary of State for near Eastern, South Asian, and African Affairs* (Washington DC: Office of the Historian, January 2, 1957), accessed 5/2/2011, http://history.state.gov/historicaldocuments/frus1955-57v13/d425

_____. *President Truman to the King of Yemen (the Imam Yehya Bin Mohamed Hamid Al-Din)* (Washington DC: Foreign relations of the U.S., November 19, 1945), accessed 6/3/2011, http://images.library.wisc.edu/FRU.S./EFacs/1945v08/reference/fr-us.frus1945-v08.i0016.pdf

_____. *Telegram from Secretary of State Rogers to the Department of State* (Washington DC: Office of the Historian, July 3, 1972), accessed 3/9/2010, http://history.state.gov/historicaldocuments/frus1969-76v24/d193

_____. *Telegram from the Department of State to the Embassy in Egypt, Embassy Requested Convey Following Message Abu Taleb for Imam from Usg* (Washington DC: Office of the Historian, March 29, 1956), accessed 2/2/2011, http://history.sta-te.gov/historicaldocuments/frus1955-57v13/d424

_____. *The Consul at Aden (Clark) to the Secretary of State* (Washington DC: Foreign relations of the U.S., January 17, 1945), accessed 12/11/2010, http://images.l-ibrary.wisc.edu/FRUS/EFacs/1945v08/reference/frus.frus1945v08.i0016.pdf

_____. *U.S. Policy toward Yemen; Policy Statement Prepared in the Department of State* (Washington DC: Foreign relations of the U.S., February 8, 1951), accessed 2/1/2011, http://images.library.wisc.edu/FRUS/EFacs2/1951v05/reference/frus.frus1-951v05.i0020.pdf

_____. *Yemen, Visit of Prince Saif Al-Islam Abdullah to the United States, Editorial Note* (Washington DC: Foreign relations of the U.S., 1947), accessed 2/1/2011,

http://images.library.wisc.edu/FRUS/EFacs/1947v05/reference/frus.frus19
47v05.i0019.pdf

U.S. House of Represetative Committe on Foreign Affairs. *Proposed Arms
Transfers to the Yemen Arab Republic: Hearing March 12,
1979* (Washington DC: U.S. Govt. Print, 1979).

USAID: Strategic Planning and Analysis Division. *Yemen Gap
Analysis* (Washington, DC: United States Agency, April 25, 2011),
accessed 3/2/2012, http://www.usai-
d.gov/locations/europe_eurasia/wp/mcp_gap_analysesyemen_april_2011.
pdf

Reports

Almarkaz Ala'am Llelderast wa Albh'oth wa Alesdar. "Annual Strategic
Report: Yemen 2000." (Sana'a: Alkadasi Llteba'ah wa Alnasher, 2001).

Almarkaz Alyemeny Lelderasat wa Alabh'wth. "Yemen and the World,
Strategic Report." (Sana'a: Almarkaz Alyemeny, 2002).

_____. "Yemen Strategic Report 2003." (Sana'a: Almarkaz Alyemeny,
2004).

_____. "Yemen Strategic Report 2007." (Sana'a: Almarkaz Alyemeny,
2008).

_____. "Yemen Strategic Report 2008." (Sana'a: Almarkaz Alyemeny,
2009).

Arab Center for Research and Policy Studies. "The Yemeni Revolution:
Replacing Ali Abdullah Saleh, or Replacing Obsolete Institutions?." by al-
Qarawi, Hisham. (May, 2011).

BP Organization. "Bp Statistical Review of World Energy." (London: BP
Amoco, 2012), accessed 20/7/2012,
http://www.bp.com/assets/bp...review_of_world_energy-
_full_report_2012.pdf

Canadian Defence and Foreign Affairs Institute. "The New Terrorism:
Understanding Yemen." by Carment, David B. (Calgary), accessed
1/7/2012, http://www4.carleton.ca-/cifp/app/serve.php/1349.pdf

Carleton University. "Yemen: A Risk Assessment Report." by Alie,
Nicole, Mahsa Hedayati, Amy Keuhl and Nathan Lysons. (Calgary: 2007),
accessed 7/1/2011, http://www4.carleto-n.ca/cifp/app/serve.php/1251.pdf

Congressional Research Service. "Yemen: Background and U.S. Relations 2010." by Sharp, Jeremy. (Washington DC: CRS Report for Congress, July 28, 2010).

_____. "Terrorist Attack on USS Cole: Background and Issues for Congress." by Perl, Raphael, and Ronald O'Rourke. (Washington DC: CRS, January 30, 2001).

_____. "U.S. Democracy Promotion Policy in the Middle East: The Islamist Dilemma." by Sharp, Jeremy M. (Washington DC: CRS, June 15, 2006).

_____. "Yemen: Background and U.S. Relations 2008." by Sharp, Jeremy. (Washington DC: CRS, June 10, 2008).

_____. "Yemen: Background and U.S. Relations 2009." by Sharp, Jeremy. (Washington DC: CRS, July 7, 2009).

_____. "Yemen: Background and U.S. Relations 2010." by Sharp, Jeremy. (Washington DC: CRS, January 13, 2010).

_____. "Yemen: Background and U.S. Relations 2011." by Sharp, Jeremy. (Washington DC: CRS, 2011), accessed 3/1/2012, www.fas.org/sgp/crs/mideas-t/RL34170.pdf

_____. "Yemen: Background and U.S. Relations 2012." by Sharp, Jeremy. (Washington DC: CRS, 2012), accessed 2/5/2012, http://www.fas.org/sgp/crs/mid-east/RL34170.pdf

_____. "Yemen: Current Conditions and U.S. Relations." by Prados, Alfred B., and Jeremy M. Sharp. (Washington DC: CRS, January 4, 2007).

Council on Foreign relations. "In Support of Arab Democracy: Why and How." by Albright, Madeleine K. and Vin Weber Co Chairs. (New York: 2005), accessed 31/8/2012, http://www.cfr.org/content/publications/attachments/Arab_Democracy_T-F.pdf

CSIS Middle East Program. "Trouble in the Backyard: Yemen and the GCC." (March 10, 2010), accessed 7/1/2011, www.csis.org/mideast.

Department of Defense. "National Military Strategic Plan for the War on Terrorism." (Washington DC: Council on Foreign Relations, February 1, 2006).

EIU. "Country Report: Yemen at a Glance: 2005-06." (London: EIU, August 2005), accessed 1/1/2011, http://www.mophp-ye.org/DocDB/docs/MoPHP_224_544.pdf

_____. "Country Report: Yemen." (London: November 2009), accessed 1/7/2011, http://www.europarl.europa.eu/meetdocs/2009_2014/document s/darp/dv/darp20091203_08_/darp20091203_08_en.pdf

FOI, Swedish Defence Research Agency. "Yemen in Crisis – Consequences for the Horn of Africa." by Atarodi, Alexander. (Stockholm: Division of Defence Analysis, March, 2010), accessed 6/1/2011, http://www.nai.uu.se/research/naifoi%20lectures/Y-emenIn-Crisis_AlexanderAtarodi.pdf

Graduate Institute of International and Development Studies. "Completing the Count Civilian Firearms." (Geneva: 2007), accessed 9/12/2011, http://www.sma-llarmssurvey.org/fileadmin/docs/A-Yearbook/2007/en/full/Small-Arms-Survey-2007-Chapter-02-EN.pdf

John F. Kennedy School of Government, Harvard University. "Combating Terrorism in the Horn of Africa and Yemen." by West, Deborah L.

(Cambridge, Massachusetts: 2005).

London School of Economics and Political Science. "Changing Donor Policy and Practice on Civil Society in the Post-9/11 Aid Context." by Howell, Jude, and Jeremy Lind. (London: July, 2008), accessed 9/1/2011, http://www2.lse.ac.uk/international-Development/research/NGPA/publications/WP25_Donors_HowellLind_Web.pdf

Ministry of Interior. "Yemen's Efforts Fight against Terrorism." (Sana'a: 2009), accessed 1/7/2010, http://www.moi.gov.ye/moi1/GetFile.aspx?aliaspath=%2fFi....-pdf

Ministry of Planning and Development and UNDP. "Yemen Human Development Report 2000-2001." (Sana'a: The Human Development Report CD-ROM, 2001).

_____. "Yemen Human Development Report 2003." (Sana'a: UNDR, 2003).

National Council on U.S.-Arab Relations. "10th Anniversary of the Attack on the USS Cole in Yemen: A Retrospective." by Anthony, John Duke. (Washington: October 12, 2010), accessed 8/2/2011, http://ncusar.org/publications/Publications/2010-10-12-Cole-Investigation-Retrospective.pdf

National Defence Research Institute, "Politics and the Soviet Presence in the People's Democratic Republic of Yemen: Internal Vulnerabilities and Regional Challenges." by Mylroie, Laurie. (Santa Monica: RAND

Corporation, 1983), accessed 22/2/2010,
http://www.rand.org/pubs/notes/N2052.

_____. "Regime and Periphery in Northern Yemen: The Houthia
Phenomenon." by Barak Salmoni, Bryce Loidolt and Madeleine Wells.
(Santa Monica: RAND Corporation, 2010).

Senate Foreign Relations Committee. "Testimony of Gregory D. Johnsen."
(Washington DC: U.S. Congress, January 20, 2010), accessed 1/7/2011,
http://www.fo-reign.se-
nate.gov/imo/media/doc/JohnsenTestimony100120a1.pdf

The Fund for Peace Publication. "Failed States Index 2011." (Foreign
Policy, 2011, 2010 and 2009), accessed 6/9/2012,
http://www.foreignpolicy.com/articles/2011/06/1-
7/2011_failed_states_index_interactive_map_and_rankings.

The Heritage Foundation. "2012 Index of Economic Freedom (Yemen)."
(2012), accessed 1/7/2012, http://www.heritage.org/index/country/yemen.

The Senlis Council. "Chronic Failures in the War on Terror: From

Afghanistan to Somalia." (London: MF Publishing Ltd, May 2008),
accessed 19/4/2011,
http://www.icosgroup.net/static/reports/chronic_failures_war_terror.pdf.

The U.S. State Department. "U.S. State Department Report on Terrorism
for 2007; Yemen." (2007), accessed 2/6/2011,
http://photos.state.gov/libraries/yemen-/231771/PDFs/2007.pdf.

_____. "U.S. State Department Report on Terrorism for 2008; Yemen."
(2008), accessed 9/6/2011, http://photos.state.gov/libraries/yemen-
/231771/PDFs/2008.pdf.

_____. "Advancing Freedom and Democracy Report." (Washington
DC: The Bureau of Democracy and Labor, May 23, 2008), accessed
9/12/2010 http://photos.state.g-
ov/libraries/yemen/231771/PDFs/advancing-freedom-and-demo-cracy-
reports--2008.pdf.

Transparency International. "Corruption Perceptions Index 2011
(Yemen)." (2012), accessed 1/7/2012,
http://cpi.transparency.org/cpi2011/results/#CountryResults.

United Nations. "Yemen, Country Profile: Human Development
Indicators." (2011), accessed
29/3/2012, http://hdrstats.undp.org/en/countries/profiles/YEM_print.html

U.S. Government Printing Office. "Reliable, Affordable, and Environmentally Sound Energy for America's Future." (Washington DC: US Gov., 2001).

Wakalt al-Anbaa al-Yemenia, Saba. "Al-Yemen Fi Ma'et A'mm." (Sana`a: Markez Al-Bah'ath wa Al-Derasat Saba, 2000).

Thesis

Al-faqih, Abdullah M. "The Struggle for Liberalization and Democratization in Egypt, Jordan and Yemen." (PhD Thesis, Northeastern University, 2003).

Al-Jahny, Shiry. "South Yemen and the Soviet Union, 1967-1986: A Study of a Small Power in an Alliance." (PhD Thesis, George Washington University, 1991).

Al-Khraisha, Mohammed Jamal. "Evaluating Theories of Liberal Hegemony and Small States in U.S.-Jordanian Relations since 2000." (PhD Thesis, Nottingham Trent University, 2010).

Al-Sadsy, Noha Abdullah. "Ath'er Th'aherat Al-Erhab Aldoaly A'la Alsyasah Al-Yemeniah Ak'ab Ah'dath' Alhadie Ashar Men September."

(Master Thesis, Cairo University, 2005).

Al-Shameri, Abad al-Ghany. "Alsiasah Alk'argiah Tegah Altagrabah Aldemok'ratiah Alyemeniah 1990-2006." (Master Thesis, Sana'a University, 2008).

Al-Zandani, Ahmed. "Political Discourse of George W. Bush and Its Impact on the Policies of Selected Arab Countries of the Middle East, 2001-2005." (PhD Thesis, International Islamic University Malaysia, 2009).

Al-Zandani, Bakeel A. "The Bush Doctrine, the War on Terror, and American Promotion of Democracy in the Middle East: The Cases of Egypt and Yemen." (PhD Thesis, University of Nebraska, 2010).

———, "U.S.-Yemen Relations in a Changing World: A Study of Four Major Events in U.S.-Yemen Relations." (Master Thesis, Long Island University, 2003).

Al-Zandani, Mansoor. "Al-Alakit Al-Yemeni Maa Al-Qwatine Al-Odhmaiene, 1962-1988." (PhD Thesis, Jaimat al-Qahera, 1988).

Charrett, Catherine. "Taking on the Normative Dilemma of Writing Securitization: A Critical Approach." (Masters Dissertation, London School of Economics, 2008).

Choi, Insu. "Small States and the Balance of Power." (Master Thesis, Naval Postgraduate School, 1995).

Dammag, Salwa A. "A Study Yemen United States Relations 1990-2002." (Master Thesis, University of Malaya, 2005).

Ferris, Jesse. "Egypt, the Cold War, and the Civil War in Yemen, 1962 - 1966." (PhD Thesis, Princeton University, 2008).

Folensbee, Fatma Izri. "Spreading Democracy, Supporting Dictators: Pragmatism and Ideology in U.S. Foreign Policy in the Global War on Terror." (Master Thesis, Georgetown University, 2009).

Ga'id, Mohamed Aglan. "Al-Alaqat Al-Yemenia Al-Ameicia 1990-1998." (Master Thesis, Baghdad University 1999).

Hiepko-Odermann, Kari M. "Latvian-American Relations in the 20th Century: The Study of a Great Power and a Small State." (PhD Thesis, Freie Universität, 2009).

J.P, James E.R. Unsworth. "The Global Political System: The Demise of the Westphalian Era Post- 9/11." (PhD Thesis, International Islamic University, 2008).

Mahanty, Daniel R. "The Aid for Security Dilemma: The Distortive Impact of U.S. National Security Interests on Development Assistance." (Master Thesis, Georgetown University, 2010).

Motah'er, Najwa Abdul Altif. "Se'ra'a Alk'how'a Ala'a Tehama (1818-1849)." (Master Thesis, University Sana'a, 2005).

Nitz, Eric Richard "Does Democracy Influence the Export of Terrorism?." (Master Thesis, Georgetown University, 2010).

Nowicki, Daniel E. "Assessing the Effectiveness of the U.S. Counter-terrorism Assistance Program to the Republic of Yemen." (Master Thesis, Georgetown University, 2011).

Rosthauser, Richard "Terrorism Conflict: How the United States Responds to Al-Qaeda Violence and Expressed Grievances." (Master Thesis, University of Denver, 2010).

Saltzman, B. Chance. "Liberty and Justice for All: The Democracy Project and the Global War on Terrorism." (Dissertation, Air University, May 2005).

Tetenburg, Stefanie. "Diplomacy in the Post 9/11 Era: an Examination of the Role of Diplomacy in Containing the Terrorist Threat." (Dissertation, King's College London, 2009).

Conference Papers

"Understanding Modern Piracy: Terrorists and Their Maritime Campaign." In *10th Annual Maritime Homeland Security Summit 2012* (Sheraton Norfolk Waterside, Norfolk, VA: GreySide Group, 2012).

AbdulGhani, Ahmad Mohamed. "Wark'a K'odemat Ela Nidowit Al-Alak'at Al-Yemeni Al-Americiah." In *Althadiat Alrahenh Amam al-Alak'at al-Yemeni al-Americiah* (Sana'a, 2001).

Algamh'y, Saeed Obaid. "Almujahdeen Fi Alyemen." In *Mostak'bal Ala'lakat bain Algama'at Aleslamiah wa Alhkomah Alyamniah* (Sana'a, 2003).

Al-Qirbi, Abu Bakr. "U.S. Wa Masirat' Aldomkra'tiah in Yemen." In *Had'er wa Mostak'bal Alalakat Al-Yemeniah Al-Americiah*, edited by Fares Alsakaf. (Sana'a: Markaz Drasat al-Mostkabal, 2002).

Al-Zandani, Mansour. "Almasaleh Alamericieah Kabl Almbadea." In *Had'er wa Mostak'bal Alalakat Al-Yemeniah Al-Americiah*, edited by Fares Alsakaf. (Sana'a: Markaz Drasat al-Mostkabal, 2002).

Carvajal, Fernando. "Imamic Yemen's Sacred National Charter (1948): Failed Interpretations of an Established Social Compact." In *Middle East PhD Students International Conference State, Society and Economy in the Modern Middle East* (London: SOAS, May 7-8, 2011).

Corry, Olaf. "Securitzation and 'Riskization': Two Grammars of Security." In *7th Pan-European International Relations Conference* (Stockholm: Standing Group on International Relations, September, 2010).

Duncan, Hon Alan. "Yemen: Political Dynamics and the International Policy Framework." In *Yemen: Political Dynamics and the International Policy Framework* (London: Chatham House, 2010).

Hoffman, Bruce. "Al-Qaeda, Trends in Terrorism and Future Potentialities: An Assessment." In *The Middle East After Afghanistan and*

Iraq; 3rd Annual Conference (Geneva: the RAND Center for Middle East Public Policy and Geneva Center for Security Policy, 5 May 2003).

Kasem, Kaled. "Economic Challenges." In *Altah'dieat alYemeniah fi*

faterat al-Raeasah al-Gadidah (Sana'a: Political Development Forum, 2006).

Petřík, Jaroslav. "Securitization of Official Development Aid: Analysis of Current Debate." In *International Peace Research Conference* (Leuven, Belgium: Conflict Resolution and Peace-Building Commission, July14-19, 2008).

Republic of Yemen. "Yemeni Experience in Counter-Terrorism." In *International Conference on Counter-Terrorism* (Riyadh, 2005).

Newspapers and Magazines

"A Guide to the United States' History of Recognition, since 1776: Yemen." *Office of the Historian* (2011), accessed 3/6/2012, http://history.state.gov/countries/yemen

"Al-Qaeda Claims Parcel Bomb Plot." *Al-Jazeera English* (2010), accessed 12/9/2011, http://www.aljazeera.com/news/middleeast/2010/11/20101152 04329353739.html

"Ambassador Gerald Firestein, Interview with Yemen News Agency (Saba)." *U.S. Embassy in Sana'a* (Mach 7, 2011), accessed 10/2/2012, https://yemen2-ar.cms.getusinfo.com/fis.html

"Background." *Indian Ocean Rim Association for Regional Cooperation* (2012), accessed 5/1/2012, http://www.iorarc.org/about-us/background.aspx

"History of Embassy." *Embassy of the Russian Federation in the Republic*

of Yemen (2011), accessed 7/7/2012, http://www.rusemb-ye.org/oldsite/content/view/38/lang,en/

"International Laws." *Security Council, Counter-Terrorism Committee* (2011), accessed 12/7/2012, http://www.un.org/en/sc/ctc/laws.html

"Interview with Ahmad Mansor, the Official Media to Al-Qaeda in Yemen." *Alwasat News* (January 30, 2008).

"Interview with U.S. Ambassador in Sana'a Gerald Firestein by Middle East News." *Mareb Press*, accessed 8/6/2012, http://marebpress.net/articles.php?id=16346&lng=a-rabic

"Maritime Chokepoints Critical to Petroleum Markets." *Today in Energy* (March 2, 2011), accessed 3/7/2011, http://205.254.135.7/todayinenergy/detail.cfm?id=330

"Middle East Overview." *Patterns of Global Terrorism* (1992), accessed 2/3/2010, http://www.fas.org/irp/threat/terror_92/mideast.html

"Remarks with Yemeni President Ali Abdullah Saleh after Their Meeting" *U.S. Embassy in Sana'a* (2011), accessed 5/6/2012, http://yemen.usembassy.gov/ryp.html

"Secretary Clinton's Town Hall in Sana'a, Yemen." *U.S. Embassy in Sana'a* (2011) accessed 3/4/2012, http://yemen.usembassy.gov/sth.html

"Statement by U.S. Assistant Secretary of State Jeffrey Feltman at the Friends of Yemen Conference." *U.S. Embassy in Sana'a* (May, 2012), accessed 29/5/2012, http://yem-en.usembassy.gov/ffyc.html

"Tfasiel Gadidah Lemhawlat Eghteial Mohamed Ben Naif." *Al- Sharq Alawsat* (2011), accessed 2/5/2011, http://www.aawsat.com/details.asp?section=4&issueno=11733&-article=603489&feature=

"The Interview with President Saleh by Al-Jazeera TV, Weekly Program - without Borders'" *National Information Center in Yemen* (October, 2000), accessed 4/3/2011, http://www.yemen-nic.info/presidency/detail.php?ID=6800

"The Oil and Gas Producing Countries of North Africa and the Middle East," *IFP Energies Nouvelles* (2012), accessed 21/6/2012, http://www.ifpenergiesnouvelles.c-om/publications/notes-de-synthese-panorama/panorama-2012

"Weekly Address: President Obama Outlines Steps Taken to Protect the Safety and Security of the American People." *The White House*, accessed 23/4/2012, http://www.whitehouse.gov/the-press-office/weekly-address-president-obama-outlines-steps-taken-protect-safety-and-security-ame

"Wikileaks Cble: Discussion with Dr. Prince Turki, Saudi Ministry of Foreign Affairs." *WIKILEAKS* (2009), accessed 4/1/2012, http://www.washingtonpost.com/wpsrv/spec-ial/world/wikileaks-yemen/cable6.html

"Wikileaks Cble: Oman's Ali Majid Warns Yemen on the Brink."
WIKILEAKS, accessed 4/1/2012, http://www.washingtonpost.com/wp-srv/special/world/wikileaks-yemen/cable8.html

"Wikileaks Cble: Prime Minister: Qatar Deeply Concerned About Yemen." *WIKILEAKS*, accessed 4/1/2012,
http://www.washingtonpost.com/wpsrv/special/wor-ld/wikileaks-yemen/cable10.html

"Wikileaks Cble: Yemen - Another Insider Speaks Out: "He Won't Listen to Anyone." *The Washington Post*, accessed 1/2/2012,
http://www.washingtonpost.com/wp-srv/special/world/wikileaks-yemen/cable4.html

"Yemen F'i Al-A'ser Al-H'adith," *Algomhoriah News* (2010), accessed 6/2/2011, http://www.algomhoriah.net/atach.php?id=32076

"Yemen Warns Iran to Avoid Interference." *Al-jazeera.Net* (2012),
accessed 20/7/2012, http://www.aljazeera.net/news/pages/9303c95c-ca21-45a2-885c-fd510956ddd5?GoogleStatID=1

"Yemen: Maps of Conflict/Crisis." *The Project on Middle East Democracy (POMED)*, accessed 8/9/2012,
http://pomed.org/blog/2011/04/yemen-maps-of-conflictcrisis.ht-ml/#.UCLDMKNE7Kg

"Yemeni Tourism Sector Loses USD 10 Billion." *Ministry of Commerce People's Republic of China*, accessed 6/21/2012,
http://english.mofcom.gov.cn/aarticle/.....d-africareport/201010/20101007195417.html

"Counter-terrorism Committee." *UN,* accessed 12/1/2012,
http://www.un.org/-en/sc/ctc/l-aws.html

"Maritime Chokepoints Critical to Petroleum Markets." *Today in Energy* (2011), accessed 3/7/2011,
http://205.254.135.7/todayinenergy/detail.cfm?id=330

Ala'ahmadi, Mohamed. "Ala'alakat Alyemeniah Alemerciah Bad Ah'dath 11 September." *Al-Moslim* (September, 2003), accessed 23/6/2011,
http://almoslim.ne-t/node/85268

Aldein, Maysa Shoga'a. *Ala'alakat Alyemeniah Alemerciah Wa Azmat Alta'awn* (2002), accessed 6/2/2011,
http://www.onislam.net/arabic/newsanalysis/analysis-opinions/eur-ope-north-america-australia/85815-2002-09-07%2000-00-00.html

Al-Faqiah, Abd Allah. "Al-A'lak'at Al-Yemeniah Al-Americiah Bein Alastemrar Wa Altaghieer." *Alwasa't News* (24/5/2006).

Alk'ader, Nizar. "Alalakat Alyemeniah Alemrekiah Fi D'oa Althwapet Alwataniah." *26 September* (December 12, 2002), accessed 5/9/2010, http://www.26sep.net/newswe-ekartic-le.php?lng=arabic&sid=2253

Al-Majeed, Najmey Abd. "Almo'arek'h Hamzah Ali Lok'man W'a Eshamateh F'i Ketabat Tarik'h Aden." *14 October News* (May 19, 2006).

Alrefaei, Moath A. "Hatheh Alh'rb Alea'alamiah Wa Aba'adaha." *26 September* (June 3, 2004), accessed 8/7/2011, http://www.26sep.net/newsweekarticle.php?lng=ara-bic&sid=10164

Amine, Adel. *Men Moa'tamer Landan Ela Riyadh* (January, 2010), accessed 8/4/2011, http://www.alshibami.net/saqifa//showthread.php?t=79917

Anthony, John Duke. *Yemen and the USS Cole Investigation in Context: A Regional Perspective* (November 11, 2000), accessed 1/2/2011, http://ncusar.org/publicatio-ns/Publications/2000-11-25-Cole-Investigation-In-Context.pdf

Dilanian, Ken. "Yemen Hasn't Received as Much U.S. Aid as Its Neighbors." *USA Today News* (2010), accessed 2/1/2011, http://www.usatoday.com/news/world/2010-01-05-yemen-aid_N.htm

Hamdan, Ahmed. "Lemath'a Tada'am Alwelayat Almotahedah Israel." *26 September News* (February 25, 2012).

Hardy, Roger. "Kelaf Emraiki Yemeni H'aol Tahkikat Almodamerak Cool." *BBC Online Network* (2001), accessed 6/6/2011, http://news.bbc.co.uk/hi/arabic/news/n-ewsid_1504000/1504744.stm

Kelemen, Michele. "Clinton: Yemen Instability Threatens World." *NPR news* (January 4, 2010), accessed 12/3/2011, http://www.npr.org/templates/story/story.php?sto-ryId=122226355

Kellner, Douglas. "September 11, Terror War, and Blowback." *Columbia University* (2005), accessed 16/6/2011, http://www.gseis.ucla.edu/faculty/kellner/kellner.html

Naits, Maickl. "Alyemen Moltaka Alerhabeen Alalemeen." *Althawry News* (27/4/2006).

Phillips, Sarah. "What Comes Next in Yemen? Al-Qaeda, the Tribes, and State-Building." *Carnegie* (March, 2010), accessed 1/8/2012, www.CarnegieEndow-ment.org/

Rash'ied, Fayz. "America, Israel Man Yah'kom Man." *Al-Tajreed Al-Arabi* (November, 2010), accessed 2/1/2011, http://www.arabrenewal.info/2010-06-11-14-11-19/4255

Schanzer, Jonathan. "Yemen's War on Terror." *Pundicity, Information & Review* (Summer, 2004), accessed 6/7/2012, http://schanzer.pundicity.com/827/yem-ens-war-on-terror

Shuster, Mike. "The Middle East and the West: The U.S. Role Grows." *NPR: National Public Radio* (August, 2004), accessed 29/9/2010, http://www.npr.org/templates/st-ory/story.php?storyId=3865983

Stein, Sam. "Lieberman: The United States Must Pre-Emptively Act in Yemen." *HUFF POST* (2010), accessed 23/7/2012,

http://www.huffingtonpost.com/2009/1-2/27/li-eberman-the-united-stat_n_404241.html

Zakarya, Mohammed. "Al-Sera'a Alothmani Alinglizy F'i Al-Yemen." *14 Octoper News* (April 2,2007).

Websites

"A Focus on Yemen." *The George Washington University*, accessed 4/3/2012, http://-elliott.gwu.edu/news/events/mepf/gnehm_kuawit_chair_0310_yemen-transcript.cfm.

Google Maps, accessed 1/8/2012, https://maps.google.com

"Statement Adopting the Madrid Bombings by Ktae'b Abo H'afss Almasry." accessed 29/1/2010, http://www.paldf.net/forum/showthread.php?p=84314

"The New Steel Silk Road." *Resource Investor; News That Trades*, accessed 2/3/2012, http://www.resourceinvestor.com/2011/11/03/the-new-steel-silk-road.

The Defense Manpower Data Center (DMDC). *Flg as Sep* (2011), accessed 10/1/2012, http://www.bbc.co.uk/news/world-us-canada-16433138

"USA: You're either with us or against us Al-Qaeda: Yes, We're with You." accessed 31/5/2012, http://multipletext.com/2012/2-you_are_either_with_us_or_against_us.html

"Wilson's Fourteen Points an Address to a Joint Session of Congress,

January 8, 1918." accessed
3/5/2011, http://www.cosmopolitikos.com/DigitalLibrary/Wilson%20-%20Fourteen%20Points%20(1918).pdf

"Wordpress." accessed 12/11/2011, http://bobblincoe.files.wordpress.com/2011/05/fr-enchcolonial.jpg.

Appendix

APPENDIX A:
MAP OF BAB EL MANDEB IN THE RED SEA

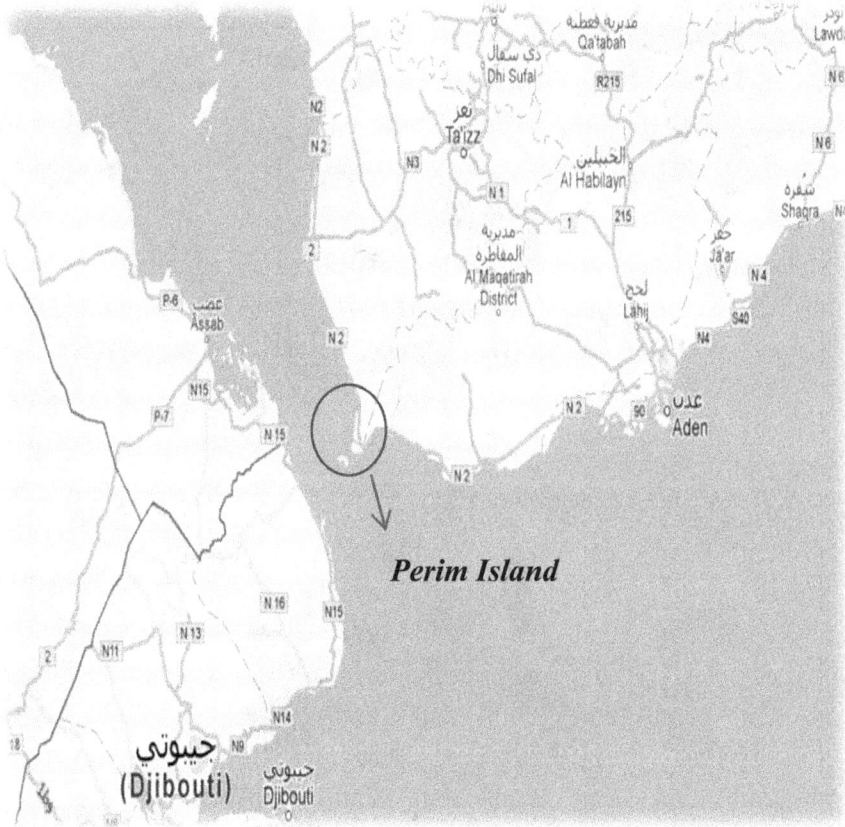

Perim Island

APPENDIX B:
MAP OF TRADE ROUTES BETWEEN THE INDIAN OCEAN,
RED SEA, AND MEDITERRANEAN

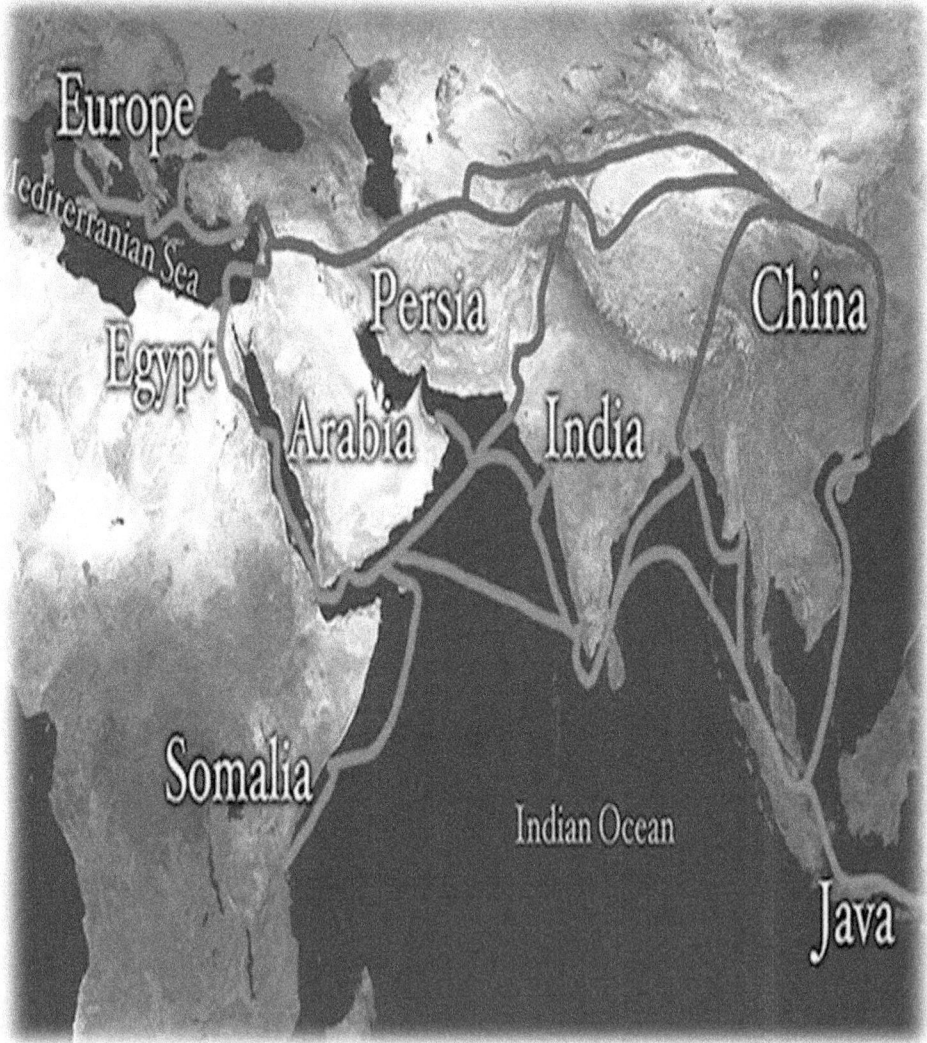

Source: Resource Investor: News That Trades, accessed 2/3/2012
http://www.resourceinvestor.com/2011/11/03/the-new-steel-silk-road.

APPENDIX C:
FIGURE OF THE WORLD OIL RESERVE 2012

- Middle East
- S. & Cent. America
- North America
- Europe & Eurasia
- Africa
- Asia Pacific

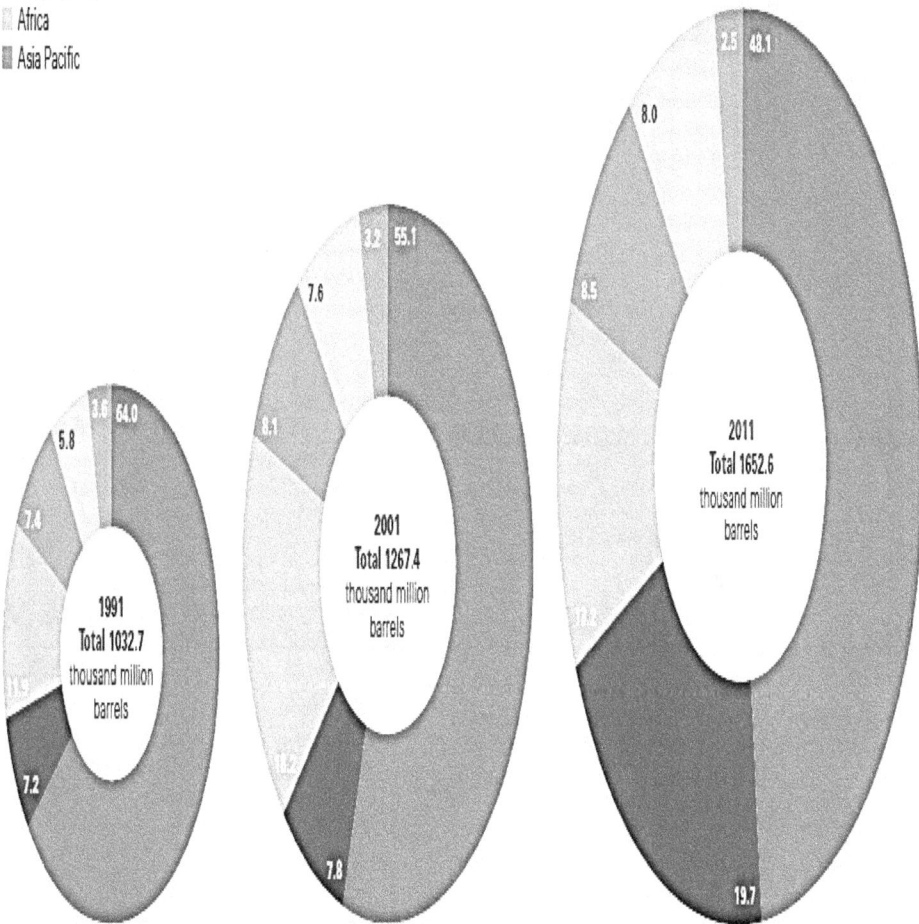

1991
Total 1032.7
thousand million
barrels

3.6 64.0
5.8
7.4
7.2

2001
Total 1267.4
thousand million
barrels

3.2 55.1
7.6
8.1
7.8

2011
Total 1652.6
thousand million
barrels

2.5 48.1
8.0
8.5
19.7

Source: BP Organization. "Bp Statistical Review of World Energy." (London: BP Amoco, 2012).

APPENDIX D:

TABLE OF HUMANITARIAN CONVENTIONS RATIFIED BY YEMEN

No	Approval Date	Convention Name	Content
1	18/10/1972	International Convention on the Elimination of All Forms of Racial Discrimination	Under the Convention, state parties are obliged to condemn racial discrimination and undertake to pursue by all appropriate means without delay a policy of eliminating racial discrimination in all its forms.
2	17/8/1978	The Convention on the Suppression and Punishment of the Crime of Apartheid	Under the Convention, state parties will declare that apartheid is a crime against humanity. One of the crimes that violate the principles of international law.
3	9/2/1978	The International Covenant on Civil and Political Rights	Whereby states parties undertake to respect the rights with regard to the political and civil sides and ensure to all individuals without discrimination.
4	9/2/1978	International Covenant on Economic, Social and Cultural Rights	Covenant focuses on the principle of the right to self-determination of all peoples and the pursuit of economic growth and social and cultural cooperation with countries pledged to make the exercise of these rights is innocent of racial discrimination
5	9/2/1978	Convention for the Prevention and Punishment of the Crime of Genocide	In order to get rid of this odious scourge and the losses inflicted on humanity by the United Nations approved the convention on the prevention of genocide and punishment
6	9/2/1978	Convention on the Non-Applicability of Statutory Limitations to War Crimes and Crimes Against Humanity	The agreement does not apply to any statute of limitations on war crimes and crimes against humanity

7	30/5/1984	Convention on the Elimination of All Forms of Discrimination against Women	The agreement emphasizes that discrimination against women violates the principles of equality of .rights and respect for human dignity
8	9/2/1987	International Convention on the Political Rights of Women	The signing of this agreement works on the principle of equality between men and women in the rights contained in the Charter of the UN.
9	9/2/1987	Convention on Consent to Marriage, Minimum Age for Marriage and Registration of Marriages	It is the application of Article (16) of the Universal Declaration of Human Rights states that the men and women of full age have the right to marry and raise a family and also included an agreement on the principle of consent between the two parties if the marriage is in the .presence of witnesses
10	9/2/1987	International Convention on slavery	Under the agreement, it is pledged that the High Contracting Parties are to prevent the slave trade and punishment and work as quickly as possible to eliminate slavery in all its .forms
11	6/4/1989	Convention for the Suppression of the Traffic in Persons and of the Exploitation of the Prostitution of Others	The agreement aims to complete the United Nations procedures practices with human dignity because of prostitution and trafficking in persons is incompatible with human .dignity and ability
12	1/5/1991	Convention on the Rights of the Child	Include the convention on the fundamental rights of the child for which states parties undertake to .protect those rights
13	5/11/1991	Convention Against Torture And Other Cruel, Inhuman or Degrading Treatment or Punishment	Under the agreement, states parties are obliged to take all legislative or administrative action effective for the prevention of torture in its territory and make the perpetrators accountable.
14	29/9/1994	The Universal Declaration of Human Rights	Whereby states agree on the right of everyone to the enjoyment of all rights and freedoms without distinction of any kind
		Source: Table's designing and assembling by researcher	

APPENDIX E:
TABLE OF THE 16 INTERNATIONAL LEGAL INSTRUMENTS

No	Data	Convention Name	Status
1	4 December 1969	Convention on Offences and Certain Other Acts Committed On Board Aircraft	185 Parties
2	14 October 1971	Convention for the Suppression of Unlawful Seizure of Aircraft	185 Parties
3	26 January 1973	Convention for the Suppression of Unlawful Acts Against the Safety of Civil Aviation	188 Parties
4	20 February 1977	Convention on the Prevention and Punishment of Crimes against Internationally Protected Persons, including Diplomatic Agents	172 Parties
5	3 June 1983	International Convention Against the Taking of Hostages	167 Parties
6	8 February 1987	Convention on the Physical Protection of Nuclear Material	144 Parties
7	8 July 2005, Vienna	Amendments to the Convention on the Physical Protection of Nuclear Material	47 Parties
8	6 August 1989	Protocol for the Suppression of Unlawful Acts of Violence at Airports Serving International Civil Aviation, Supplementary to the Convention for the Suppression of Unlawful Acts against the Safety of Civil Aviation, done at Montreal on 23 September 1971	171 Parties
9	1 March 1992	Convention for the Suppression of Unlawful Acts Against the Safety of Maritime Navigation	156 Parties
10	14 October 2005	Protocol to the Convention for the Suppression of Unlawful Acts Against the Safety of Maritime Navigation	20 Parties
11	1 March 1992	Protocol for the Suppression of Unlawful Acts Against the Safety of Fixed Platforms Located on the Continental Shelf	144 Parties

12	14 October 2005	Protocol to the Protocol for the Suppression of Unlawful Acts Against the Safety of Fixed Platforms Located on the Continental Shelf	15 Parties
1 3	21 June 1998	Convention on the Marking of Plastic Explosives for the Purpose of Detection	147 Parties
14	23 May 2001	International Convention for the Suppression of Terrorist Bombings	164 Parties
15	10 April 2002	International Convention for the Suppression of the Financing of Terrorism	173 Parties
16	7 July 2007	International Convention for the Suppression of Acts of Nuclear Terrorism	77 Parties

Source: UN, Counter-terrorism Committee, accessed 12/1/201,2
http://www.un.org/en/sc/ctc/laws.html.

Appendix F:
Map of U.S. Military Bases around the World

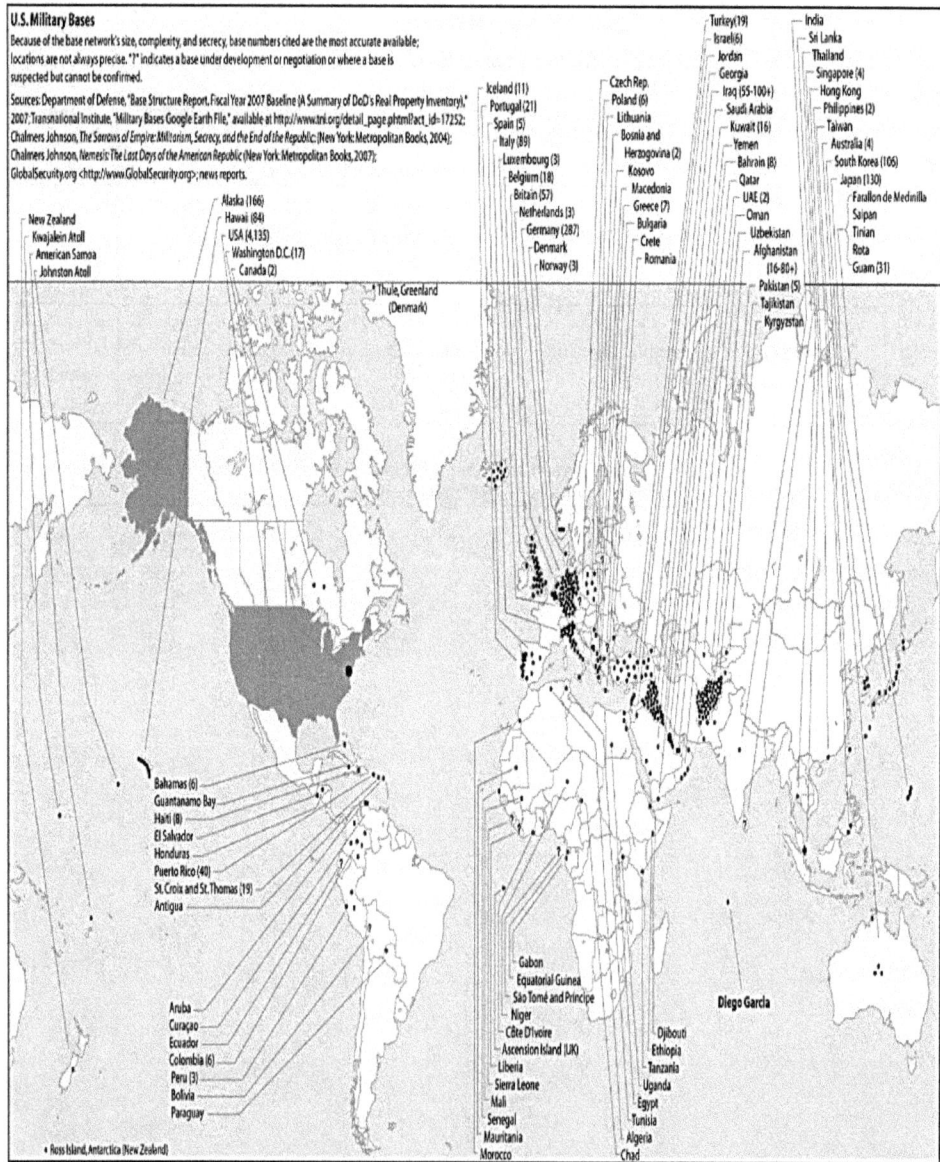

U.S. Military Bases

Because of the base network's size, complexity, and secrecy, base numbers cited are the most accurate available; locations are not always precise. "?" indicates a base under development or negotiation or where a base is suspected but cannot be confirmed.

Sources: Department of Defense, "Base Structure Report, Fiscal Year 2007 Baseline (A Summary of DoD's Real Property Inventory)," 2007. Transnational Institute, "Military Bases Google Earth File," available at http://www.tni.org/detail_page.phtml?act_id=17252; Chalmers Johnson, The Sorrows of Empire: Militarism, Secrecy, and the End of the Republic (New York: Metropolitan Books, 2004); Chalmers Johnson, Nemesis: The Last Days of the American Republic (New York: Metropolitan Books, 2007); GlobalSecurity.org <http://www.GlobalSecurity.org> news reports.

New Zealand
Kwajalein Atoll
American Samoa
Johnston Atoll

Alaska (166)
Hawaii (84)
USA (4,135)
Washington D.C. (17)
Canada (2)

Iceland (11)
Portugal (21)
Spain (5)
Italy (89)
Luxembourg (3)
Belgium (18)
Britain (57)
Netherlands (3)
Germany (287)
Denmark
Norway (3)

Czech Rep.
Poland (6)
Lithuania
Bosnia and Herzegovina (2)
Kosovo
Macedonia
Greece (7)
Bulgaria
Crete
Romania

Turkey (19)
Israel (6)
Jordan
Georgia
Iraq (55-100+)
Saudi Arabia
Kuwait (16)
Yemen
Bahrain (8)
Qatar
UAE (2)
Oman
Uzbekistan
Afghanistan (16-80+)
Pakistan (5)
Tajikistan
Kyrgyzstan

India
Sri Lanka
Thailand
Singapore (4)
Hong Kong
Philippines (2)
Taiwan
Australia (4)
South Korea (106)
Japan (130)
Farallon de Medinilla
Saipan
Tinian
Rota
Guam (31)

Thule, Greenland (Denmark)

Bahamas (6)
Guantanamo Bay
Haiti (8)
El Salvador
Honduras
Puerto Rico (40)
St. Croix and St. Thomas (19)
Antigua

Aruba
Curaçao
Ecuador
Colombia (6)
Peru (3)
Bolivia
Paraguay

Gabon
Equatorial Guinea
São Tomé and Principe
Niger
Côte D'Ivoire
Ascension Island (UK)
Liberia
Sierra Leone
Mali
Senegal
Mauritania
Morocco

Djibouti
Ethiopia
Tanzania
Uganda
Egypt
Tunisia
Algeria
Chad

Diego Garcia

• Ross Island, Antarctica (New Zealand)

Source: Vine, D. Island of Shame: The Secret History of the U.S. Military Base on Diego Garcia (New Jersey: Princeton University Press, 2009).

APPENDIX G:
YEMEN IN THE HUMAN DEVELOPMENT INDEX:
TRENDS 1995 – 2011.

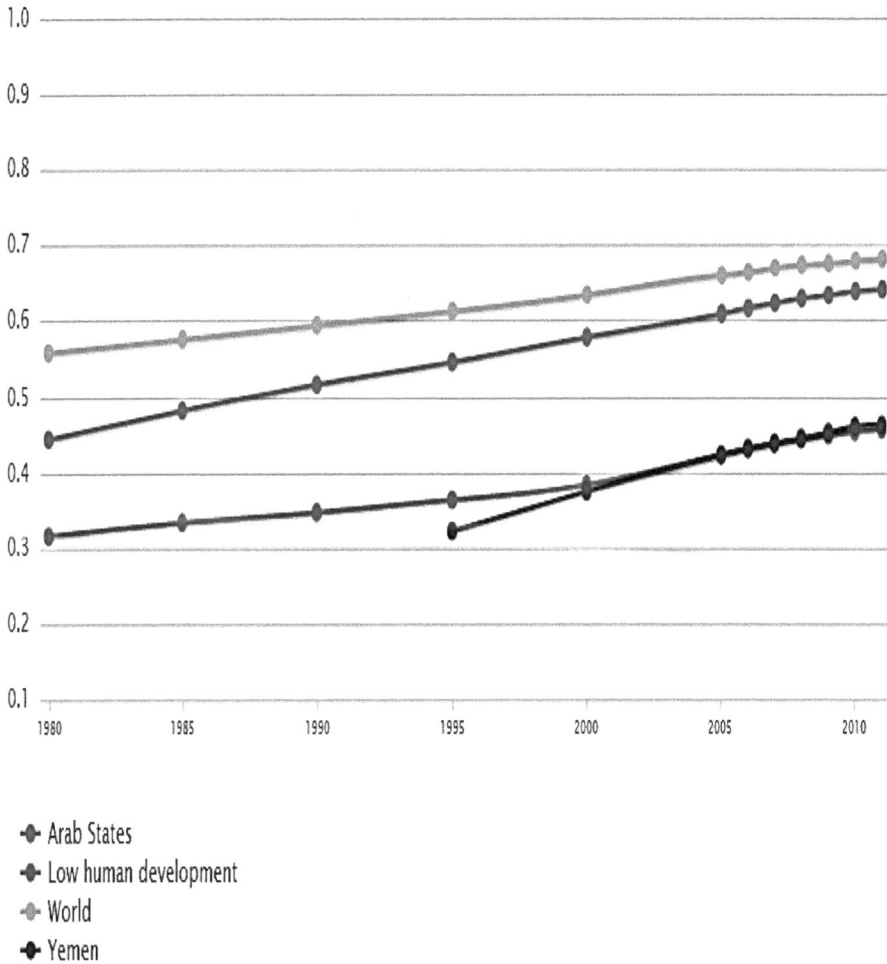

- Arab States
- Low human development
- World
- Yemen

Source: United Nations. "Yemen, Country Profile: Human Development
  Indicators." (2011), accessed 29/3/2012 http://hdrstats.undp.org/en/coun-
  tries/profiles/YEM_print.html

APPENDIX H: TABLE OF YEMEN'S VOTE ON THE UN RESOLUTIONS CONCERNING IRAQ

Resolution number	Date	Issue	Yemen's position
660	8/2/1990	Denunciation of the Iraqi invasion of Kuwait and the demand to withdrew forces.	Absent
661	8/6/1990	Economic sanctions.	Abstain
662	8/9/1990	Considering the annexation of Kuwait by Iraq illegal.	Agree
664	8/18/1990	Calling on Iraq to allow foreigners to leave Iraq and Kuwait.	Abstain
665	8/25/1990	Imposing a maritime Embargo	Abstain
666	9/13/1990	The expansion of economic sanctions to include food and medicine.	Disagree
667	9/16/1990	Protesting Iraq's closure of diplomatic missions in Kuwait	Agree
669	9/24/1990	Empowering the Committee on sanctions to compensate affected countries.	Agree
670	29/25/1990	Air embargo	Agree
674	10/29/1990	Assigning responsibility to Iraq for the destruction of Kuwait	Abstain
677	11/28/1990	Condemning the Iraqi attempt to alter the demographics of Kuwait.	Agree
678	11/29/1990	Authorizing the use of force to liberate Kuwait	Disagree
686	3/2/1991	Terms of ceasefire	Abstain.
687	4/3/1991	Ceasefire	Abstain

Source: Al-Mutawakel 2002; United Nations 2003.

APPENDIX I: TABLE IDENTIFYING YEMEN IN THE FAILED STATES INDEX 2009- 2011

Performance by Indicator	2011	2010	2009
Rank	13	15	18
Total	100.3	100	190.1
Demographic Pressures	8.7	8.6	8.8
Refugees and IDPs	8.4	8.3	7.9
Group Grievance	8.6	8.2	7.7
Human Flight and Brain Drain	6.9	7.2	7.4
Uneven Economic development	8.3	8.6	8.9
Economy and Poverty	7.7	7.9	8.2
Legitimacy of the State	8.6	8.7	8.3
Public Services	8.7	8.6	8.5
Human Rights and Rule of Law	7.7	8	7.7
Security Apparatus	9.3	8.9	8.4
Factionalization of Elites	9.3	9.2	9
External Intervention	8.2	7.8	7.3

For further reading about the table's indicators, see: The Fund for Peace Publication. "Failed States Index 2011." (Foreign Policy, 2011,2010 &2009), accessed6/9/2012, http://www.foreignpo

APPENDIX J: SECURITY COUNCIL RESOLUTION NO. 2014, (2011)

Adopted by the Security Council at its 6634th meeting,
on 21 October 2011

The Security Council, Recalling its Press Statements of 24 September 2011, 9 August 2011, and 24 June 2011,

Expressing grave concern at the situation in Yemen,

Reaffirming its strong commitment to the unity, sovereignty, independence and territorial integrity of Yemen,

Welcoming the Secretary-General's statement of 23 September 2011 urging all sides to engage in a constructive manner to achieve a peaceful resolution to the current crisis,

Welcoming the engagement of the Gulf Cooperation Council, and reaffirming the support of the Security Council for the GCC's efforts to resolve the political crisis in Yemen,

Welcoming the continuing efforts of the Good Offices of the Secretary-General, including the visits to Yemen by the Special Adviser,

Taking note of the Human Rights Council resolution on Yemen (A/HRC/RES/18/19), and *underlining* the need for a comprehensive, independent and impartial investigation consistent with international standards into alleged human rights abuses and violations, with a view to avoiding impunity and ensuring full accountability, and *noting* in this regard the concerns expressed by the United Nations High Commissioner for Human Rights,

Welcoming the statement by the Ministerial Council of the Gulf Cooperation Council on 23 September 2011 which called for the immediate signing by President Saleh and implementation of the Gulf Cooperation Council initiative, condemned the use of force against unarmed demonstrators, and called for restraint, a commitment to a full and immediate ceasefire and the formation of a commission to investigate the events that led to the killing of innocent Yemeni people,

Expressing serious concern at the worsening security situation, including armed conflict, and the deteriorating economic and humanitarian situation due to the lack of progress on a political settlement, and the potential for the further escalation of violence,

Reaffirming its resolutions 1325 (2000), 1820 (2008), 1888 (2009), 1889 (2009) and 1960 (2010) on women, peace, and security, and reiterating the need for the full, equal and effective participation of women at all stages of peace-processes given their vital role in the prevention and resolution of conflict and peace building, *reaffirming* the key role women play in re-establishing the fabric of society and stressing the need for their involvement in conflict resolution in order to take into account their perspective and needs,

Expressing serious concern also about the increasing number of internally displaced persons and refugees in Yemen, the alarming levels of malnutrition caused by drought and soaring fuel and food prices, the increasing interruption of basic supplies and social services, and increasingly difficult access to safe water and health care,

Expressing further serious concern at the increased threat from Al-Qaida in the Arabian Peninsula and the risk of new terror attacks in parts of Yemen, *and reaffirming* that terrorism in all forms and manifestations constitutes one of the most serious threats to international peace and security and that any acts of terrorism are criminal and unjustifiable regardless of their motivations,

Condemning all terrorist and other attacks against civilians and against the authorities, including those aimed at jeopardizing the political process in Yemen, such as the attack on the Presidential compound in Sana'a on 3 June 2011, *Recalling* the Yemeni Government's primary responsibility to protect its population,

Stressing that the best solution to the current crisis in Yemen is through an inclusive and Yemeni-led political process of transition that meets the legitimate demands and aspirations of the Yemeni people for change, *Reaffirming* its support for the Presidential decree of 12 September which is designed to find a political agreement acceptable to all parties, and to ensure a peaceful and democratic transition of power, including the holding of early Presidential elections,

Stressing the importance of the stability and security of Yemen, particularly regarding overall international counter-terrorism efforts, *Mindful* of its primary responsibility for the maintenance of international peace and security under the Charter of the United Nations, and emphasizing the threats to regional security and stability posed by the deterioration of the situation in Yemen in the absence of a lasting political settlement,

1. *Expresses* profound regret at the hundreds of deaths, mainly of civilians, including women and children;

2. *Strongly condemns* the continued human rights violations by the Yemeni authorities, such as the excessive use of force against peaceful protestors as well as the acts of violence, use of force, and human rights abuses perpetrated by other actors, and *stresses* that all those responsible for violence, human rights violations and abuses should be held accountable;

3. *Demands* that all sides immediately reject the use of violence to achieve political goals;

4. *Reaffirms* its view that the signature and implementation as soon as possible of a settlement agreement on the basis of the Gulf Cooperation Council initiative is essential for an inclusive, orderly, and Yemeni-led process of political transition, *notes* the signing of the Gulf Cooperation Council initiative by some opposition parties and the General People's Congress, *calls on* all parties in Yemen to commit themselves to implementation of a political settlement based upon this initiative, *notes* the commitment by the President of Yemen to immediately sign the Gulf Cooperation Council initiative and encourages him, or those authorized to act on his behalf, to do so, and to implement a political settlement based upon it, and *calls* for this commitment to be translated into action, in order to achieve a

peaceful political transition of power, as stated in the Gulf Cooperation Council initiative and the Presidential decree of 12 September, without further delay;

5. *Demands* that the Yemeni authorities immediately ensure their actions comply with obligations under applicable international humanitarian and human rights law, allow the people of Yemen to exercise their human rights and fundamental freedoms, including their rights of peaceful assembly to demand redress of their grievances and freedom of expression, including for members of the media, and take action to end attacks against civilians and civilian targets by security forces;

6. *Calls* upon all concerned parties to ensure the protection of women and children, to improve women's participation in conflict resolution and encourages all parties to facilitate the equal and full participation of women at decision-making levels;

7. *Urges* all opposition groups to commit to playing a full and constructive part in the agreement and implementation of a political settlement on the basis of the Gulf Cooperation Council initiative, and *demands* that all opposition groups refrain from violence, and cease the use of force to achieve political aims;

8. *Further demands* that all armed groups remove all weapons from areas of peaceful demonstration, refrain from violence and provocation, refrain from the recruitment of children, and *urges* all parties not to target vital infrastructure;

9. *Expresses* its concern over the presence of Al-Qaida in the Arabian Peninsula, and its determination to address this threat in accordance with the Charter of the United Nations and international law including applicable human rights, refugee and humanitarian law;

10. *Encourages* the international community to provide humanitarian assistance to Yemen, and in this regard requests all parties in Yemen to facilitate the work of the United Nations agencies and other relevant organizations, and ensure full, safe and unhindered access for the timely delivery of the humanitarian aid to persons in need across Yemen;

11. *Requests* the Secretary-General to continue his Good Offices, including through visits by the Special Adviser, and to continue to urge all Yemeni stakeholders to implement the provisions of this resolution, and encourage we all States and regional organizations to contribute to this objective;

12. *Requests* the Secretary-General to report on implementation of this resolution within 30 days of its adoption and every 60 days thereafter;

13. *Decides* to remain actively seized of the matter.

APPENDIX K:
THE GCC PROPOSAL TO SOLVE YEMEN'S POLITICAL CRISES

The Agreement between Yemen's Ruling Party And The

Opposition

*Basic Principles.

- The resolution of the agreement will lead to safety, security, stability and unity of Yemen.

- The agreement will achieve Yemen's people ambitions in change and reform.

- The agreement will achieve peaceful transition of power, and avoid Yemen entering chaos and violence and this will be within a national agreement.

- Both sides are obligated to defuse all elements of political and security tension.

- Both sides are obligated to stop all sorts of revenge and persuing of the other in appliance to the guarantees and pledges offered by this proposal.

*Executive Steps:

- From the first day to the agreement, the President of the Republic instructs the opposition to form a national government 50% for the ruling party, 40% for the opposition, and 10 % from other political powers.

- The government will be formed during the seven days from the date of signing   the   agreement.
  - The new government will create the suitable atmosphere to achieve

the national agreement and defuse all elements of political and security tension.

- On the 29th day of the signing of the agreement, the parliament including the opposition will issue a law which will grant President and those who served under his rule Immunity from law and judicial prosecution.

- In the 30th day after the signing of the agreement, and after the president and his aides in rule are granted Immunity from prosecution, the president will hand over his resignation to parliament, and his vice president becomes the new president after parliament approves Saleh's resignation.

- The new president (former Vice President) forms a constitutional committee to supervise to prepare a new constitution.

- After the constitution being finished, a referendum will take place to accept the new constitution.

- When the constitution is approved by the people, it is important to offer a timetable for the new parliamentary elections according to the constitution.

- After the parliamentary elections are complete, the winning party with majority of seats in parliament will be asked to form a new government.

The GCC, EU, and US will be witnesses to this agreement.

Signature

The President of Yemen Republic

Yemeni Opposition

The GCC

The US

The EU

APPENDIX L:
US EXECUTIVE ORDER NO. 13611, (2012)

Blocking Property of Persons Threatening the Peace, Security,
or Stability of Yemen

By the authority vested in me as President by the Constitution and the laws of the United States of America, including the International Emergency Economic Powers Act (50 U.S.C. 1701 *et seq.)* (IEEPA), the National Emergencies Act (50 U.S.C. 1601 *et seq.)* (NEA), and section 301 of title 3, United States Code,

I, BARACK OBAMA, President of the United States of America, find that the actions and policies of certain members of the Government of Yemen and others threaten Yemen's peace, security, and stability, including by obstructing the implementation of the agreement of November 23, 2011, between the

Government of Yemen and those in opposition to it, which provides for a peaceful transition of power that meets the legitimate demands and aspirations of the Yemeni people for change, and by obstructing the political process in Yemen. I further find that these actions constitute an unusual and extraordinary threat to the national security and foreign policy of the United States, and I hereby declare a national emergency to deal with that threat. I hereby order:

Section 1. All property and interests in property that are in the United States, that hereafter come within the United States, or that are or hereafter come within the possession or control of any United States person, including any foreign branch, of the following persons are blocked and may not be transferred, paid, exported, withdrawn, or otherwise dealt in: any person determined by the Secretary of the Treasury, in consultation with the Secretary of State, to:

(a) have engaged in acts that directly or indirectly threaten the peace, security, or stability of Yemen, such as acts that obstruct the implementation of the agreement of November 23, 2011, between the Government of Yemen and those in opposition to it, which provides for a peaceful transition of power in Yemen, or that obstruct the political process in Yemen;

(b) be a political or military leader of an entity that has engaged in the acts described in subsection (a) of this section;

(c) have materially assisted, sponsored, or provided financial, material, or technological support for, or goods or services to or in support of, the acts described in subsection (a) of this section or any person whose property and interests in property are blocked pursuant to this order; or

(d) be owned or controlled by, or to have acted or purported to act for or on behalf of, directly or indirectly, any person whose property and interests in property are blocked pursuant to this order.

Sec. 2. I hereby determine that the making of donations of the type of articles specified in section 203(b)(2) of IEEPA (50 U.S.C. 1702(b)(2)) by, to, or for the benefit of any person whose property and interests in property are blocked pursuant to section 1 of this order would seriously impair my ability to deal with the national emergency declared in this order, and I hereby prohibit such donations as provided by section 1 of this order.

Sec. 3. The prohibitions in section 1 of this order include but are not limited to:

(a) the making of any contribution or provision of funds, goods, or services by, to, or for the benefit of any person whose property and interests in property are blocked pursuant to this order; and

(b) the receipt of any contribution or provision of funds, goods, or services from any such person.

Sec. 4. The prohibitions in section 1 of this order apply except to the extent provided by statutes, or in regulations, orders, directives, or licenses that may be issued pursuant to this order, and notwithstanding any contract entered into or any license or permit granted prior to the effective date of this order.

Sec. 5. Nothing in section 1 of this order shall prohibit transactions for the conduct of the official business of the United States Government by employees, grantees, or contractors thereof.

Sec. 6. (a) Any transaction that evades or avoids, has the purpose of evading or avoiding, causes a violation of, or attempts to violate any of the prohibitions set forth in this order is prohibited.

(b) Any conspiracy formed to violate any of the prohibitions set forth in this order is prohibited.

Sec. 7. For the purposes of this order:

(a) the term "person" means an individual or entity;

(b) the term "entity" means a partnership, association, trust, joint venture, corporation, group, subgroup, or other organization; and

(c) the term "United States person" means any United States citizen, permanent resident alien, entity organized under the laws of the United States or any jurisdiction within the United States (including foreign branches), or any person in the United States.

Sec. 8. For those persons whose property and interests in property are blocked pursuant to this order who might have a constitutional presence in the United States, I find that because of the ability to transfer funds or other assets instantaneously, prior notice to such persons of measures to be taken pursuant to this order would render those measures ineffectual. I therefore determine that for these measures to be effective in addressing the national emergency declared in this order, there need be no prior notice of a listing or determination made pursuant to section 1 of this order.

Sec. 9. The Secretary of the Treasury, in consultation with the Secretary of State, is hereby authorized to take such actions, including the promulgation of rules and regulations, and to employ all powers granted to the President by IEEPA as may be necessary to carry out the purposes of this order. The Secretary of the Treasury may redelegate any of these functions to other officers and agencies of the United States Government consistent with applicable law. All agencies of the United States Government are hereby directed to take all appropriate measures within their authority to carry out the provisions of this order.

Sec. 10. The Secretary of the Treasury, in consultation with the Secretary of State, is hereby authorized to submit the recurring and final reports to the Congress on the national emergency declared in this order, consistent with section 401(c) of the NEA (50 U.S.C. 1641(c)) and section 204(c) of IEEPA (50 U.S.C. 1703(c)).

Sec. 11. This order is not intended to, and does not, create any right or benefit, substantive or procedural, enforceable at law or in equity by any party against the United States, its departments, agencies, or entities, its officers, employees, or agents, or any other person.

THE WHITE HOUSE,
May 16, 2012

www.ingramcontent.com/pod-product-compliance
Lightning Source LLC
Chambersburg PA
CBHW081149270326
41930CB00014B/3094